Patricia Smith's
DOLL VALUES
Antique to Modern
Seventh Series

COLLECTOR BOOKS
A Division of Schroeder Publishing Co., Inc.

The current values in this book should be used only as a guide. They are not intended to set prices, which vary from one section of the country to another. Auction prices as well as dealer prices vary greatly and are affected by condition as well as demand. Neither the Author nor the Publisher assumes responsibility for any losses that might be incurred as a result of consulting this guide.

Additional copies of this book may be ordered from:

Collector Books
P.O. Box 3009
Paducah, KY   42002-3009

@ $12.95 add $2.00 for postage and handling.

Copyright: Patricia Smith, 1991

Printed by IMAGE GRAPHICS, INC., Paducah, Kentucky

CREDITS

We thank the following for their help in making this volume possible: Gloria Anderson, Sandy Johnson-Barts, Shirley Bertrand (Shirley's Doll House, Wheeling, IL), Sally Bethscheider, Margaret Biggers, Arthur Bouliette, Candy Brainard, Kay Bransky, Joanna Brunkin, Elizabeth Burke, Barbara Earnshaw-Cain (P.O. Box 14381; Lenexa, KS 66215), Bessie Carson, Lee Crane, Renie Culp, Bonnie Chichura, Millie Chappelle, Marlowe Cooper, Durham Arts (36429 Row River Rd.; Cottage Grove, OR), Marie Ernst, Frasher Doll Auctions (Rt. 1, Box 72; Oak Grove, MO 64075), Sally Freeman, Maureen Fukushima, Hagele Collection, Karen Heidemann, Martha Gragg, Anne Grauls, Genie Jinright, Cheryl & Wayne Koenig, Diane Kornhauser, Mary Koshuta, Liza Lineberger, Margaret Mandel, Patty Martin, Jeannie Mauldin, Mary McArthur, Marge Meisinger, A.P. Miller, Jay Minter, Lynn Motter, Shirley Puertzer, Henri Starzel, June Schultz, Paul Spencer (1414 Cloverleaf; Waco, TX 76705), Bonnie Stewart, Phyllis Teague, Pat Timmons, Turn of Century Antiques (1415 S. Broadway; Denver, CO 80220 – Photos by Moto-Photo of Denver), Marjorie Uhl, "Dutch" Voss, Jane Walker, Mary Williams, Glorya Woods.

Cover photo credit:
Frasher Doll Auctions
Rt. 1, Box 72; Oak Grove, MO 64075.

PRICES

This book is divided into "Antique" and "Modern" sections, with the older dolls in the first section and the newer dolls in the second section. Each section lists the dollmaker, type of material or name of doll alphabetically. (Example: Bye-lo or Kewpie.) This is done to try to make a quick reference for the reader. An index is provided for locating a specific doll.

The condition of the doll is the uppermost concern in pricing. An all original modern doll in excellent condition will bring a much higher price than listed in a price guide. A doll that is damaged or without original clothes, is soiled and dirty, will bring far less than the top price listed. The cost of doll repairs and cleanup has soared, and it is wise to judge the damage and estimate the cost of repairs before you attempt to sell or buy a damaged doll.

With antique dolls, the condition of the bisque, or material the head is made from, is the uppermost importance, as is the body in that it does not need repairs and is correct to the doll. Antique dolls must be clean, nicely dressed and ready to place into a collection and have no need of repair in any way for them to bring book price. An all original doll with original clothes, marked shoes and original wig will bring a lot more than any price listed. Boxes are very rare, so here again, the doll will have a higher price.

It is very important to show the "retail" price of dolls in a price guide and to try to be as accurate as possible for insurance reasons. This can be referred to as "replacement cost" as an insurance company or a postal service must have some means to appraise a damaged or stolen doll for the insuree, and the collector must have some means to judge their own collections to be able to purchase adequate amounts of insurance.

No one knows your collection better than yourself and in the end, in relation to what to pay for a doll, you must ask yourself if the doll is affordable to you and do you want it enough to pay the price. You will buy the doll, or pass it up - it is as simple as that!

Prices shown are for dolls that are clean, undamaged, well-dressed and in overall excellent condition with many prices listed for soiled, dirty, redressed dolls also.

ANTIQUE AND OLDER DOLLS

French all bisque dolls will be jointed at the necks, shoulder and hips. They have slender arms and legs, glass eyes and most have kid-lined joints. The majority of the heads have a sliced pate with a tiny cork pate. French all-bisque dolls have finely painted features with outlined lips, well tinted bisque, and feathered eyebrows. They can have molded-on shoes, high top boots with pointed toes, high top buttoned boots with four or more painted straps. They can also be barefooted or just have stockings painted onto the legs. Any French bisque should be in very good condition, not have any chips, breaks, nor should there be any hairline cracks to bring the following prices:

Swivel Neck: (Socket head.) Molded shoes or boots. 5" - $800.00; 7" - $1,000.00.

Bare Feet: 5-6" - $1,000.00; 8-9" - $1,700.00; 11" - $2,700.00.

With Jointed Elbows: 5½-6" - $2,300.00.

With Jointed Elbows and Knees: 5½-6" - $3,400.00.

S.F.B.J., UNIS, or other late French all bisques: 5-6" - $450.00; 7" - $600.00.

Lower left: 5½" French all bisque with swivel head, glass eyes, closed mouth, ball jointed at elbows, and flat bare feet. Right: 5½" all bisque Oriental, glass eyes, closed mouth, and painted-on slippers. Original. Upper: 8" all bisque by Kestner with closed mouth, glass eyes, extra joint at knees, and painted-on boots. Courtesy Frasher Doll Auctions. 5½" - $2,300.00; 5½" Oriental - $950.00; 8" - $2,500.00 up.

German-made all bisque dolls run from excellent to moderate quality. The following prices are for excellent quality and condition with no chips, cracks, breaks or hairlines. Dolls should be nicely dressed and can have molded hair or a wig. They generally have painted-on shoes and socks.

Swivel Neck, Glass Eyes: Open or closed mouth, good wig, nicely dressed, painted-on shoes and socks. 5" - $465.00; 6" - $525.00; 8" - $750.00; 10" - $950.00 up. Jointed knees or elbows: 6" - $2,000.00; 8" - $3,000.00.

Swivel Neck, Painted Eyes: Open or closed mouth, one-strap shoes and painted socks. Nice clothes and wig. 4" - $250.00; 6" - $300.00; 8" - $485.00; 10" - $700.00 up.

One-Piece Body and Head, Glass Eyes: Excellent bisque, open or closed mouth with good wig and nicely dressed. 4" - $285.00; 7" - $475.00; 9" - $600.00; 11" - $1,000.00.

One-Piece Body and Head, Painted Eyes: Open or closed mouth with good wig or molded hair and nicely dressed. 2" - $85.00; 5" - $195.00; 6" - $225.00; 8" - $300.00; 10" - $900.00.

Marked: 155, 156, 162: Smiling, closed or open/closed mouth, glass eyes and swivel head. 7" - $800.00.

Molded-on Clothes or Underwear: Jointed at shoulders only or at shoulders and hips. No cracks, chips or breaks. 4" - $165.00; 5" - $225.00; 7" - $375.00.

Marked: 100, 125, 225: (Made by Alt, Beck and Gottschalck.) Closed mouth or open/closed, sleep or inset glass eyes, chubby body and limbs and molded-on one-strap shoes with painted socks. No chips, cracks or breaks. Has one-piece body and head: 5" - $235.00; 6½" - $365.00; 8" - $500.00; 10" - $800.00.

Marked 150: (Made by Kestner or Bonn.) One-piece body and head, painted-on one strap shoes with painted socks. Glass eyes, not damaged and nicely dressed. 4" - $275.00; 6" - $385.00; 9" - $875.00.

Marked 150: With painted eyes and molded hair. 4" - $250.00; 7" - $325.00; 11" - $1,200.00.

Marked 150: With swivel neck and glass eyes. 5" - $485.00; 9" - $950.00 up.

Mold 155: Smile face, glass eyes. 5½" - $565.00. Painted eyes: 5½" - $350.00.

Molded Hair: One-piece body and head, painted eyes, painted-on shoes and socks. Excellent quality bisque and artist workmanship. No chips, cracks and nicely dressed: 5" - $200.00; 6½" - $350.00.

Marked: 886, 890: (Made by Simon and Halbig.) Or any all bisque with marks S&H. Painted-on high-top boots with four or five straps. No damage and nicely dressed. 6" - $975.00; 8" - $1,500.00.

Black or Brown All Bisque: see Black Section.

Molded-on Hat or Bonnet: All in perfect condition. 6" - $450.00 up; 8" - $600.00 up.

With Long Stockings: (To above the knees.) Glass eyes, open or closed

5" all bisque jointed at shoulders and hips only. Glass eyes, one stroke eyebrows. Painted-on white ribbed socks and high-top boots. Original wig and old clothes. Made in Germany. Courtesy Joanna Brunkin. 5" - $325.00.

mouth; jointed at neck and stockings will black, blue or green. Perfect condition: 6" - $650.00; 8" - $850.00.

Flapper: One-piece body and head, wig, painted eyes, painted-on long stockings and has thin limbs, fired-in tinted bisque, one-strap painted shoes. 6" - $365.00; 8" - $485.00. Same, but with molded hair: 6" - $325.00; 8" - $425.00. Same, but medium quality bisque and artist workmanship: 6" - $185.00; 8" - $275.00.

Marked With Maker: (S&H, JDK, A.B.G., etc.) Closed mouth, early fine quality face. 8" - $1,300.00; 11" - $1,600.00 up. Same, with open mouth and later quality bisque: 6" - $500.00; 8" - $700.00; 10" - $900.00.

Pink Bisque: 1920's and 1930's. Jointed shoulders and hips with painted features, can have molded hair or wig. All in excellent condition: 3" - $80.00; 5" - $100.00; 7" - $185.00.

Bathing Dolls: see that section.

ALL BISQUE - BABIES

All bisque babies were made in both Germany and Japan, and dolls from either country can be excellent quality or poor quality. Prices are for excellent workmanship to the painting and quality of bisque. There should be no chips, cracks, or breaks. Dressed or nude.

11" rare size all bisque "All Boy" with glass eyes, smile open/closed mouth. Incised "833-14 Germany." Courtesy Turn of Century Antiques. 11" - $1,400.00 to $1,800.00.

Germany (Jointed Necks, Shoulders and Hips): Can have glass eyes or painted eyes, wigs or painted hair. 3½" - $175.00; 6" - $285.00; 8½" - $425.00.

Germany (Jointed at Shoulders and Hips Only): Well-painted features, free-formed thumbs and many have molded bottle in hand. Some have molded-on clothes. 3½" - $95.00; 6" - $175.00.

Germany (Character Baby): Jointed shoulders and hips, molded hair, painted eyes with character face. 4" - $185.00; 6" - $300.00. Glass eyes: 4" - $325.00; 6" - $400.00. Swivel neck, glass eyes: 6" - $525.00; 10" - $1,000.00 up.

Germany (Toddler): Jointed neck, glass eyes, perfect condition. 7" - $600.00; 9" - $900.00; 11" - $1,400.00.

Japan: Of poor to medium quality. 3½-5" - $5.00-40.00. Very nice quality: 3½-5" - $15.00 to $65.00.

"Candy Babies": (Can be either German or Japanese.) Generally poorly painted with high bisque color. Were given away at candy counter with purchase. 1920's. 4" - $60.00; 6" -$80.00.

Pink Bisque Baby: Jointed at shoulders and hips, painted features and hair, bent baby legs. 1920's and 1930's. 2" - $50.00; 4" - $75.00; 8" - $135.00.

All bisque with character faces or stances were made both in Germany and Japan. The German dolls have finer bisque and workmanship of the painted features. Most character all bisque dolls have jointed shoulders only, with some having joints at the hips and a very few have swivel heads. They can have molded-on shoes or be barefooted. Prices are for dolls with no chips, cracks, hairlines or breaks.

Baby Bo Kaye: Made by Alt, Beck & Gottschalck. Marked with mold number "1394." 6-6¼" - $1,800.00.

Baby Peggy Montgomery: Made by Louis Amberg and marked with paper label. 6" - $550.00.

Bonnie Babe: Made by Georgene Averill. Has paper label. 5" - $750.00; 7" - $1,000.00.

Bye-Lo. Made J.D. Kestner. Has paper label. Jointed neck, glass eyes, solid dome. 4" - $525.00; 6" - $700.00. Jointed neck, wig, glass eyes: 5" - $700.00; 7-8" - $1,200.00. Painted eyes, molded hair and one-piece body and head: 5" - $385.00; 7-8" - $650.00.

Campbell Kids: Molded-on clothes, "Dutch" hairstyle. 5" - $265.00.

Chi Chi: Made by Orsini. 5-6" - $1,500.00.

Chin-Chin: Made by Heubach. 4½" - $325.00.

Didi: Made by Orsini. 5-6" - $1,500.00.

Googly: Glass eyes: 6" - $625.00. Painted eyes: 4" - $300.00; 6" - $485.00. Glass eyes, swivel neck: 6" - $700.00; 8" - $900.00 Jointed elbow and/or knees: 6" - $2,100.00; 7-7½" -$2,400.00. *Marked with maker (example K*R): 6½-7" - $2,400.00.

Grumpy Boy: Marked "Germany": 4" - $185.00. Marked "Japan": 4" - $85.00.

Happifats: Boy or girl. 5" - $350.00 each and up.

Hebee or Shebee: 4¼" - $300.00-$350.00.

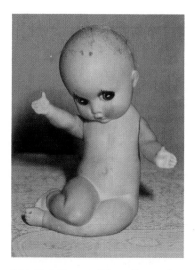

6" all bisque sitting figure has jointed shoulders and solid dome head that should have wig. Large painted "googly" (to side) eyes with heavy painted upper lashes. Unmarked, looks like a "Baby Betty Boop." Very detailed modeling. Courtesy Joanna Brunkin. 6" - $200.00 up.

3½" all bisque known as "The Medic" was made in Germany. It has bare feet, molded on clothes and the Red Cross symbol is on cap, sleeveband, and medical case. The 4½" all bisque "Happifats," made in Germany for the Horsman Doll Co., has jointed shoulders and painted-on clothes. Courtesy Frasher Doll Auctions. 3½" - $225.00; 4½" - $350.00.

Heubach: Molded hair, side glance eyes: 6½" - $775.00. Molded ribbon: 6½" - $850.00. Wigged: 7" - $925.00. **Bunny Boy or Girl figurine:** 5" - $575.00. **Little Imp:** Has hoofed feet. 6½" - $550.00. **Kestner:** Marked mold number 257, 262, etc. 10" - $900.00; 12" - $1,300.00. **Mibs:** Made by Louis Amberg. May be marked "1921" on back and have paper label with name. 3½" - $250.00; 5" - $375.00.

Mimi: Made by Orsini. 6" - $1,500.00. **Molded-on Clothes:** Made in Germany. Unjointed, painted features. 4" - $200.00; 7" - $345.00. Jointed at shoulder: 4" - $275.00; 7" - $485.00. **Orsini:** Head tilted to side, made in one piece and hands hold out dress. 2½-3" - $450.00. **Our Fairy:** Molded hair and painted eyes. 9" - $1,600.00. Wig and glass eyes: 9" - $1,900.00. **Our Mary:** Has paper label. 4½" - $475.00. **Peek-a-boo:** By Drayton. 4" - $285.00. **Peterkin:** 9" - $450.00. **Peterkin, Tommy:** Horsman. 4" - $275.00. **Quesue San Baby:** Various poses. 5" - $300.00. **Scootles:** Made by Cameo. 6" - $950.00 up. **Sonny:** Made by Averill. 5" - $850.00. **Teenie Weenie:** Made by Donahey. Painted one-piece eyebrows and features. 4½" - $225.00. **Tynie Baby:** Made by Horsman. 9" - $1,700.00. **Wide Awake Doll:** Germany. 7½" - $325.00. **Japan:** 7½" - $125.00. **Veve:** Made by Orsini. 6" - $1,600.00. **"Wrestler":** (so called.) Fat legs, painted high-top boots, glass eyes, closed or open mouth, no damage. 8" one-piece body and head - $950.00. 8" swivel neck - $1,400.00 up. Bare feet: 8" - $1,800.00 up; 11" - $2,600.00 up.

7¼" **"Wrestler"** has bent left arm, swivel neck and in original box with clothes. Open mouth with two upper teeth. Ears pierced through head. Courtesy Turn of Century Antiques. 7½-8" - $1,800.00 up; with box/wardrobe - $2,500.00.

"Knotter's" are called "Nodders" as when their heads are touched, they "nod." The reason they should correctly be called "knotters" is due to the method of stringing. The string is tied through a hole in the head, and they can also be made with cutouts on the bodies to take a tiny rod that comes out of the side of the neck. Both styles were made in Germany and Japan.

Santa Claus: 6" - $145.00.
Teddy Bear: 6" - $145.00.
Other Animals: (Rabbit, dog, cat, etc.) 3½-5" - $40.00-85.00.
Comic Characters: 3½-5" - $125.00 up.
Children/Adults: Made in Germany. 4½-5½" - $65.00-100.00.
Japan/Nippon: 4½" - $25.00; 5½" - $35.00.
Sitting Position: 8" - $300.00.

ALL BISQUE - JAPAN

All bisque dolls from Japan vary a great deal in quality. Jointed at shoulders (may have other joints). Good quality bisque and well painted with no chips or breaks. (Also see all bisque characters and nodder sections.)
Marked Nippon: 4" - $35.00; 6" - $80.00.
"Betty Boop": Style with bobbed hair, large painted eyes to side and one-piece body and head. 4" - $25.00; 7" - $45.00.
Child: With molded clothes. 4½" - $40.00; 6" - $55.00.

Comic Characters: See "All bisque - Comic Characters" section.
Occupied Japan: 3½" - $15.00; 5" - $20.00; 7" - $35.00.
Figurines: Called "Immobilies" (no joints). Children: 3" - $30.00. Teddy Bears: 3" - $60.00. Indians, Dutch, etc: 2½" - $25.00. Santa Claus: 3½" - $85.00. Adults: 5" - $85.00.
Bent Leg Baby: May or may not be jointed at hips and shoulders. See "All Bisque - Babies" sections.

ALL BISQUE - COMIC CHARACTERS

Annie Rooney: Made in Germany. 4" - $325.00.
Betty Boop: With musical instrument. Made in Japan. 3½" - $60.00 up.
Betty Boop: Fleisher Studios. Made in Japan. 3½" - $55.00 up.
Dick Tracy: Made in Germany. 4" - $265.00.
Johnny: "Call for Phillip Morris." Made in Germany. 5" - $135.00.
Max or Moritz (K star R): 5-5½", each - $1,000.00 up
Mickey Mouse: Walt Disney.

5" - $200.00 up.
Mickey Mouse: With musical instrument. $200.00 up.
Minnie Mouse: Walt Disney. $200.00 up.
Moon Mullins and Kayo: 4" - $85.00.
Orphan Annie: 3½" - $65.00. Nodder - $90.00 up.
Mr. Peanut: Made in Japan. 4" - $45.00.
Our Gang: Boys: 3½" - $75.00. Girls: 3½" - $80.00.

Popeye: 3" - $95.00 up.
Seven Dwarfs: Walt Disney. 3½" - $85.00 each.
Skeezix: 3½" - $75.00.

Skippy: 5" - $100.00.
Snow White: 5½" - $100.00. In box with Dwarfs: $800.00.

5" and 5½" "Max and Moritz" with bisque swivel heads on five-piece all bisque bodies have intaglio eyes, closed grinning mouths. They are wearing old clothes and have painted hair and shoes. Made for Kammer & Reinhardt with 19" Tete Jumeau with closed mouth. Courtesy Frasher Doll Auctions. 5-5½" - $1,000.00 up each. 19" Tete Jumeau - $4,400.00.

7½" all bisque "Mama Katzenjammer" and 8" and 4" "Uncle Ben" comic characters with painted features. Clothes are molded and painted. Made in Germany. Courtesy Frasher Doll Auctions. 7½" - $95.00; 8" - $90.00; 4" - $45.00.

ALL BISQUE - PAINTED BISQUE

Painted bisque has a layer of paint over the bisque which has not been fired. Molded hair, painted features, painted-on shoes and socks. Jointed at shoulder and hips. All in good condition with no paint chips.

Boy or Girl: 4" - $55.00; 6" - $85.00.
Baby: 4" - $70.00; 6" - $90.00.

Alt, Beck & Gottschalck was located near Ohrdruf at Nauendorf, Germany. The firm was the maker of both the "Bye-lo" baby and "Bonnie Babe" for the distributor, George Borgfeldt. The leading authorities in Germany, and now the United States, have assigned nearly all the turned-head dolls as being made by Alt, Beck & Gottschalck, with the bodies being made by Wagner & Zetzsche. It is claimed that this firm produced dolls with tinted bisque and molded hair (see that section of this book), as well as wigged turned head and shoulder head dolls and also dolls made of china. There is a vast variation to the eyebrows among these dolls, which is just one variation listed here, but "officially" almost all these dolls are being lumped under Alt, Beck & Gottschalck.

Marks:

![AB monogram mark]

A B·C

698 ✕ 9

1235 # No 10.

Babies: After 1909. Open mouth, some have pierced nostrils, bent leg baby body and are wigged. Prices will be higher if on toddler body or has flirty eyes. Allow more for toddler body. Clean, nicely dressed and with no cracks, chips or hairlines. 12-13" - $400.00; 17" - $565.00; 21" - $800.00; 25" - $1,400.00.

Child: Socket head on jointed composition body, sleep or set eyes. No crack, chips or hairlines. Clean and nicely dressed. 12" - $425.00; 14" - $450.00; 17" - $500.00; 21" - $600.00; 25" - $750.00; 31" - $1,100.00; 36" - $1,800.00; 40-42" - $2,700.00.

Character Child: Ca. 1910 on. Socket head on jointed composition body, sleep or set eyes, open mouth. Nicely dressed with good wig or molded hair with no hairlines, cracks or chips. **#1322:** 15" - $500.00; 19" - $700.00. **#1352:** 12" - $400.00; 16" - $525.00; 21" - $850.00. **#1357:** 14" - $650.00; 18" - $900.00. **#1358, 1359, 1362:** 14" - $1,800.00; 18" - $2,900.00. **#1361:** 12" - $395.00; 16" - $495.00; 21" - $750.00.

Turned Shoulder Head: Bald head or plaster pate, closed mouth, glass eyes, kid body with bisque lower arms. All in good condition with no chips, hairline and nicely dressed. Ca. 1870's and 1880's. Some have the Wagner & Zetzsche mark on head or paper label

19" turned shoulder head, glass eyes, closed mouth and on kid body with bisque lower arms. Courtesy Frasher Doll Auctions. 19" - $900.00.

inside top of body. Some mold numbers include: 639, 698, 870, 911, 916, 1044, 1123, 1127, 1234, 1235. 16" - $775.00; 20" - $900.00; 24" - $1,300.00.
Turned Shoulder Head: Same as above, but with open mouth. 16" - $485.00; 20" - $600.00; 24" - $750.00.

34" is marked "S&H (Simon & Halbig) 1079" and has jointed body and open mouth. 24" with open mouth is marked "A.B.&G." and is on fully jointed body. Made by Alt, Beck and Gottschalck. Courtesy Frasher Doll Auctions. 24" - $925.00; 34" - $1,600.00

AMBERG, LOUIS & SONS

Louis Amberg & Sons were in business from 1878 to 1930 in New York City and Cincinnati, Ohio.

Marks:

L.A. & S. 1926

AMBERG
DOLLS
THE WORLD
STANDARD
MADE
IN
U.S.A.

AMBERG
L.A. & S. 1928

Prices for dolls in perfect condition, no cracks, chips or breaks, clean and nicely dressed.

Baby Peggy (Montgomery): 1923 and 1924. Closed mouth, socket head. Mold numbers 973 or 972: 18" - $3,000.00; 22" - $3,300.00.
Baby Peggy: Shoulder head. Mold numbers 983 or 982: 18" - $3,000.00; 22" - $3,300.00.
Baby Peggy: All bisque. See "All Bisque" section.
Baby Peggy: Composition head and limbs with cloth body, painted eyes, closed mouth, molded brown short bobbed hairdo. 1923. 12" - $375.00; 16" - $575.00; 19" - $850.00.
Charlie Chaplin: 1915-1920's. Portrait head of composition with painted features, composition hands, cloth body and legs. Black suit and white shirt. Cloth tag on sleeve or inside seam of coat. 13-14" - $500.00.
Newborn Babe: Bisque head with cloth body and can have celluloid, composition or rubber hands. Lightly painted

hair, sleep eyes, closed mouth with protruding upper lip. 1914 and reissued in 1924. Marks: "L.A.&S. 1914/G45520 Germany." Some will be marked "L. Amberg and Son/886" and some will be marked "Copyright by Louis Amberg." 9-10" - $475.00; 14" - $650.00; 18" - $1,200.00.

Newborn Babe: Open mouth version. Marked "L.A.&S. 371." 9-10" - $350.00; 14" - $500.00.

Mibs: Marked "L.A.&S. 1921/Germany" and can have two different paper labels with one "Amberg Dolls/Please Love Me/I'm Mibs," and some with the same label, but does not carry the name of Amberg. Molded hair with long strand down center of forehead. Composition head and limbs with cloth body, painted eyes. All in good condition. 12" - $550.00; 16-17" - $850.00.

Mibs: All bisque. See all bisque section.

Sue (or Edwina): All composition with painted features, molded hair and with a waist that swivels on a large ball attached to the torso. Jointed shoulders, neck and hips. Molded hair has side part and swirl bangs across forehead. Marked "Amberg/Pat. Pen./ L.A.&S." 1928. 14" - $475.00

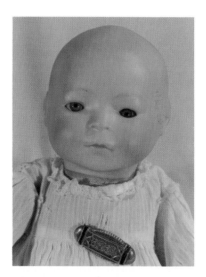

15" "Newborn Babe" with cloth body, bisque head, celluloid hands, and sleep eyes. Marked "L.A. & S. 1914 G45520 Germany." Courtesy Turn of Century Antiques. 15" - $550.00.

14" marked on head "Amberg/L.A. & S. 1928/Pat. Pend." Eyes painted straight ahead and molded hair very different than most "body twist" dolls with large ball at waist. All original clothes with tag on dress. Courtesy Mary Koshuta. 14" - $500.00.

Twist Bodies: (Tiny Tots) 1926, 1928. All composition with swivel waist made from large ball attached to torso. Boy or girl with molded hair and painted features. Tag attached to clothes: "An Amberg Doll/Body Twist/Pat. Pend. #32018." 7½"-8½" - $200.00.

Vanta Baby: Marked "Vanta Baby-Amberg." Composition head and limbs with fat legs. Cloth body, spring strung, sleep eyes, open/closed mouth with two teeth. Made to advertise Vanta baby garments. 1927. 18" - $285.00.

Vanta Baby: Same as above, but with bisque head. 22" - $1,500.00; 26" - $1,900.00.

Petite 8" all composition is marked "Pat. Applied For. L.A. & S. 1926" and has molded hair, painted features, jointed waist on large ball, and jointed shoulders. The "Campbell Kid" type is a 3½" all bisque with molded-on clothes. Courtesy Glorya Woods. 8" - $200.00; 3½" - $145.00.

ARMAND MARSEILLE

Prices are for perfect dolls with no chips, cracks, breaks or hairline cracks, and need to be clean and nicely dressed.

Armand Marseille made the majority of their dolls after the 1880's and into the 1920's, so they are some of the most often found dolls today. The factory was at Kopplesdorf, Germany. A.M. marked dolls can be of excellent to very poor quality. The finer the bisque and artist workmanship, the higher the price. This company made a great many heads for other companies also, such as George Borgfeldt, Amberg (Baby Peggy,) Hitz, Jacobs & Kassler, Otto Gans, Cuno & Otto Dressel, etc. They were marked with "A.M." or full name "Armand Marseille.

Mold #370, 326, 309, 273, 270, 375, 376, 920, 957: Kid or kidaleen bodies, open mouths. 15" - $265.00; 21" - $375.00; 26" - $600.00.

Mold #390, 266, 300, 310, (not "Googly"), 384, 391, 395: Socket head, jointed body and open mouth. 6" (closed mouth) - $250.00; 10" (crude 5-piece body) - $175.00; 10" (good quality jointed body) - $250.00; 14" - $285.00; 16" - $350.00; 18" - $425.00; 22" - $485.00; 24" - $550.00; 26" - $585.00; 28" - $675.00; 32" - $950.00. **Large Sizes Marked Just A.M.:** Jointed bodies, socket head and open mouths. 36"- $1,600.00; 38" - $1,900.00; 42" - $2,600.00.

Mold Number 1776, 1890, 1892, 1893, 1894, 1896, 1897 (which can be a shoulder head or have a socket head); **1898, 1899, 1901, 1902, 1903, 1908, 1909:** Kid or kidaleen body, open mouth. (See below for prices if on composition bodies.) 10" - $165.00; 14" - $245.00; 19" - $395.00; 23" - $425.00; 27" - $600.00.

Same as above, on composition jointed bodies: 10" - $195.00; 14" - $365.00; 19" - $525.00; 23" - $695.00; 28" - $825.00; 31" - $875.00; 35" - $1,450.00; 39" - $1,800.00.

Alma, Floradora, Mabel, Lilly, Darling, My Playmate, Sunshine, Dutchess: 1890's. Kid or kidaleen body. 10" - $185.00; 14" $235.00; 17" - $285.00; 21" - $375.00; 24" - $485.00; 29" - $825.00.

Same as above, on composition body: 15" - $300.00; 19" - $450.00; 23" - $485.00; 27" - $650.00; 30" - $900.00.

Queen Louise, Beauty, Columbia, Jubilee, Majestic, Princess, Rosebud: Kid or kidaleen body. 13" - $250.00; 17" - $325.00; 21" - $425.00; 25" - $550.00; 28" - $865.00; 32" - $1,100.00.

Same as last listing, on composition body: 15" - $300.00; 19" - $400.00; 26" - $750.00; 29" - $850.00; 32" - $985.00; 36" - $1,100.00.

Babies (infant style): Some from 1910; others from 1924. Can be on composition bodies, or have cloth bodies with curved or straight cloth legs. (Add $100.00-150.00 more for toddler babies.)

Mold #340, 341: With closed mouth (My Dream Baby, also called "Rock-A-Bye Baby.") Made for the

33" Armand Marseille, mold #390, has sleep eyes, open mouth and is on fully jointed composition body. Courtesy Gloria Anderson. 33" - $1,000.00.

Arranbee Doll Co. 6-7" - $185.00; 9" - $250.00; 12" - $365.00; 14" - $550.00; 16" - $650.00; 20" - $750.00; 24" - $1,000.00; 28" - $1,400.00.

Mold #345, 351: With open mouth. Same as above, but some will also be marked "Kiddiejoy" or "Our Pet." 7-8" - $195.00; 10" - $265.00; 14" - $550.00; 20" - $750.00; 28" - $1,400.00.

Mold #340, 341 or 345, 351: Twin puppets in basket - $850.00 up. Hand puppet, single doll - $350.00.

Mold #341, 345, 351 ("Kiddiejoy" or "Our Pet): With fired-on black or brown color. See Black section.

Babies: 1910 on. (Add $100.00-150.00 for toddler bodies.) **Mold #256, 259, 326, 327, 328, 329, 360, 750, 790, 900, 927, 971, 975, 980, 984, 985, 990, 991, 995, 996, 1321, 1333:** 9" - $250.00; 12" - $300.00; 15" - $425.00; 20" - $600.00; 23" - $685.00; 27" - $950.00. **Same mold**

numbers as above, but painted bisque: 13" - $200.00; 17" - $325.00; 20" - $450.00; 25" - $500.00

Character Babies: 1910 on. (Add $100.00-150.00 for toddler body.) Composition jointed body. Can have open mouth or open/closed mouth.

Mold #233: 9" - $300.00; 13" - $565.00; 17" - $850.00.

Mold #248: With open/closed mouth: 15" - $1,700.00. With open mouth: 15" - $800.00.

Mold #251: With open/closed mouth. 15" - $1,700.00; 17" - $1,800.00. With open mouth, 16" - $875.00.

Mold #328: 9" - $250.00; 13" - $400.00; 17" - $575.00; 21" - $750.00.

Mold #346: 16" - $600.00; 21" - $725.00; 26" - $900.00.

Mold #352: 9" - $250.00; 13" - $350.00; 17" - $525.00; 24" - $850.00.

17" smiling Armand Marseille baby, mold #352, has five-piece bent composition toddler body. Courtesy Gloria Anderson. 17" - $525.00.

Mold #355: A. Eller/3K. Closed mouth, sweet face. 11" - $765.00; 16" - $950.00.

Mold #362: 9" - $245.00; 16" - $600.00; 22" - $900.00.

Mold #410: Two rows of teeth, some are retractable. 14" - $950.00; 16" - $1,200.00.

Mold #518: 15" - $575.00; 21" - $700.00.

Mold #506a: 14" - $550.00; 19" - $850.00.

Mold #570: Open/closed mouth. 16" - $1,500.00; 20" - $1,800.00.

Mold #580: Has open/closed mouth. 18" - $1,700.00; 22" - $2,000.00.

Mold #590: Has open/closed mouth. 17" - $1,700.00; 23" - $2,200.00. Open mouth, 16" - $950.00.

Mold #970: 18" - $575.00; 22" - $800.00; 27" - $1,000.00.

Baby Gloria: Mold #240: 10" - $400.00; 14" - $600.00; 18" - $1,000.00; 24" - $1,400.00.

Baby Phyllis: Heads by Armand Marseille. Painted hair, closed mouth. 12" - $450.00; 16" - $700.00; 20" - $1,200.00.

Baby Florence: 12" - $465.00; 20" - $1,200.00.

Baby Betty: 1890's. Jointed composition child body, but few heads found on bent limb baby body. 17" - $575.00; 21" - $800.00.

Fany Baby: Mold #231 along with incised "Fany." Can be baby, toddler or child. With wig: 15" - $4,200.00; 19" - $6,800.00.

Fany Baby: Mold #230 along with incised "Fany." Molded hair. 15" - $4,500.00; 19"- $7,000.00; 25" - $8,200.00.

Melitta: Baby: 16" - $575.00; 20" - $800.00. Toddler: 20" - $1,000.00.

Character Child: 1910 on. May have wig, molded hair, glass or intaglio painted eyes and some will have fully closed mouths while others have open/closed mouth. For these prices, doll must be in excellent condition and have no damage.

Mold #250: 18" - $1,200.00.

Mold #345: 10" - $1,000.00; 18" - $2,000.00.

Mold #350: Socket head, glass eyes, closed mouth. 9" - $1,200.00; 15" - $2,200.00; 22" - $3,800.00.

Mold #360: 14" - $450.00; 18" - $800.00.

Mold #372: "Kiddiejoy." Kid body, molded hair, glass eyes. 13" - $625.00; 18" - $995.00; 22" - $1,400.00.

Mold #400: Glass eyes, socket head and closed mouth. 15" - $2,700.00; 18" - $3,300.00.

Mold #449: Painted eyes, socket head and closed mouth. 9" - $450.00; 17" - $1,100.00.

Mold #450: Socket head, glass eyes and closed mouth. 21" - $2,100.00 up.

Mold #500, 520: Molded hair, intaglio eyes, open/closed mouth. 9" - $425.00; 17" - $1,000.00; 22" - $1,600.00.

Mold #500, 520: Wigged, glass eyes and open/closed mouth. 9" - $6750.00; 17" - $1,200.00; 22" - $2,000.00.

Mold #550, 600, 640: Molded hair, painted eyes. 11" - $1,300.00; 15" - $2,100.00. Glass eyes: 12" - $1,750.00; 17" - $3,000.00; 22" $4,000.00. Closed mouth, dimples. 14" - $1,450.00.

Mold #570, 590: Open mouth: 10" - $500.00; 15" - $875.00. Open/closed mouth: 17" - $1,800.00.

Mold #700, 701, 709, 711: Glass eyes, closed mouth, sweet expression. 9" - $1,200.00; 17" - $2,900.00.

Left: 10" marked "A.M. 550/Germany." Closed mouth character child. All original on fully jointed body. Courtesy Barbara Earnshaw-Cain. 10" - $1,200.00. Right: 15" Armand Marseille, mold #590, with glass eyes, open/closed mouth, and fully jointed body. Courtesy Barbara Earnshaw-Cain. 15" - $1,700.00 up.

Mold #800, 820: Glass eyes, open/closed mouth. 18" - $2,100.00; 22" - $2,800.00.

Mold #950: Painted hair and eyes, open mouth. 10" - $400.00; 15" - $900.00.

Character with Closed Mouth Marked only "A.M.": Intaglio, 19" - $4,900.00. Glass eyes, 19" - $5,200.00.

Googly: See Googly section.

Just Me: See Googly section.

Black or Brown Dolls: See that section.

Adult Lady Dolls: 1910-1920's. Adult face with long, thin jointed limbs. Knee joint is above knee area.

Mold #300: 10" - $1,000.00.

Mold #400, 401: Closed mouth. 15" - $1,900.00; 17" - $2,400.00.

Mold #400, 401: Open mouth. 15" - $1,000.00; 17" - $1,300.00.

Painted Bisque: Mold #400, 401: 15" - $825.00; 17" $1,100.00.

Painted Bisque: Mold #242, 244, 246, etc. 15" - $325.00; 19" - $575.00; 28" - $800.00.

Biscoloid: Like painted bisque but material under paint more plastic type. **Mold #378, 966, etc.** 16" - $500.00; 18" - $750.00.

7" "Louis Bleriot," French airplane inventor and aviator, who was first to fly across the English Channel, July 25, 1909. All original with oil cloth helmet and boot tops. Flannel coat and real fur collar. Metal airplane sewn to helmet. Doll is marked "A. 10/0 M." and on five-piece papier maché body. Open mouth, painted arms and shoes. 7" - $225.00.

A. Thuillier made dolls in Paris from 1875 to 1893 and may be the maker of the dolls marked with "A.T." A.T. marked dolls can be found on wooden, jointed composition or kid bodies and can range in sizes from 14" to 30". The dolls can have closed mouths or open mouths with two rows of teeth. The following prices are for marked A.T. dolls on correct body, clean, beautiful face, dressed nicely and with no damage, such as a hairline cracks, chips or breaks.

Closed Mouth: Jointed composition body. 13" - $49,000.00 up; 19" - $56,000.00 up; 23" - $67,000.00 up. Same but with kid body, bisque lower arms. 13" - $60,000.00 up; 19" - $70,000.00 up; 23" - $80,000.00 up.

Open Mouth: Jointed composition body. 15" - $12,000.00; 19" - $16,000.00; 26" - $20,000.00.

Marks:

A.T. N°3

A N°6 T

A. 8 T.

Marked "A. 5 T." by A. Thuillier. Closed mouth and on jointed composition body with straight wrists. Courtesy Frasher Doll Auctions. 13-14" - $49,000.00 up.

12½" A. Thuillier marked "A 3 T." Large glass eyes, closed mouth and swivel head on bisque shoulder plate. Jointed kid body with bisque lower arms. Courtesy Frasher Doll Auctions. 12-14" - $60,000.00 up.

22" marked "A 10 T" on head and shoulder. Socket head on shoulder plate, kid body with bisque lower arms. Courtesy Frasher Doll Auctions. 22" - $75,000.00 up.

AVERILL, GEORGENE (MADAME HENDRON)

Georgene Averill used the business names of Madame Georgene Dolls, Averill Mfg. Co., Georgene Novelties and Madame Hendron. Averill began making dolls in 1913 and designed a great many for George Borgfeldt.

First prices are for extra clean dolls and second for dolls with chips, craze lines, dirty or soiled or with part of or none of the original clothes.

Baby Georgene or Baby Hendron: Composition/cloth and marked with name on head. 16" - $200.00, $70.00; 22" - $300.00, $100.00.

Baby Yawn: Composition with closed eyes and yawn mouth. 17" - $300.00, $100.00.

Body Twist Dolls: Composition with large ball joint at waist, painted hair and features. 15" - $400.00, $100.00.

Bonnie Babe: Bisque head; Mold #1368-140. Cloth body, open mouth/two lower teeth, molded hair and composition arms/or hands. 14" - $725.00, $350.00; 22" - $1,500.00 up, $500.00. Celluloid head: 15-16" - $500.00 up, $100.00.

Bonnie Babe: All bisque: see "All Bisque" section.

Cloth Dolls: Mask face with painted features, yarn hair, cloth body. Clean condition for first price, second for soiled dolls.

International: 12" - $95.00, $20.00; 15" - $125.00, $45.00.

Children: 15" - $165.00, $50.00; 20" - $225.00, $60.00; 25" - $275.00, $75.00.

Tear Drop Baby: One tear painted on cheek. 16" - $275.00, $65.00.

Children: Composition, cloth body. Perfect and original. 18" - $400.00; less than mint - $145.00.

Comic Characters: All cloth with mask faces and painted features. Includes Little Lulu, Nancy, Sluggo, Topsy & Eva, Tubby Tom. 1940's - 1950's. 12" - $465.00, $150.00; 14" - $550.00, $200.00.

Dolly Dingle (for Grace Drayton): All cloth. 11" - $425.00, $125.00.

Fangel, Maude Tousey: All cloth. Marked "M.T.F." on tag. 12" - $485.00, $125.00.

Dolly Record: 1922. Composition with record player in back. 26" - $600.00, $250.00.

Googly: Composition/cloth. 14" - $300.00, $85.00; 16" - $350.00, $125.00; 19" - $565.00, $165.00.

Indian, Cowboy, Sailor, Soldier: Composition/cloth, molded hair or wig, sometimes yarn hair, painted features. 14" - $300.00, $100.00.

Krazy Kat: Felt, unjointed, 1916. 14" - $300.00, $85.00. 18" - $500.00, $125.00.

Snookums: Composition/cloth. Smile face, character from George McManus's "The Newlyweds." 14" - $375.00, $125.00.

Vinyl Head, Laughing Child: With oil cloth body. 28" - $175.00, $60.00.

Whistling Dan: Sailor, cowboy, policeman, child, etc. 1925-1929. 14" - $225.00, $85.00; 16" - $285.00, $100.00.

Whistling Rufus: Black doll. 14" - $425.00, $125.00.

Whistling Dolly Dingle: 14" - $425.00, $125.00.

Babies, Infant Types: 1920's. Composition/cloth, painted hair, sleep eyes. 14-16" - $185.00, $70.00; 22-23" - $265.00, $100.00.

Left: 14" all-cloth, all original "Brownie." Mask face with painted features and floss-like hair. Courtesy Gloria Anderson. 14" - $150.00. Right: 15" cloth body "Scout" with composition shoulder, head, and limbs, painted features, and closed mouth. Marked "By Grace Corry" on shoulder plate; "Genuine Madame Hendron Doll/ made in U.S.A." stamped on cloth body. All original. Courtesy A.P. Miller. 15" - $300.00.

Bisque heads were made by Alt, Beck & Gottschalck in 1925. Celluloid heads were made in Germany, and composition heads were made in the U.S. by Cameo Doll Company. Designer of the doll was Joseph L. Kallus, owner of Cameo Doll Co.

Bisque Head: Molded hair, open mouth, glass eyes, cloth body, composition limbs, mold #1307-124. In overall good condition with no damage. 17" - $2,800.00; 20" - $3,000.00.

Celluloid Head: Same as "Bisque Head" description. 16" - $825.00.

Composition Head: Same as above description. 16" - $700.00. Light craze: 16" - $500.00. Cracks and/or chips: 16" - $200.00.

All Bisque: 4½" - $1,200.00; 6½" - $1,800.00.

BAHR & PROSCHILD

Bahr & Proschild operated at Ohrdruf, Germany from 1871 into late 1920's. They also made dolls with celluloid (1910).

Marks:

18" marked "BP/O." Made by Bahr & Proschild. Sleep eyes with open/closed mouth and two modeled upper teeth. On fully jointed body. Courtesy Frasher Doll Auctions. 18" - $4,900.00.

Character Baby: 1909 on. Bent limbs, sleep eyes, wigged and open mouths. Allow $100.00-150.00 more for toddler body. Clean, nicely dressed and no damage.

Mold #585, 586, 587, 604, 620, 624, 678, 619, 641: 14" - $550.00; 17" - $600.00; 20" - $685.00; 24" - $1,150.00.

Mold #169: 10" - $400.00; 18" - $700.00; 22" - $850.00.

Character Child: Can be on fully jointed composition body or toddler body. Ca 1910. Nicely dressed, clean and no damage. Can have molded hair or be wigged.

Mold #526, 2072, or marked B.P.: Open/closed mouth. 14" - $3,900.00; 18" - $4,900.00.

Mold # in 200 and 300 Series: Now attributed to Bahr & Proschild. Can be on French bodies. Open mouth, jointed composition bodies. Ca. 1880's.

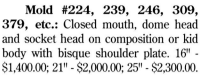

Prior to recent findings, these dolls were attributed to Kestner.
Mold #224, 239, 246, 309, 379, etc.: As described above. 14" - $700.00; 20" - $900.00; 24" - $1,200.00.
Mold #224, 239, 246, 309, 379, etc.: On kid bodies, open mouth. 18" - $500.00; 26" - $750.00; 30" - $1,200.00.

Mold #224, 239, 246, 309, 379, etc.: Closed mouth, dome head and socket head on composition or kid body with bisque shoulder plate. 16" - $1,400.00; 21" - $2,000.00; 25" - $2,300.00.
Mold #2025: Painted eyes, closed mouth. 16" - $1,200.00 up.
Mold #2072: Closed mouth, glass eyes. 22" - $4,300.00.

26" Bahr & Proschild baby marked "B.P. 585 Germany." 17" head circumference, sleep eyes, open mouth, and on five-piece bent limb baby body. Courtesy Frasher Doll Auctions. 26" - $1,200.00.

16" Bahr & Proschild baby, mold number 620. Open mouth with two teeth and on five-piece toddler body. Pristine mint old bear. Courtesy Barbara Earnshaw-Cain. 16" - $600.00 up; Bear: $1,500.00 up.

Bathing dolls can be in any position, including standing on base. They are all bisque and will have painted-on bathing costumes or be nude. They were made in Germany and some in the United States. Prices are for ones with no damage, chips or breaks, and must be clean.

Excellent quality bisque and artist workmanship: 3" - $225.00; 5-6" - $525.00; 8-9" - $800.00 up.

Fair quality of bisque and workmanship or marked Japan: 3" - $85.00; 5-6" - $125.00; 9" - $185.00.

Right: 4½" figure bathing doll on life ring marked "445 Germany" on bottom; in script on top of ring, "The girl on the buoy at Southend-on-Sea." (England resort area). 4½" - $85.00.

13" "Gertrude Ederle," first swimmer to cross the English Channel in 1926. Excellent quality to figure and swimsuit which is pebbled. Marked "R" in diamond. (Miss Ederle's record of 14 hours, 39 minutes from France to Dover, England, stood for 35 years.) Courtesy Barbara Earnshaw-Cain. 13" - $1,450.00. On the right is a close-up of the figure showing excellent detail of the features and hair.

"Belton-type" dolls are not marked or will just have a number on the head. They have a concave top to a solid uncut head with one to three holes for stringing and/or plugging in wig. The German dome heads have a full round solid uncut head, but some of these may even have one or two holes in them. This style doll was made from 1875 on, and most likely a vast amount of these dolls were actually German made, although they must be on a French body to qualify as a "Belton-type." But since these dolls are found on French bodies, it can be assumed the German heads were made for French firms.

Prices are for dolls with excellent quality bisque, bodies that are French and have a straight wrist, nicely dressed and no damage.

8" on five-piece body - $800.00; 8" on jointed body - $975.00; 13" - $1,800.00; 16" - $2,200.00; 19" - $2,600.00; 22" - $3,100.00; 25" - $3,500.00; Bru Look: 18" - $2,200.00; 22" - $3,400.00.

20" Belton type marked "204." Concave head with two holes, closed mouth with space between lips. French jointed body with straight wrists. Courtesy Frasher Doll Auctions. 20" - $2,700.00.

18" Belton type marked "10." Open/closed mouth with space between lips. French jointed body. Courtesy Barbara Earnshaw-Cain. 16" - $2,200.00; 22" - $3,100.00.

Shows true "Belton type" top of head. It can have two or three holes in concave molding. Doll was originally strung through front two holes and wig was plugged into the back hole.

BERGMANN, C.M.

Charles M. Bergmann made dolls from 1889 at both Walterhausen and Friedrichroda, Germany. Many of the Bergmann heads were made by other companies for him, such as Simon & Halbig, Kestner, Armand Marseille and others.

Marks:

C.M. BERGMANN

S. & H
C.M. BERGMANN
Walterhausen
Germany

Child: 1880's into early 1900's. On fully jointed composition bodies and open mouth. 19" - $475.00; 23" - $600.00; 29" - $950.00; 31" - $1,100.00; 39" - $2,200.00.

Character Baby: 1909 and after. Socket head on five-piece bent limb baby body. Open mouth. 10" - $350.00; 14" - $525.00; 18" - $650.00.

Mold #612 Baby: Open/closed mouth. 15" - $950.00; 19" - $1,500.00.

Lady Doll: Adult-style body with long thin arms and legs. "Flapper-style" doll. 15" - $975.00; 19" - $1,800.00; 22"- $2,200.00.

30" marked "C.M. Bergmann/Simon & Halbig." Glass eyes, open mouth and on fully jointed body. Made by Simon & Halbig for Bergmann. Courtesy Gloria Anderson. 30" - $1,000.00.

24" marked "C.M. Bergmann/Made in Germany." Sleep eyes, open mouth and on fully jointed body. Courtesy Glorya Woods. 24" - $700.00.

B.F.

The French dolls marked "B.F." were made by Ferte (Bébé Ferte), and some collectors refer to them as Bébé Française by Jumeau. They are now being attributed to Danel & Cie who also used the Bébé Française trademark. They have closed mouths and are on jointed French bodies with most having a straight wrist.

Marks:

$$B \, 6 \, F$$

Child: 14" - $2,800.00; 19" - $4,200.00; 23" - $4,600.00; 27" - $5,000.00.

This 25" doll, marked "B. 12 L.," has a closed mouth and pierced ears and is on French jointed body. Dolls marked "B.L." are referred to as "Bébé Louve," but they most likely were made by Alexandre Lefebvre, who made dolls from 1890 and by 1922 was part of S.F.B.J. 12" - $2,600.00; 20" - $3,400.00; 25" - $4,900.00; 27" - $5,300.00.

BLACK OR BROWN DOLLS

Black or brown dolls can have fired-in color or be painted bisque, composition, cloth, papier mache´ and other materials. They can range from very black to a light tan and also be a "dolly" face or have Negroid features. The quality of these dolls differ greatly and prices are based on this quality. Both the French and German made these dolls. Prices are for undamaged, nicely dressed and clean dolls.

Alabama: See Cloth Doll section.

All Bisque: Glass eyes, one-piece body and head. 4-5" - $425.00.

All Bisque: Glass eyes, swivel head. 4-5" - $800.00.

All Bisque: Painted eyes, one-piece body and head. 5" - $200.00. Swivel head: 5" - $400.00.

A.M. 341 or 351: 14" - $585.00; 17" - $950.00; 21" - $1,200.00.

A.M. 390: 12" - $400.00, 16" - $565.00; 20" - $800.00.

A.M. 390n: 15" - $550.00; 23" - $850.00.

A.M. 518, 362, 396, 513: 15"- $700.00; 21" - $1,000.00.

A.M. 451, 458 (Indians): 9" - $300.00; 12" - $450.00.

A.M. 971, 992, 995 Baby or Toddler: 9" - $265.00; 13" - $525.00; 18" - $900.00.

A.M 1894, 1897, 1912, 1914: 10" - $400.00; 16" - $700.00.

Baby Grumpy: Made by Effanbee. 10" - $250.00; 16" - $450.00. Craze, dirty: 10" - $90.00; 16" - $100.00.

Bahr & Proschild #277: Open mouth. 12" - $650.00; 16" - $850.00.

Bruckner: See Cloth Section.

Bru Jne: 18" - $30,000.00 up; 24" - $44,000.00 up.

Bru, Circle Dot or Brevette: 16" - $30,000.00 up; 20" - $38,000.00 up.

Bubbles: Made by Effanbee. 17" - $425.00; 21" - $650.00. Craze, dirty: 17" - $100.00; 20" - $200.00.

Bye-Lo: 14" - $2,900.00 up.

Candy Kid: 12" - $325.00. Craze, dirty: 12" - $145.00.

Celluloid: All celluloid (more for glass eyes.) 16" - $325.00; 19" - $600.00. Celluloid shoulder head, kid body (more for glass eyes): 16" - $265.00; 19" - $425.00.

Chase: 24" - $6,200.00; 28" - $6,900.00.

Cloth: See cloth section.

Composition: Made in Germany. 15" - $550.00; 19" - $685.00; 25" - $975.00.

E.D.: Open mouth: 17" - $2,100.00; 23" - $2,700.00.

French, Unmarked: Closed mouth, bisque head: 15" - $3,200.00; 19" - $4,300.00. Painted bisque: 15" - $975.00; 19" - $1,200.00.

French, Unmarked: Open mouth, bisque head: 10" - $500.00; 15" - $1,200.00; 22" - $1,900.00. Painted bisque: 15" - $500.00; 20" - $800.00. With Negroid features: 18" - $4,400.00.

Frozen Charlotte or Charlie: 3" - $65.00; 6" - $85.00; 8" - $100.00. Jointed shoulder: 3" - $95.00; 6" - $125.00.

German, Unmarked: Closed mouth, bisque head: 10" - $565.00; 13" - $850.00; 16" - $1,000.00. Painted bisque: 14" - $350.00; 20" - $600.00.

German, Unmarked: Open mouth, bisque head. 14" - $425.00; 17" - $575.00; 21"-$985.00. Painted bisque: 16"-$350.00; 19" - $575.00.

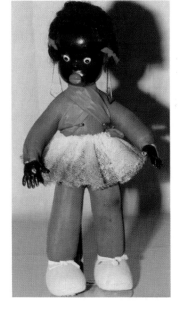

16" black celluloid head, hands and feet with wires running through limbs so they can be posed. Inset glass eyes and original clothes. Embroidered tag on foot "Made in France." 16" - $165.00.

12" "Baby Bud" has painted features and necklace and is jointed at shoulders only. Original one-piece romper; replaced shoes. Made of all composition. Courtesy Gloria Anderson. 12" - $350.00.

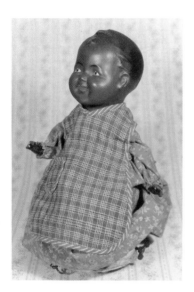 

10" painted bisque key-wound walking doll. Body is cardboard housing and mounted on two-wheeled base. Painted features, original. Courtesy Frasher Doll Auctions. 10" - $175.00.

19" black composition marked "SP" in circle "2906." Socket head on five-piece chubby toddler body. Sleep eyes. Courtesy Frasher Doll Auctions. 19" - $600.00.

18" black all composition baby with set eyes, closed mouth and bent limb baby body. Unmarked. Courtesy Frasher Doll Auctions. 18" - $425.00.

Heinrich Handwerck: Open mouth. 18" - $875.00; 22" - $1,000.00; 26" - $1,500.00.

Hanna: Made by Schoenau & Hoffmeister. 9" - $450.00; 14" - $725.00; 17" - $1,100.00.

Heubach, Gebruder Mold #7668: Wide smile mouth. 11" - $2,000.00; 13" - $2,400.00.

Heubach, Gebruder #7671: 9" - $1,000.00; 13" - $1,600.00; 16" - $2,400.00.

Heubach, Gebruder: (Sunburst mark) Boy, eyes to side. 12" - $1,900.00.

Heubach Koppelsdorf Mold #320, 339: 10" - $400.00; 13" - $500.00; 18" - $700.00; 21" - $900.00.

Heubach Koppelsdorf Mold #399: Allow more for toddler. 10" - $500.00; 14" - $600.00; 18" - $850.00. Celluloid: 14" - $265.00; 17" - $575.00.

Heubach Koppelsdorf Mold #414: 14" - $775.00; 17" - $1,300.00.

Heubach Koppelsdorf Mold #418: (Grin.) 9" - $700.00; 14" - $950.00.

Heubach Koppelsdorf Mold #463: 12" - $600.00; 16" - $950.00.

Heubach Koppelsdorf Mold #444, 451: 9" - $450.00; 13" - $800.00.

Heubach Koppelsdorf Mold #452: 10" - $375.00; 14" - $600.00.

Heubach Koppelsdorf Mold #458: 10" - $450.00; 15" - $700.00.

Heubach Koppelsdorf Mold #1900: 14" - $475.00; 17" $675.00.

Hottentot: (Kewpie) All bisque. 5" - $500.00 up. Maché: 8" - $165.00.

Kestner #134: 13-14" - $975.00.

Kestner #245, 237: Hilda. 15" - $4,600.00; 19" - $5,600.00.

Kestner: Child, no mold number. 12" - $525.00; 16" - $725.00. Five-piece body: 12" - $350.00.

Jumeau: Open mouth. 14" - $2,100.00; 17" - $2,700.00; 22" - $3,300.00.

Jumeau: Closed mouth. 14" - $4,300.00; 17" - $4,900.00; 22" - $6,300.00.

12" brown fired-in color bisque marked with incised "7." Maker unknown, possibly Jumeau. Closed mouth with rose-pink lips and jointed Jumeau-style body with straight wrists. Maybe original dress, shoes and socks. Courtesy Frasher Doll Auctions. 12" - $2,600.00.

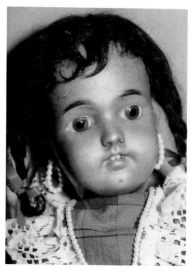

19" marked "Germany/Heinrich Handwerck/Simon & Halbig." Fired in brown color, open mouth, brown fully jointed body. Courtesy Frasher Doll Auctions. 19" - $925.00.

Jumeau: Marked "E.J." 14" - $6,800.00; 18" - $7,900.00.

K Star R: Child, no mold number. 14" - $650.00.

K Star R #100: 10" - $700.00; 14" - $1,100.00; 17" - $1,800.00.

K Star R #101: 16" - $5,300.00.

K Star R #114: 13" - $3,100.00

K Star R #116, 116a: 15" - $2,900.00; 19" - $3,400.00.

K Star R #126: Baby. 10" - $750.00; 17" - $1,100.00.

Kewpie: Composition. 12" - $300.00. Toddler, 12" - $650.00; 16" - $975.00.

KW/G (Konig & Wernicke) 18" - $650.00.

Papier Maché: Negroid features: 14" - $675.00. Others: 14" - $300.00; 24" - $500.00.

Paris Bébé: 15" - $4,200.00; 18" - $5,300.00

Recknagel: Marked "R.A." May have mold #138. 15" - $950.00; 21" - $1,900.00.

Schoenau & Hoffmeister #1909: 15" - $600.00; 19" - $800.00.

Scowling Indian: 10" - $375.00; 13" - $500.00.

Scootles: Composition: 15" - $725.00 up. Vinyl: 14" - $250.00; 19" - $425.00; 27" - $585.00.

Simon & Halbig #739: Closed mouth: 18" - $2,300.00; 21" - $3,000.00.

Simon & Halbig #939: Closed mouth: 18" - $3,200.00; 21" - $4,300.00. Open mouth: 18" - $1,800.00.

24" papier maché shoulder head, cloth body with papier maché hands and sewn on black shoes on cloth legs. Painted features, unmarked. Courtesy Frasher Doll Auctions. 24" - $350.00.

12" by Simon & Halbig, marked "S & H 939." On jointed body, open mouth and remains of original wig. Courtesy Frasher Doll Auctions. 12" - $1,200.00.

Simon & Halbig #949: Closed mouth: 18" - $2,600.00; 21" - $3,100.00. Open mouth: 18" - $1,500.00.

Simon & Halbig #1039, 1079: Open mouth: 16" - $800.00; 19" - $1,200.00.

Simon & Halbig #1302: Closed mouth, glass eyes, very character face. Black: 18" - $5,200.00. Indian: 18" - $5,300.00.

Simon & Halbig #1248: Open mouth. 14" - $750.00; 17" - $900.00.

Simon & Halbig #1358: 16" - $5,400.00; 20" - $6,500.00.

Simon & Halbig #1368: 15" - $4,200.00; 18" - $5,000.00.

S.F.B.J. #301 or 60: Open mouth. 10" - $425.00; 14" - $575.00.

S.F.B.J. #235: Open/closed mouth. 15" - $2,600.00; 17" - $2,900.00.

S.F.B.J. 34-29: Open mouth. 17" - $4,000.00 up; 23" - $5,400.00.

Sarg, Tony: Mammy Doll. Composition/cloth. 18" - $575.00. **S.P. mark:** Toddler, glass eyes, open mouth: 16" - $550.00.

Steiner, Jules: Open mouth. "A" series: 16" - $4,200.00; 19" - $4,900.00.

Steiner, Jules: Closed mouth. "A" series: 17" - $5,600.00; 21" - $6,300.00. "C" series: 17" - $5,200.00; 19" - $6,000.00.

Stockenette: Oil painted features. 18" - $2,800.00 up.

S & Q #251: 9" - $600.00; 16" - $2,100.00. **#252:** 14" - $1,700.00.

Unis #301 or 60: Open mouth. 13" - $425.00; 16" - $785.00.

Left to right: 13" "A" series Steiner, open mouth and on French fully jointed body. In foreground, 9" K star R 114 with painted features and closed mouth and five-piece body. 14" brown "Peter" mold number 101 by K star R. Painted features and fully jointed body. Courtesy Frasher Doll Auctions. 13" - $2,500.00; 9" - $2,400.00; 14" - $3,400.00 up.

BLEUETTE

The "Bleuette" doll was produced by S.F.B.J. exclusively for Gautier-Languereau and their newspaper for children, *La Semaine de Suzette.*

11½-12" "Bleuette" marked "71 Unis France 149 301" with "1½" at base of neck socket. Body marked "2" and the feet are marked "1." Sleep eyes, open mouth. Print dress and matching bloomers called "Mille Fleurs" and dates from summer 1942. Basket handbag from winter 1937-1938. Hat, shoes, and socks are authentic Gautier-Languereau accessories for "Bleuette." The deckchair goes with "Bleuette" and is called "Transatlantique," spring/summer 1938 to 1960. She holds a "Becassine" doll, an authentic "Bleuette" item from spring/ summer 1956. Courtesy Billie Boy™, Paris. 12" - $900.00.

BONNET

Pair of 9" "Dutch" Bonnet dolls. He is marked "16518" and she is "16519." Swivel heads with painted features. Cloth with wire armature to pose hands. All original. 22" Simon & Halbig with solid dome head/wig, closed mouth and set eyes. On kid body with bisque lower arms. Courtesy Frasher Doll Auctions. 9" - $765.00 each; 22" - $2,400.00.

16" Bonnet head with untinted stone bisque shoulder head with molded hair and bonnet, cloth body with bisque limbs. 8½" Bonnet shoulder head with molded-on butterfly bonnet, cloth body and bisque limbs. Courtesy Frasher Doll Auctions. 8½" - $185.00; 16" - $400.00.

BONNIE BABE

The "Bonnie Babe" was designed by Georgene Averill in 1926 with the bisque heads being made by Alt, Beck & Gottschalck and the cloth bodies made by the K & K Toy Co. (NY). The dolls were distributed by George Borgfeldt. The doll can have cloth body and legs or can have composition arms and legs.

Marks: "Copr. by Georgene Averill/Germany/1005/3652" and sometimes "1368."

Bisque head, open, crooked smile mouth: 16" - $850.00; 24" - $1,600.00.

Celluloid head: 10" - $375.00; 16" - $625.00.

All Bisque: See the All Bisque section.

Lower left: Toddler "Bonnie Babe" by Georgene Averill, mold number 1005/3652. Head circumference is 14½". Open mouth, crooked smile, sleep eyes, two lower teeth, cloth body and composition limbs. Upper: 30" Jumeau marked "1907" with open mouth. In buggy, 20" Tete Jumeau doll with open mouth. 32½" child with open mouth by Kammer & Reinhardt. Courtesy Frasher Doll Auctions. Baby - $1,400.00; "1907" - $3,600.00; Tete - $2,600.00; K star R - $1,800.00.

George Borgfeldt imported, distributed and assembled dolls in New York, and the dolls that he carried or had made ranged from bisque to composition. He had many dolls made for him in Germany.

8½" bisque head baby on five-piece papier maché bent limb baby body. Intaglio eyes, open/closed mouth with molded tongue. Brush stroke painted hair, dimple in chin. Original dress and teddy (underclothes). Marked "G 250 B/A. 7/0 M. Germany. D.R.G.M." Made for Borgfeldt by Armand Marseille. Courtesy Joanna Brunkin. 8½" - $200.00.

Marks: "G.B."

Child: Fully jointed composition body, open mouth. No damage and nicely dressed. 16" - $400.00; 19" - $525.00; 23" - $625.00; 27" - $725.00.

Baby: Five-piece bent limb baby body, open mouth. 10" - $200.00; 14" - $425.00; 17" - $600.00; 22" - $850.00; 28" - $1,500.00 up.

24" bisque head with sleep eyes and open mouth. On fully jointed body. Doll is marked "Germany/G.B." 24" - $650.00.

BOUDOIR DOLLS

Boudoir dolls are also called "Flapper" dolls and were most popular during the 1920's and early 1930's, although they were made through the 1940's. Very rarely is one of these dolls marked with the maker or country of origin, but the majority were made in the United States, France and Italy.

The most desirable Boudoir dolls are the ones from France and Italy

(Lenci, especially, see that section.) These dolls will have silk or cloth painted face mask, have an elaborate costume, and are of overall excellent quality.

The least expensive ones have a full or half-composition head, some with glass eyes, and the clothes will be stapled or glued to the body.

Boudoir Dolls: With excellent quality, finely painted features and excellent clothes. 28" - $485.00; 32" - $575.00.

Boudoir Dolls: With composition head, stapled or glued-on clothes. No damage, and original clothes. 28" - $125.00; 32" - $165.00.

Smoking Doll: Cloth: 25" - $550.00 up. Composition: 25" - $350.00; 28" - $425.00.

29" composition head with painted features and cigarette; the rest is cloth. Mohair wig and has been redressed. Courtesy Bonnie Stewart. 29" - $425.00.

Left: A beautifully modeled Boudoir doll that is all original and has an exceptional styled mohair wig. Body and limbs are cloth with free-standing thumb and stitched fingers. Head is fine papier maché with glass eyes. May have been made in France. Courtesy Bonnie Stewart. 28" - $485.00.

BRU

Bru dolls will be marked with the name Bru or Bru Jne, Bru Jne R. Some will have a circle and dot (☉) or a half circle and dot (☽). Some have paper labels - see marks. Prices are for dolls with no damage at all, very clean, and beautifully dressed.

Marks:

BEBE BRU BTE SGDG

BEBE
BREVEE SDGD
PARIS

Closed Mouth Dolls: All kid body. Bisque lower arms. 15" - $9,500.00; 17" - $11,000.00; 23" - $25,000.00; 25" - $29,000.00.

Bru Jne: Ca. 1880's. Kid over wood, wood legs, bisque lower arms. 15" - $19,000.00; 18" - $22,000.00; 21" - $25,000.00; 24" - $29,000.00; 27" - $35,000.00.

Bru Jne: All wood body. 17" - $15,000.00; 20" - $20,000.00.

Circle Dot or Half Circle: Ca. 1870's. 15" - $22,000.00; 20" - $27,000.00; 24" - $30,000.00; 27" - $34,000.00.

Brevette: Ca. 1870's. 13" - $16,000.00; 18" - $24,000.00; 23" - $29,000.00.

Open Mouth Dolls: Bru Jne R.

1890's. Jointed composition body. First price for excellent quality bisque and second for poor quality bisque. 16" - $6,500.00, $4,000.00; 19" - $7,400.00, $5,200.00; 24" - $8,300.00, $6,400.00; 29" - $10,000.00, $7,600.00.

Walker Body, Throws Kiss: 16" - $4,900.00; 20" - $6,000.00; 24" - $7,000.00.

Nursing Bru: 1878-1899. Operates by turning key in back of head. Early, excellent quality: 14" - $7,600.00; 17" - $9,500.00. Not as good quality: 14" - $5,400.00; 17" - $6,200.00. High color, late S.F.B.J. type: 14" - $2,600.00; 17" - $3,200.00.

Shoes: Marked "Bru Jne." Size 3 - $900.00 up; Size 6 - $1,100.00 up; Size 9 - $1,800.00 up.

Large 37" tall marked "Bru Jne 16." Swivel head on shoulder plate, closed mouth, kid over wood upper arms, bisque lower arms, and wooden lower legs. Courtesy Frasher Doll Auctions. 37" - $44,000.00 up

14" size 3 Bru Jne with bisque head, shoulder plate and lower arms on kid body. All original and has closed mouth. Courtesy Frasher Doll Auctions. 14" - $9,500.00.

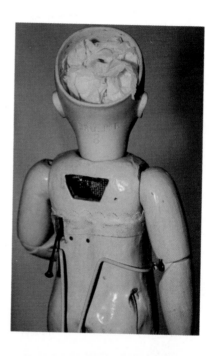

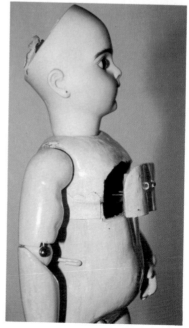

19" Bru Jne R with closed mouth and on fully jointed body. All original clothes. Has cryer strings and box, plus blows kisses and "breathes." Courtesy Barbara Earnshaw-Cain. 19" - $13,000.00.

Top right photo: Back view of 19" Bru Jne R. Lever pushes out front cutout area.

Bottom right photo: Side view shows the cutout area in front that makes dressed doll appear to "breathe-cry" when lever in back is pushed. Also raises arm to blow a kiss.

Size 0 Bébé Brevete by Casmir Bru. Marked "6/0" on head and on shoulders. 10¼". Closed mouth, all kid body and bisque lower arms. All original. Courtesy Frasher Doll Auctions. 10" - $14,000.00 up.

BYE-LO

The Bye-Lo baby was designed by Grace Storey Putnam, distributed by George Borgfeldt and the cloth bodies were made by K & K Toy Co. of NY. The bisque heads were made by Kestner, Alt, Beck & Gottschalck and others. The all bisque dolls were made by Kestner. The dolls date from 1922. Celluloid or composition hands. Prices are for undamaged, clean and nicely dressed dolls.

Marks:

1923 by
Grace S. Putnam
Made in Germany
7372145

Copy. By
Grace S. Putnam

Bye-Lo Baby
Pat. Appl'd For

All measured by head circumference.
Bisque Head: 10" - $475.00; 12"-$625.00; 15" - $1,000.00; 18" - $1,600.00.
Smiling Mouth: Bisque - very rare. 14" - $4,900.00 up.
Socket Head: Bisque head on five-piece bent limb baby body. 14" - $1,600.00; 17" - $2,000.00.
Composition Head: 10" - $345.00; 12" - $425.00; 15" - $550.00.
Painted Bisque: With cloth body, composition hands. 10" - $285.00; 13" - $425.00; 15" - $600.00.
Wood: by Schoenhut. Cloth body, wooden hands. 13" - $1,900.00.
Celluloid: All celluloid: 6" - $200.00. Celluloid head/cloth body: 10" - $425.00.
All Bisque: See All Bisque section, Characters.
Vinyl Heads: Early 1950's. Cloth/stuffed limbs. Marked "Grace Storey Putnam" on head. 16" - $300.00.

Honey Child: Bye-lo look-a-like made by Bayless Bros. & Co. in 1926. 16" - $300.00; 20" - $450.00.

Wax Bye-lo: Cloth or sateen body. 15-16" - $3,800.00.

Basket with blanket and extra clothes: Five babies in basket, bisque heads: 12" - $4,400.00 up. Composition heads: 12" - $2,700.00 up.

Fly-Lo Baby: Bisque head, cloth body, celluloid hands, glass eyes. Closed mouth, deeply molded hair. Very rare. 12" - $4,900.00; 16" - $6,000.00.

Front: Life-size Bye-Lo with 17" head circumference. Cloth body with celluloid hands. In back, sitting: an early wax head "Bye-Lo" doll with glass eyes, cloth body and marked "Grace Storey 22." In back, standing: 33" Simon & Halbig character child marked "1339 S&H/LL & S 15." Open mouth and sleep eyes. Courtesy Frasher Doll Auctions. 17" - $1,600.00; Wax - $3,000.00 up; 33" - $3,500.00.

CATTERFELDER PUPPENFABRIK

Catterfelder Puppenfabrik of Germany made dolls from 1902 until the late 1930's. The heads for their dolls were made by various German firms, including Kestner.

Marks:

CP
219
5

CP
201/40
Deponiert

Catterfelder
Puppenfabrik
45

Child: Ca. 1900's. Composition jointed body. Open mouth. **Mold #264:** Or marked "C.P." 19" - $625.00; 25" - $850.00.

Character Child: 1910 or after. Composition jointed body, closed mouth and can be boy or girl, with character face. **Mold #207:** 15" - $2,900.00. **Mold #215:** 16" - $4,000.00; 20" - $4,800.00 **Mold #219:** 15" - $3,400.00; 19" - $4,200.00.

Babies: 1909 or after. Wig or molded hair, five-piece bent limb baby body, glass or painted eyes.

Mold #262, 263, 264: 10" - $425.00; 14" - $550.00; 20" - $765.00; 24" - $1,000.00.

Mold #200, 201: 17" - $700.00.

Mold #207, 208, 209, etc.: 15" - $600.00; 20" - $825.00; 24" - $1,000.00.

Celluloid dolls date from the 1880's into the 1940's when they were made illegal in the United States because they burned or exploded if placed near an open flame or heat. Some of the makers were:

United States - Marks Bros., Irwin, Horsman, Averill, Parsons-Jackson, Celluloid Novelty Co.

France - Societe Industrielle de Celluloid (Sisoine), Petitcolin (eagle symbol), Societe Nobel Francaise (SNF in diamond), Jumeau/Unis (1950's).

Germany - Rheinische Gummi and Celluloid Fabrik Co. (turtle mark), Minerva (Buschow & Beck) (helmet symbol), E. Maar & Sohn (3 M's mark), Adelheid Nogler Innsbruck Doll Co. (animal with spread wings and a fish tail, in square), Cellba (mermaid symbol).

Prices for perfect, undamaged dolls.

All Celluloid Baby: Painted eyes: 7" - $85.00; 10" - $145.00; 14" - $185.00; 16" - $200.00; 19" - $250.00; 22" - $325.00; 26" - $450.00. Glass inset eyes: 14" - $175.00; 16" - $275.00; 19" - $345.00; 22" - $400.00.

All Celluloid Dolls: (Germany) Jointed at neck, shoulders and hips. Painted eyes: 5" - $65.00; 9" - $95.00; 12" - $145.00; 16" - $225.00; 19" - $365.00. Jointed at neck and shoulders only: 5" - $25.00; 7" - $40.00; 9" - $60.00.

All Celluloid Dolls: Same as above, but with glass eyes: 12" - $200.00; 16" - $300.00. Jointed at neck and shoulders only: 12" - $150.00.

All Celluloid Dolls: Same as above, but marked "France": 7" - $150.00; 9" - $200.00; 12" - $265.00; 19" - $425.00.

All Celluloid, Molded on Clothes: Jointed at shoulders only. 5" - $65.00; 7" - $85.00; 9" - $125.00.

12" celluloid marked with stork on head and on back with stork/Parsons & Jackson Co./Cleveland, Ohio. Spring jointed neck, shoulder and hips, painted eyes, closed mouth. Courtesy Jeannie Mauldin. 12" - $245.00.

18" and 16" all celluloid boy and baby. Painted features and jointed at neck, shoulders and hips. Both made in Germany. Courtesy Gloria Anderson. 18" - $350.00; 16" - $225.00.

All Celluloid - Black Dolls: See Black Doll section.

Celluloid Shoulder Head: Germany. Molded hair or wigged, painted eyes, open or closed mouth, kid or kidaleen bodies, cloth bodies and can have any material for arms. 14" - $185.00; 17" - $250.00; 20" - $325.00.

Celluloid Shoulder Head: Same as above, but with glass eyes: 14" - $225.00; 17" - $285.00; 20" - $385.00.

Celluloid Socket Heads: (Germany.) Glass eyes (allow more for flirty eyes). Ball-jointed body or five-piece bodies. Open or closed mouths. 15" - $365.00; 18" - $550.00; 22" - $625.00; 25" - $750.00.

Heubach Koppelsdorf Mold #399: Brown or Black. See Black section.

Kruse, Kathe: All original. 14" - $450.00; 17" - $700.00.

Kammer & Reinhardt: (K star R) Mold #700: 14"- $550.00. **Mold #701:** 12" - $800.00. **Mold #714 or 715:** 15" - $750.00. **Mold #717:** 20" - $825.00; 25" - $1,400.00. **Mold #728:** 15" - $525.00; 19" - $725.00.

Konig & Wernicke: (K&W) Toddler: 14" - $400.00; 20" - $600.00.

Japan: 5" - $30.00; 8" - $45.00; 12" - $75.00; 16" - $145.00; 19" - $250.00; 22" - $325.00; 26" - $400.00.

20" celluloid shoulder head with painted eyes and open/closed mouth. Cloth body with bisque lower arms. Unmarked, but made in Germany. 20" - $325.00.

8" and 6" all celluloid carnival dolls of early 1930's. Taller one with feathers is all original; the other, redressed. Painted features and both made in Japan. Courtesy Gloria Anderson. 6" and 8" - $60.00-70.00.

Chad Valley dolls usually will have a felt face and all velvet body that is jointed at the neck, shoulders and hips. They can have painted or glass eyes and will have a mohair wig. First prices are for those in mint condition and second price for dolls that are dirty, worn or soiled and/or do not have original clothes.

Marks: "Hygienic Toys/Made in England by/Chad Valley Co. Ltd."

"The Chad Valley Hygienic Textile/Toys/Made in England."

Child With Painted Eyes: 9" - $150.00, $45.00; 12" - $325.00, $100.00; 16" - $525.00, $200.00; 18" - $650.00, $300.00.

Child With Glass Eyes: 14" - $600.00, $150.00; 16" - $750.00, $225.00; 18" - $900.00, $400.00.

Child Representing Royal Family: (Four in set: Princess Elizabeth, Princess Margaret Rose, Prince Edward, Princess Alexandria. All four have glass eyes.) Prince Edward as Duke of Kent: 15" - $1,700.00, $600.00; as Duke of Windsor: 15" - $1,700.00, $600.00. Others: 15" - $1,400.00 up, $500.00.

Long John Silver, Captain Blye, Policeman, Train Conductor, Pirates: 20" - $900.00 up, $400.00.

Ghandi/India: 16" - $750.00 up, $350.00.

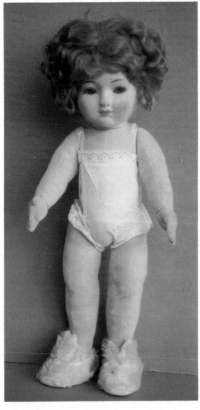

18" Chad Valley child with molded face mask, mohair wig, glass eyes and well-contoured velveteen body. Original cotton teddy and mohair slippers with felt lined ears, small pink glass eyes and cardboard inner soles. Cloth tag sewn on foot. Courtesy Margaret Mandel. 18" - $900.00 up.

Martha Jenks Chase of Pawtucket, Rhode Island began making dolls in 1893, and they are still being made my members of the family. They all have oil painted features and are made of stockenette and cloth. They will be marked "Chase Stockenette" on left leg or under the left arm. There is a paper label (often gone) on the backs with a drawn head:

The older Chase dolls are jointed at the shoulders, hips, knees and elbows where the newer dolls are jointed at the shoulders and hips with straight arms and legs. Prices are for very clean dolls with only minor wear.

Older Dolls:
Babies: 16" - $600.00; 20" - $785.00; 24" - $925.00.

Child: 13" - $485.00; 17" - $1,050.00; 21" - $2,000.00 up.

Lady: 17" - $1,900.00; 25" - $2,500.00; Life size: $2,600.00.

Man: 17" - $2,000.00; 25" - $2,600.00; Life size: $2,800.00.

Black: 24" - $6,200.00; 28" - $6,900.00.

Newer Dolls:
Babies: 14" - $185.00; 16" - $225.00; 20" - $375.00.

Child, boy or girl: 14" - $200.00; 16" - $250.00.

16" early Martha Chase baby with stockenette, oil painted head and limbs. Cloth body, jointed at shoulders, elbows, hip and knees. Original dress and bonnet. Courtesy Frasher Doll Auctions. 16" - $600.00.

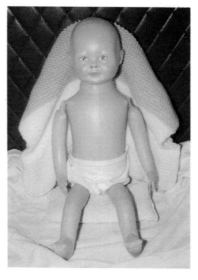

21" Chase Hospital Infant, ca. late 1940's. Pierced nostrils and ears. Oil painted on waterproof material and as heavy as life-size infant. Straight arms and legs. Courtesy Glorya Woods. 21" - $375.00.

Almost all china heads were made in Germany between 1840 and the 1900's. Most have black hair, but blondes became popular by the 1880's and by 1900, one out of every three were blonde. China dolls can be on a cloth or kid body with leather or china limbs. Generally, these heads are unmarked, but a few will have a number and/or "Germany" on the back shoulder plate. Prices are for clean dolls with no cracks, chips, or repairs on a nice body and nicely dressed.

Adelina Patti: 1860's. Center part, roll curl from forehead to back on each side of head and "spit" curls at temples and above exposed ears. 16" - $365.00; 20" - $485.00.

Bald Head/Biedermeir: Ca. 1840. Has bald head, some with top of head glazed black, takes wigs.

Excellent quality: 12" - $775.00; 16" - $950.00; 23" - $1,400.00.

Medium quality: 15" - $450.00; 22" - $1,000.00.

Glass eyes: 16" - $1,500.00; 21" - $2,400.00.

Bangs: Full across forehead, 1870's. Black hair: 14" - $250.00; 18" - $400.00; 22" - $525.00. Blondes: 15" - $275.00; 22" - $575.00; 27" - $650.00.

Brown eyes: Painted eyes, can be any hairstyle and date. 14" - $500.00; 17" - $750.00; 20" - $875.00.

Brown hair: Early hairdo with flat top or long sausage curls around head.

Left: 22" Biedermeir china with painted black spot on top of head and kid body and limbs. Right: 22" bald head Parian with original wig and clothes. She too has a black spot on top of head. Cloth body with leather arms. Courtesy Frasher Doll Auctions. 22" Biedermeir - $1,200.00; 22" Parian - $1,400.00.

Right: 18" china doll with brown eyes. White center part in flat top hairdo with sausage curls around head. Cloth body and limbs. Left: 16½" marked "DEP 154" made by Kestner. Open mouth, sleep eyes, kid body with bisque lower arms and composition lower legs. Courtesy Frasher Doll Auctions. 18" - $750.00; 16½" - $600.00.

Center part and smooth around face. 18" - $3,200.00; 22" - $4,000.00.

Bun: China with bun, braided or rolled and pulled to back of head. Usually has pink luster tint. 1830's & 1840's. Cloth body, nicely dressed and undamaged. Prices depend upon rarity of hairdo and can run from $700.00 - 3,800.00.

Early Hairdo: 7" - $825.00 up; 14" - $1,400.00 up; 17" - $1,900.00 up; 23" - $2,600.00 up.

Common Hairdo: Called "Lowbrow" or "Butterfly." Made from 1890, with most being made after 1900. Black or blonde hair. Wavy hairdo, center part with hair that comes down low on forehead. 8" - $85.00; 14" - $150.00; 17" - $225.00; 21" - $300.00; 25" - $385.00.

Child: Swivel neck, china shoulder plate and may have lower torso and limbs made of china. 12" - $2,300.00.

Child or Boy: Short black or blonde hairdo, curly with partly exposed ears. 16" - $400.00; 22" - $585.00.

22" pair of china head boys with exposed ears, cloth bodies and china limbs. Courtesy Frasher Doll Auctions. 22" - $385.00 each.

Covered Wagon: 1840's - 1870's. Hair parted in middle with flat hairstyle and has sausage-shaped curls around head. 8" - $300.00; 14" - $485.00; 18" - $600.00; 22" - $800.00.

Curly Top: 1845 - 1860's. Ringlet curls that are loose and over entire head. 18" - $700.00; 22" - $800.00.

Dolly Madison: 1870's - 1880's. Loose curly hairdo with modeled ribbon and bow in center of the top of the head. Few curls on forehead. 16" - $345.00; 19" - $500.00; 23" - $600.00; 27" - $725.00.

Early Marked China (Nurenburg, Rudustat, etc.): 14" - $2,800.00; 17" - $3,600.00.

Flat Top, Civil War: 1850 - 1870's. Black hair parted in middle, smooth on top with short curls around head. 12" - $165.00; 15" - $245.00; 18" - $295.00; 21" - $325.00; 23" - $375.00.

Glass eyes: Can have a variety of hairdos. 1840 - 1870's. 16" - $1,900.00; 19" - $2,800.00; 23" - $3,000.00.

8" and 14" "Low Brow-Butterfly" common china dolls with cloth bodies and china lower limbs. Ca. 1900-1914. Courtesy Gloria Anderson. 8" - $85.00; 14" - $150.00.

Highbrow: Like Covered Wagon, but has very high forehead, smooth on top with a center part, curls over ears and around base of neck, and has a very round face. 1860 - 1870's. 15" - $275.00; 21" - $425.00; 26" - $575.00.

Japanese: 1910 - 1920's. Can be marked or unmarked. Black or blonde and can have a "common" hairdo, or have much more adult face and hairdo. 12" - $100.00; 15" - $165.00.

Kling: Number and bell. 14" - $365.00; 17" - $475.00; 21" - $575.00.

Man or Boy: Excellent quality, early date, side part hairdo. Brown hair. 15" - $1,300.00; 17" - $2,700.00; 21" - $3,500.00.

Man or Boy: Glass eyes. 15" - $1,600.00; 17" - $3,000.00; 21" - $3,700.00.

Open Mouth: Common hairdo. 16" - $750.00; 20" - $1,000.00.

Pet Names: 1905, same as "Common" hairdo with molded shirtwaist with the name on front: "Agnes, Bertha, Daisy, Dorothy, Edith, Esther, Ethel, Florence, Helen, Mabel, Marion, Pauline. 6-7" - $115.00; 13" - $195.00; 15" - $225.00; 17" - $275.00; 19" - $325.00; 21" - $275.00; 25" - $450.00.

Pierced Ears: Can have a variety of hairstyles (ordinary hairstyle, flat top, curly, covered wagon, etc.) 15" - $575.00; 20" - $900.00.

Pierced Ears: Rare hairstyles. 16" - $975.00; 20" - $1,500.00.

Snood, Combs: Applied hair decoration. 16" - $700.00; 19" - $850.00. Grapes in hairdo: 19" - $1,600.00 up.

Spill Curls: With or without headband. Many individual curls across forehead and over shoulders. Forehead curls continued to above ears. 16" - $475.00; 19" - $650.00; 21" - $700.00.

Swivel neck: 14" - $2,600.00.

Whistle: Has whistle holes in head. 16" - $700.00; 20" - $950.00.

Wood Body: Peg wooden body, wood or china lower limbs, china head

20" "Highland Mary" china by Kling. China lower limbs and cloth body. Courtesy Turn of Century Antiques. 20" - $575.00.

18" "Spill Curl" china with molded black head band and tiny brush strokes around face. Cloth body with china lower limbs. Courtesy Frasher Doll Auctions. 18" - $625.00.

with early unusual hairdo. Fine quality and in excellent condition. 8" - $2,200.00; 12" - $2,600.00; 16" - $3,300.00. Later hairdo (such as Covered Wagon): 16" - $2,100.00.

Wood Body: Articulated with slim hips, china lower arms. 1840 - 1850's. 8" - $1,100.00; 12" - $1,500.00. Same with Covered Wagon hairdo: 8" - $975.00; 12" - $1,300.00; 16" - $1,600.00.

CLOTH DOLLS

Prices are for clean dolls with only minor scuffs or soil.

Alabama Indestructible Doll: All cloth with head molded and painted in oils, painted hair, shoes and stockings. Marked on torso or leg "Pat. Nov. 9, 1912. Ella Smith Doll Co." or "Mrs. S.S. Smith/Manufacturer and dealer/The Alabama Indestructible Doll/Roanoke, Ala./Patented Sept. 26, 1905 (or 1907)." **Child:** 19" - $2,500.00; 24" - $3,200.00.
Baby: 20" - $2,400.00.
Black Child: 19" - $3,000.00; 24" - $3,500.00.
Black Baby: 20" - $2,600.00.
Art Fabric Mills: See Printed Cloth Dolls.
Babyland: Made by E.I. Horsman from 1904 to 1920. Marked on torso or bottom of foot. Oil painted features, photographic features or printed features. With or without wig. All cloth, jointed at shoulders and hips. First price for extra clean, original dolls; second price for dolls in fair condition that show wear and have slight soil.
Oil Painted Features: 14" - $900.00, $400.00; 17" - $1,100.00, $500.00; 26" - $1,700.00, $800.00; 29" - $2,000.00, $950.00.
Black Oil Painted Features: 14" - $975.00, $450.00; 17" - $1,200.00, $550.00; 26" - $2,000.00, $950.00; 29" - $2,400.00; $1,000.00.
Photographic Face: 17" - $850.00, $400.00.
Black Photographic Face: 17" - $1,000.00, $500.00.

Printed: 18" - $600.00, $250.00; 21" - $800.00, $375.00; 26" - $950.00, $425.00.
Black printed: 18" - $800.00, $400.00; 21" - $1,000.00, $500.00; 26" - $1,200.00, $600.00.
Beecher: 1893-1910. Stuffed stockenette, painted eyes, needle sculptured features. Originated by Julia Jones Beecher of Elmira, N.Y., wife of Congregational Church pastor. Dolls made by sewing circle of church and all proceeds used for missionary work, so dolls can also be referred to as "Missionary Babies." Have looped wool hair. Extra clean: 15" - $1,400.00; 22" - $2,800.00. Slight soil and wear: 15" - $900.00; 22" - $1,500.00. Black: 15" - $1,800.00; 22" - $3,200.00.
Columbian Doll: Ca. 1890's. Sizes 15" - 29". Stamped "Columbian Doll/Manufactured by/Emma E. Adams/Oswego Centre/N.Y." After 1905-1906, the mark was "The Columbian Doll/Manufactured by/Marietta Adams Ruttan/Oswego, NY." All cloth with painted features and flesh-painted hands and feet. Stitched fingers and toes. Extra clean: 17" - $3,800.00; 21" - $4,200.00. Fair, with slight scuffs or soil: 17" - $1,800.00; 21" - $2,400.00. Columbian type: 22" - $1,200.00, $450.00.
Comic Characters: Extra clean: 15" - $450.00-500.00. Soil and wear: 15" - $165.00-200.00.
Drayton, Grace: Dolly Dingle. 1923 by Averill Mfg. Co. Cloth with printed features, marked on torso. 12" - $450.00; 16" - $650.00. **Chocolate Drop:** 1923 by Averill. Brown cloth with printed

Right: 24" papier maché with glass eyes, cloth body and leather arms, ca. 1840's. Rear: 28" Martha Chase. Cloth stockenette with oil-painted features and hair, applied ears and cotton sateen body, oil-painted limbs. 22" Rollinson doll (in black velvet). Stockenette, oil-painted features, stitched on ears, cloth body and oil-painted limbs. 21" "Philadelphia Baby" made by J.B. Sheppard Co., 1900. All cloth with oil treated shoulder head and limbs. Deeply molded eyelids, stitched fingers and toes. Center: 24" "Alabama Baby" made by Ella Smith Doll Co., ca. 1900-1924. All cloth, oil painted shoulder head and limbs, stitched fingers and painted-on boots. Courtesy Frasher Doll Auctions. 24" - $1,400.00; 28" - $1,300.00; 22" - $1,300.00; 21" - $2,700.00; 24" - $3,500.00.

features and three tuffs of yarn hair. 12" - $400.00; 16" - $600.00. **Hug Me Tight:** By Colonial Toy Mfg. Co. in 1916. One-piece printed cloth with boy standing behind girl: 12" - $275.00; 16" - $400.00. **Peek-A-Boo:** Made by Horsman in 1913-1915. All cloth with printed features: 12" - $275.00; 14" - $425.00.

Fangel, Maud Toursey: All cloth, printed features. Can have printed cloth body or plain without "undies clothes." Mitt-style hands with free-formed thumbs. Child: 9" - $350.00; 12" - $500.00; 15" - $775.00; 20" - $950.00. Baby: 14" - $600.00; 17" - $875.00.

Farnell's Alpha Toys: Marked with label on foot "Farnell's Alpha Toys/Made in England." **Child:** 15" - $450.00; 17" - $550.00. **Baby:** 14" - $465.00; 17" - $550.00. **King George VI:** 17" - $1,200.00. **Palace Guard/ Beefeater:** 17" - $725.00.

Georgene Novelities: See Averill, Georgene section.

Kamkins: Made by Louise Kampes. 1928 - 1934. Marked on head or foot, also has paper heart-shaped label on chest. All cloth with molded face mask and painted features, wigs, boy or girl. Extra clean: 20" - $1,500.00; 25" - $2,200.00. Slight wear/soil: 20" - $650.00; 25" - $800.00.

Kewpie Cuddles: See Kewpie section.

Lenci: See Lenci section.

Liberty of London Royal Dolls: Marked with cloth or paper tag. Flesh-colored cloth faces with stitched and painted features. All cloth bodies. 1939 Royal Portrait dolls are 10" and include Queen Mary, King George VI, Queen Victoria and Queen Elizabeth. Extra clean: 10" - $200.00. Slight wear/soil: 10" - $95.00. Other Historical or Coronation figures - Extra clean: 10" - $200.00. Slight wear/soil: 10" - $95.00.

Kruse, Kathe: See Kruse section.

Madame Hendron: See Averill section.

Mammy Style Black Dolls: All cloth with painted or sewn features. Ca. 1910 - 1920's. 15" - $350.00; 18" - $400.00. Ca. 1930's: 15" - $185.00.

Liberty of London Royal Dolls. Left: 10" all original "Edward VII" with painted features and glued-on beard and hair. Right: 10" all original "Mary Queen of Scots." 10" - $200.00 each.

Missionary Babies: See Beecher in this section.

Mollye: See Mollye in Modern section.

Mother's Congress Doll: Patented Nov. 1900. All cloth, printed features and hair. Mitt-style hands without formed thumbs. Designed and made by Madge Mead. Marked with cloth label "Mother's Congress Doll/Children's Favorite/Philadelphia, Pa./Pat. Nov. 6, 1900." Extra clean: 18" - $975.00 up; 23" - $1,000.00 up. Slight soil: 18" - $400.00; 23" - $475.00. Oil painted faces and hair, unidentified. Cloth body and limbs, 24" - $600.00; 29" - $900.00.

Philadelphia Baby: Also called "Sheppard Doll" as made by J.B. Sheppard in late 1890's and early 1900's. Stockenette covered body with painted cloth arms and legs. Head is modeled and painted cloth. Extra clean: 21" - $2,700.00; 26" - $3,400.00. Slight soil and wear: 21" - $900.00; 26" - $1,200.00. Very worn: 21" - $450.00; 26" - $600.00.

16" silk face mask, oil painted with floss hair in braids. Papier maché lower arms and legs with high heel feet. Eyelashes and original clothes. Tag: Au Nain Bleu 406-a-412 Rue St. Honore, Paris. (name of store purchased from). Ca. early 1930's. 16" - $300.00.

Poir, Eugenie: 1920's, made in New York and France. All cloth body with felt face and limbs or can be all felt. Painted features, majority of eyes are painted to the side, mohair wig. Stitched four fingers together with freestanding thumb. Unmarked except for paper label. Extra clean: 18" - $750.00; 25" - $1,000.00. Slight soil and wear: 18" - $350.00; 25" - $500.00. Photographic faces: (also see Babyland in this section) - Extra clean: 16" - $750.00. Slight soil and wear: 16" - $350.00.

Printed Cloth Dolls: All cloth with features and/or underwear/clothes printed. These dolls are cut and sew types **Rastus, Cream of Wheat:** 18" - $125.00. **Aunt Jemima:** Set of four dolls. $85.00 each; **Printed on underwear (Dolly Dear, Merry Marie, etc.)-** Cut: 6" - $95.00; 15" - $200.00; 18" - $250.00. Uncut: 6" - $135.00; 15" - $250.00; 18" - $325.00. **Boys and girls with printed outer clothes** - Cut: 6" - $100.00; 15" - $175.00; 18" - $245.00. Uncut: 6" - $145.00; 15" - $250.00; 18" - $325.00. **Black boy or girl:** 18" - $450.00; 22" - $600.00. **George and Martha Washington:** 1901 by Art Fabric - Cut: $450.00, set of four; Uncut: $825.00, set of four. **St. Nicholas/ Santa Claus:** Marked "Pat. Dec. 28, 1886. Made by E.S. Peck, NY." One arm stuffed with toys and other arm holds American flag. Cut: 15" - $450.00. Uncut: 15" - $800.00

Raynal: Made in France by Edouard Raynal. 1920's. Cloth body and limbs (sometimes has celluloid hands), felt mask face with painted features. Eyes painted to side. Marked on soles of shoes or will have necklace imprinted "Raynal." Original clothes generally are felt, but can have combination felt/organdy or just organdy. Extra clean: 16" - $475.00; 21" - $850.00. Slight soil and wear: 16" - $200.00; 21" - $400.00.

Russian: 1920-1930's. All cloth with stockenette hands and head. Molded face mask with painted features. Dressed in regional costumes. Marked "Made in Soviet Union." Extra clean: 10" - $85.00, 14" - $150.00. Slight soil and wear: 10" - $30.00; 14" - $75.00. **Tea Cozies:** Doll from waist up and has full skirt that is hollow to be placed over pot to keep contents warm. 17" - $145.00; 22" - $250.00; 28" - $350.00.

Rollinson Dolls: Molded cloth with painted features, head and limbs. Molded hair or wig. Designed by Gertrude F. Rollinson, made by Utley Doll Co. Marked with a stamp of doll in a diamond and printed around border "Rollinson Doll Holyoke, Ma." Molded hair, extra clean: 21" - $1,200.00 up. Molded hair slight soil and wear: 21" - $500.00. Wigged by Rollinson - Extra clean: 20" - $1,500.00 up. Wigged, slight soil and wear: 20" - $700.00.

Smith, Mrs. S.S.: See Alabama in this section.

Steiff: See Steiff section.

Walker, Izannah: Made in 1870's and 1880's. Modeled head with oil painted features. Ears are applied. Cloth body and limbs. Hands and feet are stitched and can have painted on boots. Marked "Patented Nov. 4, 1873." Brushstroke or corkscrew curls around face over ears. Fair condition: 16" - $9,500.00; 22" - $12,000.00. Very good condition: 16" - $21,000.00; 22" - $26,000.00. Two vertical curls in front of ears. Fair condition: 20"- $12,000.00; 26" - $16,000.00. Very good condition: 20" - $23,000.00; 26" - $28,000.00.

COMPOSITION DOLLS - GERMANY

Most German makers made composition-headed dolls as well as bisque and other materials. Composition dolls were made in Germany before World War I, but the majority were made in the 1920's and 1930's. They can be all composition or have a composition head with cloth body and limbs. Prices are for excellent quality and condition.

Child Doll: All composition with wig, sleep/flirty eyes, open or closed mouth and jointed composition body. Unmarked or just have numbers. 16" - $225.00; 19" - $350.00; 22" - $500.00; 25" - $625.00.

Child: Same as above, but with name of company (or initials): 16" - $265.00; 19" - $485.00; 24" - $600.00; 27" - $800.00.

Baby: All composition, open mouth. 14" - $185.00; 17" - $300.00; 19" - $400.00. Toddler: 23" - $500.00; 26" - $600.00.

Baby: Composition head and limbs with cloth body, open mouth, sleep eyes. 15" - $165.00; 19" - $285.00; 27" - $400.00.

14" German composition head toddler with glass sleep eyes, open mouth and stuffed cloth body and limbs. Stitched fingers curled except free standing index fingers. Made in Germany. Courtesy Jeannie Mauldin. 14" - $165.00.

Painted Eyes: Child: 13" - $100.00; 17" - $165.00. Baby: 15" - $135.00; 19" - $265.00.

Shoulder Head: Composition shoulder head, glass eyes, wig, open or closed mouth, cloth or kidaleen body with composition arms (full arms or lower arms only with cloth upper arms), and lower legs. May have barefeet or modeled boots. Prices for dolls in extra clean condition and nicely dressed. Unmarked.

Excellent Quality: Extremely fine modeling. 16" - $400.00; 23" - $575.00.

Average Quality: May resemble a china head doll. 14" - $185.00; 17" - $250.00; 22" - $300.00; 25" - $350.00.

Painted Hair: 10" - $185.00; 15" - $225.00; 19" - $350.00.

Swivel Neck: On composition shoulder plate. 14" - $425.00; 17" - $550.00; 23" - $700.00.

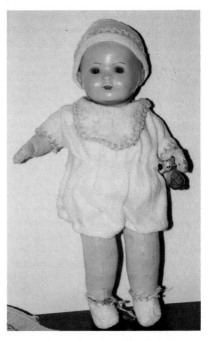

13" doll with composition head marked "135311." Glass sleep eyes, open mouth and original clothes. Cryer box in body. Straw-filled cloth body and limbs. Stitched fingers and toes. Made in Germany. Courtesy Gloria Anderson. 13" - $150.00.

DEP

Many French and German dolls bear the mark "DEP" as part of their mold marks, but the dolls referred to here are marked *only with the DEP and a size number.* They are on French bodies with some bearing a Jumeau sticker. The early 1880's DEP dolls have fine quality bisque and artist workmanship, and the later dolls of the 1890's and into the 1900's generally have fine bisque, but the color will be higher, and they will have painted lashes below the eyes with most having hair eyelashes over the eyes. The early dolls will have outlined lips where the later ones will not. Prices are for clean, undamaged and nicely dressed dolls.

Marks:

DEP
10

Open Mouth: 12" - $600.00; 15" - $850.00; 17" - $975.00; 21" - $1,200.00; 26" - $1,900.00; 32" - $2,200.00. Open mouth, very Jumeau looking, red check marks: 17" - $1,400.00; 21" - $1,800.00; 25" - $2,300.00.
Closed Mouth: 15" - $1,500.00; 19" - $2,500.00; 23" - $2,800.00; 28" - $3,200.00.
Walking, Kissing, Open Mouth: 16" - $1,100.00; 19" - $1,400.00; 23" - $1,700.00; 27" - $2,200.00.

18" French Bébé marked "DEP. 7" with red Jumeau marks. On fully jointed French body. **Courtesy Frasher Doll Auction. 18" - $1,500.00.**

31" marked "DEP-14" along with the red "Tete Jumeau" stamp. Open mouth and on French fully jointed body. Old factory-made dress. **Courtesy Frasher Doll Auctions. 31" - $2,800.00.**

35" marked "DEP-15." Sleep eyes, open mouth and on French jointed body. **Courtesy Gloria Anderson. 35" - $2,700.00.**

DOCTOR'S DOLLS

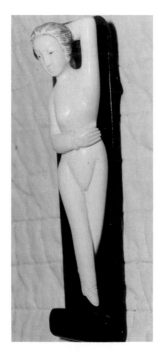

This 6" "Doctor's Doll" is an old figure (pre-1900) with bound feet and made of carved ivory. These dolls came in many sizes and positions as well as quality. The doll was sent to the doctor with a servant and a stick was used to point to area of ailment. Then the doctor prescribed medication for the servant's master. Later figures were made of bone rather than ivory. Pre-1900: 6" - $165.00; 12" - $400.00; standing, 7" - $185.00. Bone: 6" - $85.00; 12" - $200.00; standing, 7" - $90.00.

DOLL HOUSE DOLLS

Doll House Man or Lady: With molded hair/wig and painted eyes. 6-7" - $150.00 - $165.00.

Man or Woman with Glass Eyes/Wigs: 6-7" - $325.00 - $400.00.

Man or Woman with Molded Hair, Glass Eyes: 6-7" - $385.00.

Grandparents, Old People, or Molded-on Hats: 6-7" - $225.00.

Military Men, Original: 6-7" - $585.00 up.

Black Man or Women: Molded hair, all original. 6-7" - $400.00.

Swivel Neck: Wig or molded hair. 6-7" - $800.00.

6" and 7" doll house man and woman. Bisque shoulder heads and limbs with cloth bodies. 11" china head boy with center part and exposed ears. Cloth body with china lower limbs. Courtesy Turn of Century Antiques. 6" - $150.00; 7" - $165.00; 11" - $150.00 up.

Door of Hope dolls were created at the Door of Hope Mission in China from 1901 into 1910's. They have cloth bodies and head and limbs are carved of wood. The carvers came from Ning-Po Province. They usually are between 8-13" tall, and if marked, it will have label "Made in China."

Manchu: Mandarin man or woman - $450.00 up.

Mother and Baby: $500.00.

Adult: $425.00 up.

Child: $465.00 up.

11" "Door of Hope" man. Cloth body and carved wood head and limbs. All original. Unusual side part painted hair. Courtesy Barbara Earnshaw-Cain. 11" - $345.00.

DRESSEL, CUNO & OTTO

Cuno & Otto Dressel operated in Sonneberg, Thuringia, Germany and were sons of the founder. Although the firm was in business in 1700, they are not listed as dollmakers until 1873. They produced dolls with bisque heads, composition over wax, and can be on cloth, kid, or jointed composition body. Some of their heads were made for them by other German firms, such as Simon & Halbig, Heubach, etc. They registered the trademark for "Jutta" in 1906 and by 1911 were also making celluloid dolls. Prices are for undamaged, clean and nicely dressed dolls.

Babies: Marked "C.O.D." but without the word "Jutta." 12" - $365.00. 14" - $495.00; 19" - $625.00; 23" - $765.00.

Child: On jointed composition body, with open mouth. 16" - $365.00; 19" - $425.00; 23" - $500.00; 28" - $750.00; 33" - $1,000.00.

Marks:

C.O.D.

C.O.D 49 D.E.P.

Made in Germany

Child: On kid, jointed body, open mouth. 16" - $325.00; 20" - $425.00; 25" - $500.00.

Jutta: 1910-1922. **Baby:** Open mouth and five-piece bent limb body. 16" - $625.00; 19" - $800.00; 23" - $1,100.00; 25" - $1,300.00.

Toddler Body: 16" - $850.00; 19" - $1,000.00; 23" - $1,300.00; 27" - $1,900.00.

Child: Marked with "Jutta" or with S&H #1914, #1348, #1349, etc.: 15" - $600.00; 19" - $700.00; 23" - $975.00; 25" - $1,050.00; 30" - $1,200.00.

Lady Doll: 1920's with adult face, closed mouth and on five-piece composition body with thin limbs and high heel feet. Mark #1469. 16" - $4,300.00; 18" - $5,200.00.

Character Dolls: 1909 and after. Closed mouth, painted eyes, molded hair or wig. 10" - $800.00; 14" - $2,400.00; 18" - $2,900.00.

Character Dolls: Same as above, but with glass eyes. 14" - $2,400.00; 16" - $2,900.00; 18" - $3,200.00; 24" - $3,500.00.

Composition: Shoulder head of 1870's, glass or painted eyes, molded hair or wig and on cloth body with composition limbs with molded-on boots. Will be marked with Holz-Masse:

With wig: 16" - $375.00; 19" - $425.00; 23" - $525.00. Molded hair: 17" - $385.00; 24" - $485.00.

Portrait Dolls: 1896. Such as Uncle Sam, Farmer, Admiral Dewey, Admiral Byrd, Old Rip, Witch, etc. Portrait bisque head, glass eyes, composition body. Some will be marked with a "D" or "S." Heads made for Dressel by Simon & Halbig. Prices for clean, undamaged and originally dressed. **Military dolls:** 9" - $900.00; 13" - $1,800.00; 16" - $2,500.00. **Old Rip or Witch:** 9" - $750.00; 13" - $1,600.00; 16" - $1,900.00. **Uncle Sam:** 9" - $825.00; 13" - $1,675.00; 16" - $2,250.00.

19" marked "1349 Dressel S&H." Called "Jutta" and some will also be marked with the name. Open mouth, sleep eyes and on fully jointed composition body. Courtesy Frasher Doll Auctions. 19" - $625.00.

22" marked "✝ 1912.4." Made by Cuno & Otto Dressel. On fully jointed body. Sleep eyes and open mouth. Courtesy Frasher Doll Auctions. 22" - $465.00.

20" boy is marked "Jutta/Baby," made by Cuno & Otto Dressel and the girl is marked "K Star R 126," by Kammer & Reinhardt. Both are on jointed toddler bodies, sleep eyes and open mouths. Courtesy Glorya Woods. Boy - $1,000.00; Girl - $1,200.00.

Left: 19" marked "C.O.D. 9 G Dep." Shoulder head with open mouth and on kid body with bisque lower arms. Right: Marked "Dep. 154." Made by Kestner. Kid body with bisque lower arms. Baby is 15" and marked "151." Made by Hertel, Schwab & Co. Courtesy Frasher Doll Auctions. 19" - $425.00; "154" - $625.00; 15" - $550.00.

E. Denamur of Paris made dolls from 1885 to 1898. The E.D. marked dolls seem to be accepted as being made by Denamur, but they could have been made by E. Dumont, Paris. Composition and wood jointed bodies. Prices are for excellent quality bisque, no damage and nicely dressed.

Marks:

Closed Mouth: 17" - $2,600.00; 17" - $2,800.00; 23" - $3,500.00; 27" - $4,200.00.

Open Mouth: 15" - $1,500.00; 18" - $1,800.00; 22" - $2,400.00.

Black: Open mouth. 19" - $2,300.00; 25" - $2,900.00.

15" marked "E.D." with closed mouth, paperweight eyes and on French jointed body. Courtesy Barbara Earnshaw-Cain. 15" - $2,600.00.

22" closed mouth marked "E. 8 D." Fully jointed French body. Courtesy Jay Minter. 22" - $3,400.00.

EDEN BÉBÉ

Fleischmann & Bloedel of Bavaria, Furth and Oaris founded in 1873 and were making dolls in Paris by 1890, then became a part of S.F.B.J. in 1899. Dolls have composition jointed bodies and can have open or closed mouths.

Prices are for dolls with excellent color and quality bisque, no damage and nicely dressed.

Marks:

EDEN BÉBÉ PARIS

Closed Mouth: Pale bisque. 16" - $2,500.00; 20" - $3,000.00; 24" - $3,600.00; 27" - $3,900.00.
Closed Mouth: High color bisque. 16" - $1,700.00; 20" - $2,000.00; 24" - $2,300.00; 27" - $2,700.00.
Open Mouth: 16" - $1,500.00; 20" - $2,300.00; 24" - $2,800.00; 27" - $3,100.00.

Walking Kissing Doll: Jointed body with walker mechanism, head turns and one arm throws a kiss. Heads by Simon & Halbig using mold #1039 (and others). Bodies assembled by Fleischmann & Bloedel. Price for perfect, working doll. 23" - $1,400.00 up.

22" closed mouth Eden Bébé marked "Paris 8." The closed mouth versions of the Eden Bébé have a remarkable likeness to the dolls marked "F.G." and can be excellent quality or rather poor quality. Original clothes except earrings. Courtesy Gloria Anderson. 22" - $3,400.00.

Right: 20" marked "Eden Bébé/Paris 7." Closed mouth and on Jumeau marked body and is all original. Left: 21" "A" series Jules Steiner with closed mouth and on marked Steiner body. Original dress has been removed to show original underclothing. Courtesy Frasher Doll Auctions. 20" - $3,000.00; 21" - $5,600.00.

ELLIS, JOEL

Joel Ellis made dolls in Springfield, Vermont in 1873 and 1874 under the name Co-operative Manufacturing Co. All wood jointed body have tenon and mortise joints (not jointing of legs to torso, arms are jointed in same manner).

The hands and feet are made of pewter and has molded hair and painted features.
Doll in fair condition: Does not need to be dressed. 12" - $500.00. Excellent condition: 12" - $900.00; 15" - $1,100.00; 18" - $1,800.00.

Springfield Wooden Doll: It must be noted that dolls similar to the Joel Ellis ones were made in Springfield, Vt. also by Joint Doll Co. and D.M. Smith & Co. They are very much like the Joel Ellis except when standing the knee joint will be flush with the method of jointing not showing. The hips are cut out with the leg tops cut to fit the opening, and the detail of the hands are not as well done.

16" Joel Ellis "Springfield" with metal hands and feet. Fully articulated and molded hair with painted features. 16" - $1,200.00.

FASHION DOLL, FRENCH

These "adult" style dolls were made by a number of French firms from about 1860 into 1930's. Many will be marked only with a number or have a stamp on the body, although some of the stamps/labels may be the store where they were sold from and not the maker. The most available fashion doll seems to be marked F.G. dolls. Price are for dolls in perfect condition with no cracks, chips, or repairs and in beautiful old or newer clothes made of appropriate age materials.

Articulated Wood: Or blown kid bodies and limbs. Some have bisque lower arms. 16" - $3,800.00; 20" - $4,800.00.

Articulated: With bisque lower legs and arms with excellent modeling detail. 15" - $4,600.00 up; 21" - $5,800.00 up.

Marked "Bru": (Also see Smiling Mona Lisa in this section.) Kid body, fully jointed wood arms. 14" - $11,000.00; 18" - $16,000.00.

Marked "Huret": Bisque or china glazed shoulder head, kid body with bisque lower arms. Painted eyes: 14" - $6,800.00; 17" - $8,800.00. Glass eyes: 14" - $7,400.00; 17" - $9,000.00 up. Wood body: 16" - $8,800.00 up; 20" - $14,000.00 up.

Huret Child: 18" - $24,000.00; 24" - $30,000.00.

11" marked "A" called Bru fashion. Smiling closed mouth, glass eyes and all kid body with separately stitched fingers. Courtesy Frasher Doll Auctions. 11" - $2,700.00.

Marked "Rohmer": Bisque or china glazed shoulder head (can be jointed). Kid body with bisque lower arms (or china). Glass eyes: 16" - $7,500.00; 19" - $13,500.00; Painted eyes: 16" - $5,700.00; 19" - $12,000.00. Wood body: 16" - $8,000.00; 19" - $14,000.00.

Marked "Jumeau": Will have number on head and stamped body. Portrait-style head: 15" - $4,400.00; 17" - $6,200.00; 23" - $7,000.00; 26" - $8,000.00. Wood body: 18" - $9,000.00 up; 24" - $12,000.00 up.

Marked "F.G.": All kid body, one-piece shoulder and head, glass eyes. 12" - $950.00; 14" - $1,300.00; 17" - $1,800.00. Painted eyes: 12" - $950.00; 14" - $1,100.00.

Marked "F.G.": All kid body (or bisque lower arms), swivel head on bisque shoulder plate. 15" - $1,700.00; 18" - $2,400.00; 22" - $3,000.00.

Marked "F.G.": Gesland cloth-covered body with bisque lower arms and legs. 15" - $2,700.00; 18" - $3,400.00; 23" - $4,000.00; 26" - $4,600.00.

Marked "F.G.": Gesland cloth-covered body with composition or papier maché lower arms and legs. 15" - $2,450.00; 18" - $3,250.00; 23" - $3,750.00; 26" - $4,450.00.

Smiling "Mona Lisa": Now being referred to as being made by Bru. Kid body with leather lower arms, stitched fingers or bisque lower arms.

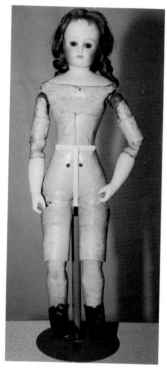

15" signed "Rohmer." Oval stamp on torso, cobalt blue glass eyes, swivel head with white bisque on bisque shoulder plate. Wood pin jointed upper arms partly covered by kid and bisque lower arms with cupped hands. Blown kid upper legs and molded kid over wood lower legs with molded calves. Courtesy Barbara Earnshaw-Cain. 15" - $8,500.00.

Marked with letter (example: E, B, D, etc.) 14" - $2,800.00; 18" - $4,000.00; 22" - $4,600.00; 26" - $5,400.00; 29" - $7,200.00.

Unmarked with Numbers Only: With one-piece head and shoulder. Extremely fine quality bisque, undamaged. 12" - $1,400.00; 14" - $1,650.00; 22" - $2,200.00; 18" - $2,600.00.

Unmarked with numbers only: Swivel neck with bisque shoulder plate. Extremely fine quality bisque and undamaged. 14" - $3,200.00; 16" - $3,800.00; 18" - $4,400.00; 20" - $4,800.00.

Unmarked: Medium to fair quality. One-piece head and shoulder: 12" - $700.00; 15" - $850.00-1,000.00. Swivel head on bisque shoulder plate: 15" - $1,000.00; 19" - $1,700.00 up.

Marked E.B. (E. Barrois): Glass eyes: 16" - $3,200.00; 20" - $4,700.00. Painted eyes: 17" - $3,200.00; 21" - $3,900.00.

Marked Simone: Glass eyes: 20" - $5,000.00; 24" - $6,000.00.

16" early French Fashion doll with swivel neck on bisque shoulder plate. All kid body. Early cobalt blue eyes. Courtesy Turn of Century Antiques. 16" - $2,600.00.

20" Simone French Fashion. Bisque swivel head on bisque shoulder plate, gusset jointed kid body with long bisque arms. Courtesy Frasher Doll Auctions. 20" - $5,000.00.

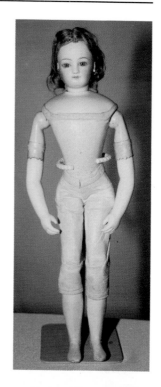

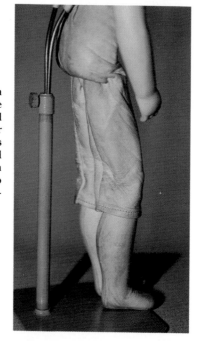

14" marked "E.B. Fashion." Swivel head on bisque shoulder plate. Made by Eugene Barrois, Paris. Top right photo: note kid covered metal upper arms and bisque lower arms. Bottom right photo: Kid baggy pants over wood upper legs. Kid very tightly molded over wood lower legs. Modeled calf with seam up back of legs. Peg hinged at hips so legs will move. Courtesy Barbara Earnshaw-Cain. Price not available.

F. Gaultier (earlier spelled Gauthier) is the accepted maker of the F.G. marked dolls. These dolls are often found on the cloth covered or all composition bodies that are marked "Gesland." The Gesland firm was operated by two brothers with one of them having the initial "F" (1887-1900).

Marks:

F. 8 G.
(block letter mark)

Child with Closed Mouth: Excellent quality bisque, no damage and nicely dressed. 15" - $2,700.00; 17" - $3,000.00; 20" - $3,600.00; 23" - $3,800.00; 27" - $4,700.00.

Child with Closed Mouth: Same as above, but with high face color, no damage and nicely dressed. 15" - $1,900.00; 17" - $2,100.00; 20" - $2,300.00; 23" - $2,700.00; 27" - $3,300.00.

Child with Open Mouth: Excellent quality bisque, no damage and nicely dressed. 15" - $1,800.00; 17" - $2,100.00; 20" - $2,900.00; 23" - $3,100.00; 27" - $3,700.00.

Child with Open Mouth: With high face color, very dark lips, no damage and nicely dressed. 15" - $775.00; 17" - $950.00; 20" - $1,200.00; 23" - $1,700.00; 27" - $2,200.00.

Marked "F.G. Fashion": See Fashion section.

Child on Marked Gesland Body: Bisque head on stockenette over wire frame body with composition limbs. Closed mouth: 17" - $4,400.00; 20" - $4,700.00; 24" - $5,200.00. Open mouth: 17" - $2,900.00; 21" - $3,500.00; 26" - $4,300.00.

Block Letter (so called) F.G. Child: Closed mouth, chunky composition body, excellent quality and condition. 17" - $3,700.00; 21" - $4,300.00; 26" - $5,400.00.

Block Letter (so called) F.G. Child: Closed mouth, bisque swivel head on bisque shoulder plate with gusseted kid body and bisque lower arms. 17" - $3,700.00; 21" - $4,300.00; 26" - $5,400.00.

13" very early marked F.G. with closed mouth, white bisque, kid body, and beautiful bisque lower arms. Swivel head on bisque shoulder plate. Courtesy Barbara Earnshaw-Cain. Price unavailable.

28" marked "F.G." with very large paperweight eyes and heavy feathered eyebrows. Closed mouth and on French jointed body. Courtesy Barbara Earnshaw-Cain. 28" - $6,500.00.

Right: 30" marked "F.G. 11." Closed mouth and on Gesland body of a jointed metal framework covered with stockenette, then padded for a soft effect. Lower arms and shoulder plate made of hardwood. Body stamped "Bébé E. Gesland. BREV. S.G.D.G." and the address of the firm. She is holding an 8" Gebruder Heubach with intaglio eyes and closed mouth, marked "7602." Courtesy Frasher Doll Auctions. 30" - $5,000.00; 8" - $800.00.

A variety of French doll makers produced unmarked dolls from 1880's into the 1920's. These dolls may only have a head size number or be marked "Paris" or "France." Many of the accepted French dolls that have a number are now being attributed to German makers and it will be questionable for some time.

Unmarked French BéBé: Closed or open/closed mouth, paperweight eyes, excellent quality bisque and artist painting on a French body. Prices are for clean, undamaged and nicely dressed dolls.

Early Desirable, Very French-style Face: 15" - $12,000.00; 19" - $17,000.00; 23" - $22,000.00; 26" - $25,000.00 up.

Jumeau Style Face: 14" - $2,800.00; 17" - $3,000.00; 23" - $4,200.00; 27" - $5,200.00.

Excellent Quality: 16" - $3,900.00; 21" - $4,900.00; 27" - $7,400.00.

Medium Quality: May have poor painting and/or blotches to skin tones: 16" - $1,400.00; 21" - $1,900.00; 26" - $2,400.00.

Open Mouth: 1890's and later. Will be on French body. Excellent quality: 15" - $1,700.00; 18" - $2,000.00; 22" - $2,500.00; 25" - $3,100.00.

Open Mouth: 1920's with high face color and may have five-piece papier maché body. 16" - $650.00; 20" - $800.00; 24" - $1,000.00.

18" unmarked French mystery doll. Closed mouth, white bisque and on Jumeau stamped body with straight wrist. May be very early Portrait Jumeau. Courtesy Frasher Doll Auctions. 18" - **$4,200.00 up.**

Left: 16½" beautiful unmarked doll with the number on head. Closed mouth and jointed body. Original chemise. Right: 14½" marked "J. Steiner/SGDG Paris Fire A 7." Closed mouth and body stamped "LePitit Parisien BEBE STEINER." Courtesy Frasher Doll Auctions. 16½" - $3,900.00; 14½" - $3,500.00.

27" marked "Paris 12." Has "Long Face" modeling, full cheeks, closed mouth and early Jumeau straight wrist body. 19" marked "ROD." Closed mouth and on French jointed body with straight wrists. Courtesy Frasher Doll Auctions. 27" - $5,000.00; 19" - $3,200.00.

20" marked "F.1." A marque-style doll; maker unknown. Closed mouth, painted eyes, cloth body with ceramic-style curved lower arms, shoes and legs to mid-thigh, painted black stock-ings. Original dress, ca. 1920's. Courtesy Frasher Doll Auctions. 20" - $3,900.00.

28" French mystery doll marked "J.D. Lilas (in shield) 10." Closed mouth and on French jointed body. Courtesy Frasher Doll Auctions. 28" - $16,000.00.

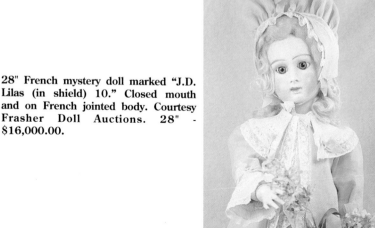

25" unmarked French with very pale bisque, almond-cut eyes, closed mouth and French jointed body with straight wrist. Smaller doll is 14½" with head marked "136" and her French jointed body with straight wrists is marked "Le Petit Parisien Bebe Steiner." Courtesy Frasher Doll Auctions. 25" - $15,000.00 up; 14½" - $2,800.00 up.

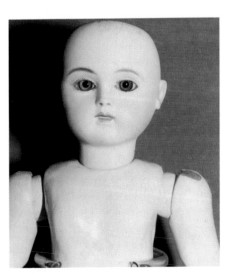

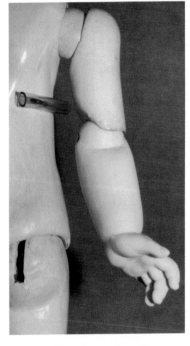

20" Belton type with paperweight eyes, closed open/closed mouth with space between lips. Marked "9J." French body is wood and composition with bisque lower arms. Right photo shows details of the doll's beautiful bisque straight wrist. Courtesy Millie Chappelle. 20" - $5,200.00.

Freundlich Novelty Company operated in New York in 1923. Most have a cardboard tag and the doll will be unmarked or may have the doll's name on the head, but no maker's name.

Baby Sandy: 1939-1942. All composition with molded hair, sleep or painted eyes. Marked "Baby Sandy" on head. Excellent condition with no cracks, craze or chips, original or appropriate clothes: 8" - $165.00; 12" - $200.00; 16" - $300.00; 19" - $500.00. With light crazing, but clean and may be redressed: 8" - $85.00; 12" - $100.00; 16" - $125.00; 19" - $200.00.

General Douglas MacArthur: Ca. 1942. Portrait doll of all composition, painted features and molded hat. Jointed shoulders and hips. Excellent condition and original. 16" - $250.00; 18" - $285.00. Light craze, clothes dirty: 16" - $100.00; 18" - $125.00.

Military Dolls: Ca. 1942 and on. All composition with painted features, molded-on hats and can be a woman or man (W.A.V.E, W.A.A.C., sailor, Marine, etc.) In excellent condition, original and no crazing: 16" - $200.00. Light craze and clothes in fair condition: 16" - $95.00.

21" composition head, cloth hands, body and legs. Painted features; all original. Tagged "The Ventriloquist Man/ Dummy Dan/ Ralph A. Freundlich." Courtesy Bonnie Stewart. 21" - $285.00 up.

FROZEN CHARLOTTE

Frozen Charlotte and Charlie figures can be china, partly china (such as hair and boots), stone bisque or fine porcelain bisque. They can have molded hair, painted bald heads or take wigs. The majority have no joints with hands extended and legs separate (some are together) and unjointed. They generally come without clothes and they can have painted-on boots, shoes and socks or be barefooted.

It must be noted that in 1976 a large amount of the 15½-16" "Charlie" figures were reproduced in Germany and are excellent quality. It is almost impossible to tell these are reproductions.

Prices are for doll figures without any damage. More must be allowed for any with unusual hairdos, an early face or molded eyelids or molded-on clothes.

All China: Glazed with black or blonde hair, excellent quality of painting and unjointed. 2" - $55.00; 5" - $95.00; 9" - $175.00. Bald head with wig: 6" - $145.00; 8" - $195.00; 10" - $275.00. **Charlie:** Molded hair, flesh tones to neck and head. 14" - $375.00; 17" - $525.00.

Untinted Bisque (Parian): Molded hair, unjointed. 4" - $140.00; 7" - $175.00.

FROZEN CHARLOTTE

Untinted Bisque: Molded hair, jointed at shoulders. 4" - $160.00; 7" - $250.00.

Stone Bisque: Unjointed, molded hair, medium to excellent quality of painting. 4" - $50.00; 8" - $70.00.

Black Charlotte or Charlie: Unjointed, no damage. 3" - $75.00; 5" - $100.00; 7" - $150.00. Jointed at shoulders: 4" - $125.00; 7" - $175.00.

Molded-on Clothes or Bonnet: Unjointed, no damage and medium to excellent quality. 6" - $400.00; 8" - $500.00.

Dressed: In original clothes. Unjointed Charlotte or Charlie. No damage and in overall excellent condition. 5" - $115.00; 7" - $150.00.

Jointed at Shoulder: Original clothes and no damage. 6" - $165.00; 8" - $265.00.

Molded-on, Painted Boots: Unjointed, no damage. 5" - $135.00; 7" - $200.00. Jointed at shoulders: 5" - $175.00; 7" - $300.00.

FULPER

Fulper Pottery Co. of Flemington, N.J. made dolls from 1918-1921. They made children and babies and used composition and kid bodies.

Marks:

Made in U.S.A.

18½" marked "Fulper Made in U.S.A." Bisque head, sleep eyes, open mouth and on fully jointed toddler body. 24" Jumeau type marked "S.F.B.J. Paris" and on Jumeau marked body. Open mouth. Courtesy Frasher Doll Auctions. 18½" - $600.00; 24" - $2,200.00.

Child: Fair to medium quality bisque head painting. No damage, nicely dressed. Composition body, open mouth: 15" - $450.00; 17" - $565.00; 21" - $675.00. Kid body, open mouth: 15" - $400.00; 17" - $500.00; 21" - $625.00.

Child: Poor quality (white chalky look, may have crooked mouth and be poorly painted.) Composition body: 16" - $350.00; 21" - $450.00. Kid body: 16" - $200.00; 21" - $365.00.

Baby: Bent limb body. Fair to medium quality bisque, open mouth, no damage and dressed well. Good artist work on features. 19" - $650.00; 26" - $1,000.00.

Toddler: Same as baby but has toddler jointed or straight leg body. 17" - $700.00; 26" - $1,200.00.

Baby: Poor quality bisque and painting. 17" - $225.00; 26" - $475.00.

Toddler: Poor quality bisque and painting. 17" - $345.00; 26" - $700.00.

GANS & SEYFORTH

Dolls with the "G.S." or "G & S" were made by Gans & Seyforth of Germany who made dolls from 1909 into the 1930's. Some dolls will be marked with the full name.

Child: Open mouth, composition body. Good quality bisque, no damage and nicely dressed. 14" - $295.00; 17" - $350.00; 21" - $485.00; 27" - $700.00.

Baby: Bent limb baby body, in perfect condition and nicely dressed. 16" - $425.00; 19" - $600.00.; 23" - $700.00; 26" - $850.00. (Add more for toddler body.)

GERMAN DOLLS, MAKER UNKNOWN

Some of these unmarked dolls will have a mold number and/or a head size number and some may have the mark "Germany."

Closed Mouth Child: 1880-1890's. Composition jointed body, no damage and nicely dressed. 12" - $1,200.00; 15" - $1,500.00; 20" - $2,100.00; 24" - $2,600.00.

Closed Mouth Child: On kid body (or cloth). May have slight turned head, bisque lower arms. 12" - $600.00; 15" - $775.00; 20" - $1,000.00; 24" - $1,200.00.

Open Mouth Child: Late 1880's to 1900. Excellent pale bisque, jointed composition body. Glass eyes, no damage and nicely dressed. 15" - $450.00; 20" - $550.00; 23" - $625.00; 26" - $800.00; 30" - $1,300.00.

Open Mouth Child: Same as above, but on kid body with bisque lower arms. 15" - $350.00; 20" - $450.00; 23" - $525.00; 26" - $675.00; 30" - $900.00.

Open Mouth Child: 1900 to 1920's. With very "dolly" type face. Overall excellent condition, composition jointed body. 15" - $350.00; 18" - $485.00; 22" - $625.00.

Open Mouth Child: Same as above, but with kid body and bisque lower arms. 15" - $300.00; 18" - $425.00; 22" - $500.00.

Bonnet or Hatted: Bisque head with modeled-on bonnet or hat, molded hair and painted features. Cloth body with bisque limbs. No damage and nicely dressed. Dates from about 1880's into 1920's.

Bisque: 12" - $400.00 up; 16" - $600.00 up.

Stone Bisque: Whitish and more porous than bisque. 11" - $250.00; 15" - $475.00.

Glass Eyes, Closed Mouth: Excellent overall quality. 16" - $2,400.00; 19" - $3,000.00; 23" - $3,800.00.

All Bisque: See "All Bisque - German" section.

Molded Hair: See that section.

Infants: Bisque head, molded/painted hair, cloth body with composition or celluloid hands, glass eyes. No damage. 12" - $385.00; 16" - $625.00; 20" - $765.00.

Babies: Solid dome or wigged, glass eyes, five-piece baby body, open mouth, nicely dressed and no damage. (Allow more for closed or open/closed mouth or very unusual face and toddler doll.) 14" - $500.00; 17" - $600.00; 22" - $750.00.

Babies: Same as above, but with painted eyes. 14" - $450.00; 17" - $525.00; 22" - $625.00.

Tiny Unmarked Doll: Head is bisque of good quality on five-piece pa-pier maché or composition body, glass eyes, open mouth. No damage. 6" - $245.00; 9" - $300.00; 12" - $425.00.

Tiny Doll: Same as above, but on full jointed composition body. 6" - $295.00; 9" - $400.00; 12" - $525.00.

Tiny Doll: Closed mouth, jointed body. 6" - $350.00; 9" - $450.00; 12" - $650.00. Five-piece body: 6" - $275.00; 9" - $375.00; 12" - $445.00.

Character Child: Unidentified, closed mouth, very character face, may have wig or solid dome, glass eyes, closed or open/closed mouth. Excellent quality bisque, no damage and nicely dressed. 16" - $3,600.00; 20" - $4,500.00.

Character: Closed mouth, mold numbers 111, 128, 134, and others of this quality. 16" - $7,500.00 up; 22" - $10,000.00 up.

German maker unknown, marked "S 811." Closed mouth 20" tall, set eyes and jointed body with straight wrists. 17" early Kestner marked "V111." Closed mouth and on jointed body with straight wrists. Courtesy Frasher Doll Auctions. 20" - $2,900.00; 17" - $2,600.00.

16" marked "17." White bisque head with glass eyes and closed mouth. On fully jointed German body. Old clothes. Courtesy Barbara Earnshaw-Cain. 16" - $2,400.00.

19" German marked "B-8." Sleep eyes with lashes, open mouth and on five-piece toddler body. Courtesy Frasher Doll Auctions. 19" - $775.00.

20" unmarked German child on German jointed body with straight wrists. Open/closed mouth. Courtesy Barbara Earnshaw-Cain. 20" - $2,900.00.

11" marked "S.P. 23. Germany 6/Ox." Maker unknown. Sleep eyes, open mouth. Body jointed at shoulders, hips, neck and wrists. Has molded on, painted Mary Jane shoes and blue socks. Original factory dress. Courtesy Frasher Doll Auctions. 11" original - $500.00; 11" - $300.00.

8" "Flapper" with bisque head on five-piece body with painted-on shoes and socks. All original. Open mouth with four teeth. Head marked "155" followed by line and "410/Made in Germany." Original box marked "Ges. Gesch/ULLA/ Puppe." In box is catalog showing 24 outfits and different hair bows with one dressed as boy. Courtesy Jeannie Mauldin. 8" - $425.00.

16" beautiful smiling Eskimo. Ceramic-style material head with open/closed mouth and molded teeth. Molded hair and painted eyes. Rest of doll is cloth and felt; all original. Marked "784." Made in Germany. All original. 16" - $200.00.

19" all original "Gladdie" by Helen Jensen and made in Germany. Ceramic-type head, open/closed mouth with modeled teeth and tongue, sleep eyes, cloth body and composition limbs. Shown with 26" Simon & Halbig mold number 939 with closed mouth. 19" ceramic - $1,200.00 up; 19" bisque - $3,500.00 up; 26" - $3,700.00.

GOEBEL

The Goebel factory has been operating since 1879 and is located in Oeslau, Germany. The interwoven W.G. mark has been used since 1879. William Goebel inherited the factory from his father, Granz Detley Goebel. About 1900, the factory only made dolls, dolls heads and porcelain figures. They worked in both bisque and china glazed items.

Marks:

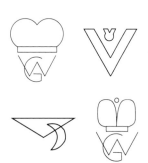

Child: 1895 and later. Open mouth, composition body, sleep or set eyes with head in perfect condition, dressed and ready to display. 16" - $375.00; 20"- $475.00; 24" - $595.00.

Character: After 1910. Molded hair that can be in various styles, with or without molded flowers or ribbons, painted features and on five-piece papier maché body. No damage and nicely dressed. 7" - $365.00; 9" - $465.00; 12" - $575.00.

Character Baby: After 1909. Open mouth, sleep eyes and on five-piece bent limb baby body. No damage and nicely dressed. 13" - $425.00; 16" - $575.00; 20" - $675.00; 25" - $925.00.

Molded-on Bonnet: Closed mouth, five-piece papier maché body, painted features and may have various molded-on hats or bonnets and painted hair. 7" - $375.00; 9" - $500.00; 12" - $625.00.

15" rare Goebel child with modeled hair, intaglio eyes and open/closed smiling mouth. On full jointed German body. Marked "☗ Germany." Courtesy Barbara Earnshaw-Cain. 15" - $3,000.00.

GOOGLY

Bisque head with glass or set eyes to the side, closed smiling mouth, impish or watermelon-style mouth, original composition or papier maché body. Molded hair or wigged. 1911 and after. Not damaged in any way and nicely dressed.

All Bisque: See All Bisque section.

Armand Marseille: #200: 8" - $1,500.00; 12" - $2,500.00. **#210:** 9" - $2,300.00; 11" - $2,900.00. **#223:** 6" - $825.00; 9" - $1,100.00. **#240, 241:** 10" - $1,400.00; 13" - $2,800.00. **#248:** 9" - $1,100.00. **#252:** 7" - $695.00. **#253:** 6" - $750.00; 8" - $900.00; 12" - $1,300.00. **#254:** 9" - $975.00. **#255-#310:** (Just Me) 8" - $1,200.00; 11" - $1,500.00. **#310** with painted bisque: 8" - $700.00; 12"- $1,000.00. **#320:** 9" - $1,300.00. **#323:** fired-in color: 6" - $650.00; 9" - $900.00; 12" - $1,400.00. On baby body: 13" - $1,300.00. Painted bisque: 8" - $500.00;

12" - $775.00. **#325:** 8" - $750.00; 11" - $950.00.

B.P. (Bahr & Proschild) #686: 12" - $2,500.00; 14" - $2,900.00 Baby: 12" - $1,300.00.

Demalcol: 10" - $650.00; 14" - $850.00.

Hertel Schwab: See that section.

Heubach Einco: 15" - $7,500.00; 17" - $8,200.00.

Heubach (marked in square): 8" - $950.00; 12" - $1,800.00. **#9573:** 9" - $1,800.00; 12" - $2,200.00. **#9578, 11173:** 8" - $1,200.00 up.

Heubach Koppelsdorf: #318: 8" - $1,200.00; 13" - $2,000.00. **#319:** 7" - $650.00; 11" - $1,200.00. **#417:** 8" - $550.00; 12" - $1,100.00.

Kestner: #163, 165: (This number now attributed to Hertel & Schwab): 14" - $4,700.00; 16" - $5,600.00. **#172-173** (Attributed to Hertel & Schwab):

14" - $5,600.00; 16" - $6,400.00. **#217, 221:** 6" - $1,200.00; 10" - $3,400.00; 12" - $4,200.00; 14" - $4,900.00; 16" - $5,400.00; 17" - $5,600.00.

Kammer & Reinhardt (K star R): 9" on five-piece body: $2,700.00. **#131:** 10" - $5,200.00; 14" - $7,000.00.

Oscar Hitt: 13" - $6,000.00; 16" - $8,000.00.

P.M. (Otto Reinecke): #950: 9" - $1,400.00; 14" - $2,600.00.

S.F.B.J.: #245: 9" on five-piece body - $1,600.00. 12" on fully jointed body: 12" - $2,800.00; 15" - $5,800.00.

Steiner, Herm: 9" - $875.00; 12" - $975.00.

Composition Face: Very round composition face mask or all composition head with wig, glass eyes to side and closed impish watermelon-style mouth. Body is stuffed felt. In original clothes and all in excellent condition.

7" - $450.00; 11" - $675.00; 13" - $900.00; 15" - $1,100.00; 19" - $1,600.00. Fair condition, cracks or crazing, nicely redressed: 7" - $175.00; 11" - $325.00; 13" - $450.00; 15" - $525.00; 19" - $750.00.

Painted Eyes: Composition or papier maché body with painted-on shoes and socks. Bisque head with eyes painted to side, closed smile mouth and molded hair. Not damaged and nicely dressed (such as A.M. 320, Goebel, R.A., Heubach, etc.): 6" - $300.00; 8" - $400.00; 12" - $650.00.

Disc Eyes: Bisque socket head or shoulder head with molded hair (can have molded hat-cap), closed mouth and inset celluloid disc in large googly eyes. 10" - $650.00; 14" - $900.00; 17" - $1,300.00; 21" - $1,800.00.

Molded-on Hat: Marked "Elite." 12" - $2,800.00; 16" - $4,400.00.

Left to right: 9" "Just Me" googly by Armand Marseille. All original and on five-piece body. 5¾" Kewpie "Thinker." 15" marked "J.D.K. 211 ges. Gesch." googly with large round eyes, on jointed toddler body. German wind-up toy. 11" "Our Fairy" googly that is marked "222" and made by Hertel & Schwab for Louis Wolf. All bisque. Courtesy Frasher Doll Auctions. 9" - $1,500.00; 5¾" - $365.00; 15" - $5,100.00; Toy - $700.00 up; 11" - $2,300.00.

11" marked "Demalcol 5/0." Round googly eyes, closed smiling mouth and on five-piece composition body. Courtesy Frasher Doll Auctions. 11" - $650.00.

7" googly marked "A 11/0 M. Germany." Made by Armand Marseille. Intaglio eyes, closed smiling mouth and on five-piece papier maché body with painted-on shoes and socks. 9" marked "1900-15/0." Open mouth, set eyes and on five-piece body, painted-on knee high boots. Original fur-like outfit. Maker unknown. Courtesy Frasher Doll Auctions. 7" - $650.00 up; 9" - $265.00 up.

12" marked "DEP. ELITE." Soldier with modeled on helmet, glass eyes and open/ closed mouth. On fully jointed body and all original. Courtesy Barbara Earnshaw-Cain. 12" - $2,800.00.

Ludwig Greiner of Philadelphia, PA made dolls from 1858 into the 1800's. The heads are made of papier maché, and they can be found on various bodies, can be all cloth (many homemade), many have leather arms or can be found on Lacmann bodies that have stitched joints at the hips and the knees and are very wide at the hip line. The Lacmann bodies will be marked "J. Lacmann's Patent March 24th, 1874" in an oval. The Greiner heads will be marked "Greiner's Patent Doll Heads/ Pat. Mar. 30, '58." Also "Greiner's/Improved/Patent Heads/Pat. Mar. 30, '58." The later heads are marked "Greiner's Patent Doll Heads/Pat. Mar. 30, '58. Ext. '72."

Greiner Doll: Can have black or blonde molded hair, blue or brown painted eyes and be on a nice homemade cloth body with cloth arms or a commerical cloth body with leather arms. Dressed for the period and clean, with head in near perfect condition with no paint chips and not repainted.

With '58 Label: 17" - $875.00; 23" - $1,200.00; 26" - $1,400.00; 29" - $1,650.00; 34" - $1,900.00; 37" - $2,300.00. With chips and flakes or repainted: 17" - $350.00; 23" - $475.00; 26" - $575.00; 29" - $700.00; 34" - $950.00; 37" - $1,400.00.

With '72 Label: 18" - $650.00; 24" - $1,000.00; 29" - $1,300.00; 35" - $1,500.00. With chips and flakes or repainted: 18" - $300.00; 25" - $400.00; 29" - $600.00; 35" - $800.00.

Glass Eyes: 22" - $2,200.00; 27" - $2,700.00. With chips and flakes or repainted: 22" - $775.00; 27" - $1,000.00.

**26" papier maché marked " '58 Pat.";
label on shoulder plate. Painted hair
and features, all cloth body. Courtesy
Frasher Doll Auctions. 26" - $1,400.00.**

34" "H." made in 1882 by Halopeau. This doll is early prototype of the later "H" dolls. Halopeau was the successor of the Eugene Barrois firm that made beautiful quality fashion dolls in the 1880's. Courtesy Frasher Doll Auctions. 20" - $85,000.00 up; 26" - $97,000.00 up; 34" - $125,000.00 up. Unmarked: 20" - $28,000.00; 26" - $38,000.00. * *22" - $100,000 at auction.*

Half dolls can be made of any material including bisque, papier maché and composition. Not all half dolls were used as pin cushions. They were also used for powder box tops, brushes, tea cozies, etc. Most date from 1900 into the 1930's, and the majority were made in Germany, but many were made in Japan. Generally they will be marked with "Germany" or "Japan." Some have numbers and others may have the marks of companies such as William Goebel Ⓦ or Dressel, Kister & Co. ⁾.

The most desirable are the large ones, or any size for that matter, that have both arms molded away from the body, or are jointed at the shoulder.

Arms/Hands: Completely away from figure. China or bisque: 3" - $125.00 up; 5" - $250.00 up; 8" - $425.00 up; 12" - $900.00 up.

Arms Extended: But hands attached to figure. China or bisque: 3" - $65.00; 5" - $75.00; 8" - $95.00. Papier maché or composition: 5" - $25.00; 7" - $65.00.

12" bisque half doll with bald head, original wig, fired-in color mask and beauty mark. Both arms modeled away from body and holds fan. Made by Goebel; marked ♉. 12" - $950.00.

4½" tall half doll with arms widely extended. Modeled on necklace and braclets. Marked "17039" on base. Made in Germany. 4½" - $200.00.

Common Figures: With arms and hands attached. China: 3" - $25.00; 5" - $35.00; 8" - $50.00. Papier maché or composition: 3" - $18.00; 5" - $22.00; 8" - $30.00.

Jointed Shoulders: China or bisque: 5" - $95.00; 8" - $115.00; 10" - $135.00. Papier maché: 4" - $28.00; 7" - $70.00. Wax over papier maché: 4" - $38.00; 7" - $95.00.

Children or Men: 3" - $45.00; 5" - $70.00; 7" - $95.00. Jointed shoulders: 3" - $60.00; 5" - $90.00; 7" - $145.00.

Japan marked: 3" - $15.00; 5" - $28.00; 7" - $45.00.

Background: 4" on pincushion base that uses lace to make bodice; also has velvet ribbon added to hair. Left: 2½" with flowers in hair, has legs with gold shoes attached to base. Right: 3" pink ribbon in hair, base has legs attached that have painted shoes. Courtesy Frasher Doll Auctions. 4" - $70.00; 2½" - $55.00; 3" - $60.00. (Add more for hose/legs.)

Back row: 3¾" marked "720" and green stamp "Made in Germany." 3½" marked "Germany 5590." 2" child marked "Germany." Lower row: 2¾" on brush, 4" marked "3033 Germany." 3" with black bobbed hairdo. Center front: 2" marked "14621 Germany." Mardi Gras child. Courtesy Frasher Doll Auctions. 3¾" - $60.00; 3½" - $30.00; 2¾" brush - $65.00; 4" - $65.00; 3" - $30.00; 2" - $45.00.

Heinrich Handwerck began making dolls and doll bodies in 1876 at Gotha, Germany. Majority of their heads were made by Simon & Halbig. In 1897 they patented, in Germany, a ball jointed body #100297 and some of their bodies will be marked with this number.

Mold numbers include: 12x, 19, 23, 69, 79, 89, 99, 100, 109, 118, 119, 124, 125, 139, 152, 189, 199, 1001, 1200, 1290.

Sample mold marks:

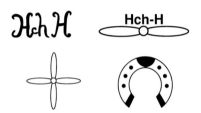

Child: After 1885. Open mouth, sleep or set eyes, on ball jointed body. Bisque head with no cracks, chips or hairlines, good wig and nicely dressed. 14" - $395.00; 17" - $485.00; 21" - $575.00; 24" - $695.00; 28" - $1,000.00; 32" - $1,400.00; 37" - $1,900.00; 41" - $2,500.00.

Kid Body: Bisque shoulder head, open mouth. All in good condition and nicely dressed. 15" - $350.00; 20" - $475.00; 24" - $600.00; 26" - $800.00.

Closed Mouth: Marked with company name and sometimes with Simon & Halbig. May have mold numbers 79 or 89. 12" - $1,300.00; 16" - $1,700.00; 20" - $2,100.00; 24" - $2,600.00.

27" marked "119-13 Handwerck." Sleep eyes, open mouth and on fully jointed body. Courtesy Frasher Doll Auctions. 27" - $975.00.

30" marked "109-15 DEP. Germany Handwerck." Open mouth and on fully jointed body. Courtesy Gloria Anderson. 30" - $1,200.00.

Max Handwerck started making dolls in 1900 and his factory was located at Walterhausen, Germany. In 1901, he registered "Bébé Elite" with the heads made by William Goebel. The dolls from this firm are marked with the full name, but a few are marked with "M.H."

Child: Bisque head, open mouth, sleep or set eyes, on fully jointed composition body, no damage and nicely dressed. **Mold #287, etc.:** 15" - $400.00; 19" - $500.00; 23" - $625.00; 27" - $775.00; 34" - $1,400.00; 39" - $2,100.00.

Bébé Elite: Bisque heads with no cracks or chips, sleep or set eyes, open mouth. Can have a flange neck on cloth body with composition limbs or be on a bent leg composition baby body. Upper teeth and smile: 16" - $465.00; 20" - $665.00. Toddler: 16" - $600.00; 20" - $800.00; 25" - $1,200.00. Socket head on fully jointed body: 16" - $585.00; 20" - $800.00.

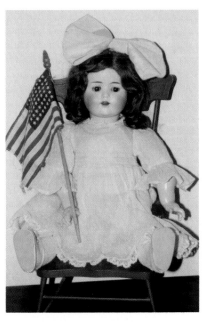

15" marked "Bébé Elite/Max Handwerck." Toddler jointed body. Original clothes. **Courtesy Gloria Anderson. 15" - $600.00.**

HERTEL, SCHWAB & CO.

Hertel, Schwab & Co. has been recognized as the maker of many dolls that were attributed to other companies all these years (by the German authors Jurgen and Marianne Cieslik.) There does not seem to be a "common denominator" to Hertel, Schwab line of dolls and can include any style.

Babies: Bisque head, molded hair or wig, open or open/closed mouth, sleep or painted eyes, bent limb baby body. No damage and all in good condition.

Mold numbers: 130, 142, 150, 151, 152, 153, 154: 11" - $400.00; 14" - $525.00; 18" - $625.00; 23" - $825.00.

Child: Bisque head, painted or sleep eyes, closed mouth, jointed composition body, no damage and nicely dressed. **#134, 141, 149:** 15" - $5,000.00; 19" - $7,200.00. **#154 with Closed Mouth:** 17" - $2,400.00; 23" - $2,700.00. Open Mouth: 18" - $950.00; 22" - $1,200.00. **#169:** 21" - $3,700.00; 24" - $4,200.00. Toddler: 21" - $3,850.00; 24" - $4,350.00.

All Bisque: One-piece body and head, glass eyes, closed or open mouth. All in perfect condition. **Prize Baby (mold #208):** 6" - $350.00; 8" - $550.00. Swivel Neck: 6" - $485.00; 8" - $750.00; 10" - $875.00. (See #222 under Googly.)

Googly: Wig or molded hair. Large, side glance sleep or set eyes. Closed mouth, no damage and nicely dressed. **#163:** 11" - $3,000.00; 15" -

$5,400.00. **#165:** 11" - $3,000.00; 15" - $5,400.00; **#172, 173:** 11" - $4,000.00; 15" - $6,000.00 **#222 (Our Fairy):** Painted eyes, molded hair. 9" - $1,400.00. Wig and glass eyes. 9" - $1,800.00; 11" - $2,300.00.

17½" rare pouty character doll marked "149." Attributed to Hertel & Schwab. Closed mouth, glass eyes and on fully jointed body. Shown with 24" smiling doll, mold number 520 Kley & Hahn with closed mouth and painted eyes. Fully jointed body. Courtesy Frasher Doll Auctions. 17½" - $6,600.00; 24" - $5,100.00.

13" Hertel, Schwab & Co. baby marked "154." Sleep eyes and open/closed mouth. All original. Courtesy Gloria Anderson. 13" - $500.00.

The Heubach Brothers (Gebruder) made dolls from 1863 into the 1930's at Lichte, Thur, Germany. They started producing character dolls in 1910. Heubach dolls can reflect almost every mood and are often found on rather crude, poor quality bodies, and many are small dolls.

Marks:

Character Dolls: Bisque head, open/closed or closed mouth, painted eyes (allow more for glass eyes), on kid, papier maché or jointed composition bodies. Molded hair or wig. No damage and nicely dressed. **#2850:** Open/closed mouth, two rows teeth. Molded braided hair, blue ribbon bow. 16" - $3,000.00 up; 20" - $5,000.00 up. **#5636:** Laughing child, intaglio painted eyes. 9" - $850.00; 12" - $1,100.00. Glass eyes: 12" - $1,600.00. **#5689:** Open mouth, smiling. 15" - $1,800.00; 19" - $2,500.00; 26" - $4,200.00. **#5730 (Santa):** 15" - $2,500.00; 19" - $3,000.00; 28" - $3,500.00. **#5777, #9355 (Dolly Dimples):** Ball jointed body. 15" - $1,600.00; 21" - $2,700.00; 25" - $3,200.00. **#6692:** Shoulder head, smiling, intaglio eyes. 16" - $950.00. **#6736, #6894:** Laughing, wide open/closed mouth, molded lower teeth. 9" - $850.00; 15" - $1,700.00. **#6896:** Pouty, jointed body. 16" - $875.00; 20" - $1,200.00. **#6969, #6970, #7246, #8017, #8420:** Pouty boy or girl, jointed body, painted eyes. 10" - $900.00; 12" - $1,000.00; 15" -

$1,700.00; 19" - $2,100.00. Toddler: 20" - $2,500.00; 24" - $2,900.00. Glass eyes: 15" - $2,500.00; 19" - $2,900.00; 23" - $3,300.00. Toddler, glass eyes: 19" - $3,400.00; 24" - $4,000.00. **#7172, #7550:** 15" - $1,500.00. **#7448:** Open/closed mouth, eyes half shut. 15" - $2,700.00. **#7602:** Painted eyes and hair, long face pouty, closed mouth. 15" - $2,700.00; 21" - $3,100.00 up. Glass eyes: 15" - $3,500.00; 21" - $3,700.00 up. **#7604:** Laughing, jointed body, intaglio eyes. 10" - $475.00; 13" - $700.00. Baby: 15" - $800.00. **#7616:** Open/closed mouth with molded tongue. Socket or shoulder head. Glass eyes: 13" - $1,500.00; 16" - $2,000.00. **#7622:** Molded hair, intaglio eyes, closed mouth and light cheek dimples. 14" - $800.00; 17" - $1,200.00. **#7623:** Molded hair, intaglio eyes, open/closed mouth, molded tongue, on bent limb baby body. 11" - $725.00; 15" - $1,100.00. Jointed

26" marked "12/sunburst mark/5689" character by Heubach." Open mouth with defined lower lip, set glass eyes and on fully jointed body. Courtesy Barbara Earnshaw-Cain. 26" - $4,200.00.

body: 16" - $1,600.00; 20" - $1,900.00. **#7634:** Crying, squinting eyes. 13" - $1,000.00; 16" - $1,600.00. **#7636:** 12" - $900.00. **#7644:** Laughing, socket or shoulder head, intaglio eyes. 14" - $775.00; 17" - $900.00. **#7679:** Whistler, socket head. 15" - $1,300.00; 17" - $1,600.00. **#7701:** Pouty, intaglio eyes. 16" - $1,600.00; 19" - $2,000.00. **#7711:** Open mouth, jointed body. 12" - $425.00; 15" - $775.00; 21" - $825.00; 23" - $1,000.00. **#7661, 7686:** Black, wide open/closed mouth, deeply molded hair. 10" - $800.00; 13" - $2,400.00; 16" - $3,200.00. **#7768, #7788:** "Coquette," tilted head, molded hair and can have ribbon modeled into hairdo. 10" - $725.00; 12" - $975.00; 14" - $1,100.00; 17" - $1,800.00. **#7849:** Closed mouth, intaglio eyes. 12" - $700.00. **#7852 or #119:** Braids coiled around ear (molded), intaglio eyes. 16" - $2,700.00 up; 18" - $3,200.00 up.

#7925, #7926: Adult, painted eyes: 16" - $3,400.00 up. Glass eyes: 18" - $4,600.00. **#7959:** Intaglio eyes, molded on bonnet and deeply molded hair, open/closed mouth. 16" - $3,500.00; 20" - $4,600.00 up. **#7977, #7877:** "Stuart Baby," molded baby bonnet. Painted eyes: 10" - $950.00; 13" - $1,300.00; 15" - $1,700.00; 17" - $2,000.00. Glass eyes: 14" - $1,900.00; 16" - $2,200.00. **#8053:** Round cheecks, closed mouth, painted eyes to side, large ears. 20" - $3,400.00. **#8145:** Closed smile mouth, painted eyes to side, painted hair. Toddler: 15" - $1,500.00 up; 18" - $1,800.00 up. **#8191:** Smiling openly, jointed body. 13" - $1,000.00; 15" - $1,200.00; 18" - $1,500.00. **#8192:** Open/closed smiling mouth with tongue molded between teeth. 16" - $1,400.00; 23" - $2,500.00.

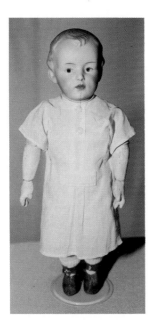

12" Heubach mold number 7622. Intaglio eyes, open/closed mouth and slight cheek dimples. Original clothes and on fully jointed body. Courtesy Barbara Earnshaw-Cain. 12" - $650.00.

11" Gebruder Heubach marked "2/0, sunburst mark, 7644." Intaglio eyes, open/closed smiling mouth with molded tongue. 19½" marked "A.B.G. 1362." Made by Alt, Beck & Gottschalck. Sleep eyes, open mouth and on fully jointed body. Courtesy Frasher Doll Auctions. 11" - $500.00; 19½" - $575.00.

Open mouth: 15" - $675.00; 18" - $1,000.00. Jointed body: 15" - $675.00; 18" - $1,000.00. **#8316:** Open/closed mouth, molded teeth, smile, glass eyes, wig. 16" - $1,800.00 up; 19" - $2,400.00 up. Painted eyes: 14" - $1,200.00 up. **#8381:** Closed mouth, pensive expression, painted eyes, molded hair, ribbon around head with bow, exposed ears. 17-18" - $3,400.00 up. **#8420:** Pouty, painted eyes. 15" - $750.00; 18" - $900.00. Glass eyes: 16" - $1,150.00; 20" - $2,300.00. **#8459, 8469:** Wide open/closed laughing mouth, glass eyes. 12" - $2,700.00; 15" - $3,300.00. **#8556, 8590:** Closed mouth smile. Googly: 14" - $1,200.00; 17" - $1,800.00. Baby: 14" - $1,000.00; 16" - $1,500.00. **#8596:** Smile, intaglio eyes. 15" - $750.00; 17" - $900.00. **#8774:** "Whistling Jim," eyes to side and mouth modeled as if whis-

tling. 14" - $1,000.00; 17" - $1,500.00. **#8868:** Molded hair, glass eyes, closed mouth, very short chin. 16" - $1,800.00; 20" - $2,400.00. **#9355:** Shoulder head. 17" - $950.00; 23" - $1,700.00. **#10532:** Open mouth, jointed body. 10" - $395.00; 14" - $625.00; 17" - $800.00; 20" - $1,200.00. **#10586, #10633:** Child with open mouth, jointed body. 17" - $600.00; 22" - $850.00; 26" - $1,200.00. **#11173:** Glass eyes, five-piece body, pursed closed mouth with large indented cheeks. Called "Tiss-Me." 8" - $1,500.00 up.

Child with Dolly-type Face (non-character): Open mouth, glass sleep or set eyes, jointed body, bisque head with no damage and nicely dressed. 14" - $450.00; 17" - $575.00; 21" - $800.00; 25" - $950.00.

Googly: Marked with a Heubach mark. Glass eyes: 8" - $950.00; 12" - $1,800.00; 14" - $2,400.00.

Indian Portrait: Man or woman. 14" - $3,400.00 up.

Left: "Whistling Jim" by Heubach, marked "8774/Heubach" in square. Molded hair, intaglio eyes and pursed, open mouth. Cloth body with toddler jointed hips and composition arms and lower legs. Right: 12½" Kley & Hahn marked "K&H 525." Painted hair and eyes, open/closed mouth and on jointed body. Courtesy Frasher Doll Auctions. 17" - $1,500.00; 12½" - $700.00.

18" Heubach mold number 8868 with painted hair, large glass eyes and closed mouth. Very small chin. On fully jointed body. Courtesy Barbara Earnshaw-Cain. 18" - $2,000.00.

Babies or Infants: Bisque head, wig or molded hair, sleep or intaglio eyes, open/closed pouty-type mouths. **Mold #6894, #6898, #7602:** 6" - $265.00; 9" - $400.00; 13" - $495.00; 16" - $600.00; 19" - $800.00; 24" - $1,100.00; 28" - $1,500.00.

16½" "Dolly Dimple" by Gebruder Heubach, marked "5," "Heubach" in square, "Germany." Shoulder head, sleep eyes, open mouth, dimples and on jointed kid body with bisque lower arms. Courtesy Frasher Doll Auctions. 16½" - $1,900.00.

22" marked "10532 10" and "Heubach" in a square. Socket head on jointed body, open mouth. Courtesy Frasher Doll Auctions. 22" - $1,300.00.

Ernst Heubach began making dolls in 1887 in Koppelsdorf, Germany and the marks of this firm can be the initials "E.H." or the dolls can be found marked with the full name Heubach Koppelsdorf, or:

Some mold numbers from this company: 27X, 87, 99, 230, 235, 236, 237, 238, 242, 250, 251, 262, 271, 273, 275, 277, 283, 300, 302, 312, 317, 320, 321, 330, 338, 339, 340, 342, 349, 350, 367, 399, 407, 410, 417, 438, 444, 450, 452, 458, 616, 1310, 1900, 1901, 1906, 1909, 2504, 2671, 2757, 3027, 3412, 3423, 3427, 7118, 32144.

Child: Mold #250, 302 etc. After 1888. Jointed body, open mouth, sleep or set eyes. No damage and nicely dressed. 8" - $175.00; 10" - $195.00; 14" - $295.00; 18" - $400.00; 22" - $500.00; 26" - $685.00; 30" - $900.00; 35" - $1,100.00.

Child: On kid body with bisque lower arms, bisque shoulder head, some turned head, open mouth. No damage and nicely dressed. 15" - $195.00; 19" - $225.00; 23" - $325.00; 28" - $750.00.

Child: Painted bisque. 8" - $130.00; 12" - $190.00.

Babies: 1910 and after. On five-piece bent limb baby body, open mouth with some having wobbly tongue and pierced nostrils. Sleep eyes. No damage and nicely dressed. 6" - $265.00; 10" - $300.00; 14" - $385.00; 19" - $525.00; 25" - $875.00.

18" marked "250-4/0 Koppelsdorf. Germany." Open mouth and on fully jointed body. 16" Martha Chase, oil painted stockenette head and limbs, cloth body, jointed at shoulders, hips, elbows and knees. Courtesy Frasher Doll Auctions. 18" - $400.00; 16" - $600.00.

27" marked "Heubach 302.8 Koppelsdorf Germany." Sleep eyes, open mouth and on fully jointed body. Maybe original clothes. Courtesy Frasher Doll Auctions. 27" - $700.00.

22" Heubach Koppelsdorf mold number 320-7. Pierced nostrils, open mouth, sleep eyes and on five-piece baby body. Courtesy Gloria Anderson. 22" - $650.00.

26" Heubach Koppelsdorf mold number 342-10. Big, flirty eyes and open mouth. On five-piece, chunky toddler body. Courtesy Gloria Anderson. 26" - $1,100.00.

Baby on Toddler Body: Same as above, but on a toddler body. 15" - $575.00; 18" - $650.00; 22" - $875.00; 25" - $975.00.

Baby, Painted Bisque: Baby, 12" - $245.00; 15" - $325.00. Toddler, 16" - $500.00.

Infant: 1925 and after. Molded or painted hair, sleep eyes, closed mouth, flange neck bisque head on cloth body with composition or celluloid hands. No damage and nicely dressed. **#338, #340:** 12" - $600.00; 14" - $850.00. **#339, #349, #350:** 12" - $585.00; 14" - $785.00. **#399** (White only): 12" - $345.00.

Infant: Same as above but with fired-in tan or brown color. 12" - $525.00; 14" - $600.00.

#452: Tan/brown fired-in color bisque head with same color toddler body, open mouth, painted hair. Earings. No damage and originally dressed or redressed nicely. 12" - $525.00; 14" - $600.00.

Black or Dark Brown: #320, #339, #399: Painted bisque head, on five-piece baby body or toddler cut body. Sleep eyes, painted hair or wig. No damage and very minimum amount of paint pulls (chips) on back of head and none on face. 12" - $475.00; 14" - $565.00; 17" - $650.00; 21" - $900.00.

Character Child: 1910 on. Molded hair, painted eyes and open/ closed mouth. No damage. **#262, #330 and others:** 12" - $500.00; 15" - $950.00.

JULLIEN

Jullien marked dolls were made in Paris, France from 1875 to 1904. The heads will be marked Jullien and a size number. In 1892, Jullien advertised "L'Universal" and the label can be found on some of his doll bodies.

Child: Closed mouth, paperweight eyes, French jointed body of composition, papier maché with some having wooden parts. Undamaged bisque head and all in excellent condition. 16" - $3,600.00; 19" - $4,100.00; 21" - $4,600.00; 23" - $4,800.00; 27" - $5,200.00.

Child: Same as above, but with open mouth. 16" - $1,700.00; 19" - $2,100.00; 21" - $2,400.00; 23" - $2,600.00; 27" - $3,000.00.

28" marked "Jullien" on head. Open mouth, dimple in chin and heavy feathered eyebrows. On French fully jointed body. 28" - $3,000.00.

JUMEAU

Tete Jumeau: 1879-1899 and later. Marked with red stamp on head and oval sticker on body. Closed mouth, paperweight eyes, jointed body with full joints or jointed with straight wrists. Pierced ears with larger sizes having applied ears. No damage at all to bisque head, undamaged French body, dressed and ready to place into collection. 9-10" - $3,700.00 up; 12" - $3,000.00; 14" - $3,300.00; 16" - $3,800.00; 18" - $4,300.00; 20" - $4,600.00; 22" - $5,200.00; 24" - $5,600.00; 28" - $6,500.00; 30" - $7,200.00.

Tete Jumeau on Adult Body: 19-20" - $6,200.00.

Tete Jumeau: Same as above, but with open mouth. 14" - $1,800.00; 16" -

Left: All original marked "Jumeau size 1." 10" tall with open/closed mouth, straight wrists and marked body and head. Right: 10½", tiny size 2, marked "E.J." Open/closed mouth, straight wrists and marked body. Courtesy Frasher Doll Auctions. 10" - $3,700.00 (original - $5,200.00); 10½" E.J. - $5,500.00.

$2,300.00; 19" - $2,500.00; 20" - $2,600.00; 22" - $3,000.00; 24" - $3,400.00; 28" - $3,900.00; 30" - $4,100.00.

1907 Jumeau: Incised 1907, sometimes has the Tete Jumeau stamp. Sleep or set eyes, open mouth, jointed French body. No damage, nicely dressed. 14" - $1,500.00; 16" - $2,100.00; 19" - $2,500.00; 22" - $2,800.00; 25" - $3,300.00; 29" - $3,500.00.

E.J. Child: Ca. early 1880's. Head incised "Depose/E.J." Paperweight eyes, closed mouth, jointed body with straight wrist (unjointed at wrist). Larger dolls will have applied ears. No damage to head or body and nicely dressed in excellent quality clothes. 10" - $5,500.00 up; 14" - $5,800.00; 16" - $6,400.00; 18" - $6,600.00; 22" - $7,500.00; 24" - $9,500.00.

23" marked "Tete Jumeau" with closed mouth and on fully jointed Jumeau body. Courtesy Turn of Century Antiques. 23" - $4,900.00.

E.J./A Child: 25" - $20,000.00 up.

Depose Jumeau: (Incised) 1880. Head will be incised "Depose Jumeau" and body should have Jumeau sticker. Closed mouth, paperweight eyes and on jointed body with straight wrists, although a few may have jointed wrists. No damage at all and nicely dressed. 16" - $5,700.00; 19" - $6,400.00; 23" - $7,400.00; 26" - $8,500.00.

Long Face (Triste Jumeau): 1870's. Closed mouth, applied ears, paperweight eyes and straight wrists on Jumeau marked body. Head is generally marked with a size number. No damage to head or body, nicely dressed. 20-21" - $23,000.00 up; 25-26"- $25,000.00 up; 29-30" - $26,000.00 up.

Portrait Jumeau: 1870's. Closed mouth, usually large almond-shaped eyes and jointed Jumeau body. Head marked with size number only and body has the Jumeau sticker or stamp. 10" - $5,700.00; 12" - $4,700.00; 15" - $6,000.00; 21" - $7,700.00; 25" - $8,800.00; 28" - $9,600.00.

27" marked "Tete Jumeau" with closed mouth, applied ears and on early Jumeau body with straight wrists. May be original clothes. Courtesy Gloria Anderson. 27" - $6,400.00.

Phonograph Jumeau: Bisque head with open mouth. Phonograph in body. No damage, working and nicely dressed. 20" - $8,000.00; 25" - $12,000.00 up..

Wire Eye (Flirty) Jumeau: Lever in back of head operates eyes. Open mouth, jointed body, straight wrists: 18" - $6,200.00; 21" - $7,500.00; 26" - $9,000.00.

Celluloid Head: Incised Jumeau. 14" - $675.00 up.

Mold Number 200 Series: (Example: 201, 203, 205, 211, 214, 223) *Very character faces* and marked Jumeau. Closed mouth. No damage to bisque or body. 22" - $50,000.00 up.

Mold Number 200 Series: Open mouth. 14" - $6,200.00 up; 20" - $12,000.00 up.

S.F.B.J. or Unis: Marked along with Jumeau. Open mouth, no damage to head and on French body. 16" - $1,400.00; 20" - $1,800.00. Closed mouth: 16" - $2,400.00; 20" - $3,000.00.

30" Jumeau marked "14." Open mouth with six teeth. All original in Bébé Jumeau box. Long, thick human hair wig. Courtesy Frasher Doll Auctions. 30" - $4,100.00; Original/box - $5,400.00.

Two-Faced Jumeau: Has two different faces on same head, one crying and one smiling. Open/closed mouths, jointed body. No damage and nicely dressed. 14" - $10,000.00 up.

Fashion: See Fashion section.

Mold 221: Ca. 1930's. Small dolls (10") will have a paper label "Jumeau." Adult style bisque head on five-piece body with painted-on shoes. Closed mouth and set glass eyes. Dressed in original ornate gown. No damage and clean. 10" - $1,000.00.

Mold 306: Jumeau made after formation of Unis and mark will be "Unis/France" in oval and "71" on one side and "149" on other, followed by "306/Jumeau/1939/Paris." Called "Princess Elizabeth." Closed mouth, flirty or paperweight eyes. Jointed French body. No damage and nicely dressed. 20" - $2,200.00; 30" - $3,600.00.

24" Jumeau marked "Depose E.11J." Closed mouth with almond-shaped eyes, applied ears, and on Jumeau marked body with straight wrists. Original dress and marked shoes. Courtesy Frasher Doll Auctions. 24" - $7,500.00.

Right: 20" marked "E 9 J." All original with open/closed mouth and almond-shaped cut eyes. Jumeau marked body with straight wrists. Left: Shows original wig and celluloid hairband. Courtesy Barbara Earnshaw-Cain. 20" - $7,000.00; Original - $13,000.00.

13" "A.T." looking Portrait Jumeau marked "4 size Jumeau." Jumeau body with straight wrists. Courtesy Barbara Earnshaw-Cain. 13" - $6,500.00

22½" incised "203" and in red "Depose Tete Jumeau Bte SGDG 10." Open/ closed smiling mouth with modeled teeth, glass eyes and marked Jumeau body with straight wrists. Courtesy Frasher Doll Auctions. "203" - $50,000.00 up.

23" "Portrait Jumeau" with very pale bisque and extreme almond-shaped eyes, closed mouth and on Jumeau jointed body with straight wrists. Courtesy Frasher Doll Auctions. 23" - $8,200.00.

On left, incised "211" and on right, "208." Character Jumeau also marked in red "Depose Tete Jumeau Bte SGDG 9. Both are 20½" tall. Glass eyes and on fully jointed marked Jumeau bodies. Both have old clothes and original wigs and shoes. Courtesy Frasher Doll Auctions. "211" - $50,000.00 up; "208" - $50,000.00 up.

Kammer and Reinhardt dolls generally have the Simon and Halbig name or initials incised along with their own name or mark, as Simon & Halbig made most of their heads. They were located in Thur, Germany at Walterhausen and began in 1895, although their first models were not on the market until 1896. The trademark for this company was registered in 1895. In 1909, a character line of fourteen molds (#100-#114) were exhibited at the Leipzig Toy Fair.

Marks:

Character Boy or Girl: Closed or open/closed mouth, on jointed body or five-piece body. No damage and nicely dressed. **#101:** 8" boy "Peter"; girl "Marie" on five-piece body - $1,500.00; 8" on fully jointed body - $1,700.00; 14" - $2,500.00; 18" - $3,500.00; 22" - $4,400.00. Glass eyes: 17" - $5,000.00; 21" - $7,000.00. **#102:** Boy "Karl," extremely rare. 12" - $10,000.00 up; 15" - $20,000.00. Glass eyes: 17" - $23,000.00; 22" - $25,000.00 up. **#103:** Closed mouth, sweet expression, painted eyes **or #104:** Open/closed mouth, dimples, mischievous expression, painted eyes, extremely rare. 18" - $55,000.00 up. **#105:** Extremely rare. Open/closed mouth and much modeling around intaglio eyes. 21" - $65,000.00 up. **#106:** Extremely rare. Full round face, pursed closed full lips, intaglio eyes to side and much chin modeling. 21" - $50,000.00 up. **#107:** Pursed, pouty mouth, intaglio eyes. 15" - $16,000.00; 22" - $24,000.00. Glass eyes: 18" - $28,000.00. **#109:** Very rare. 14" - $15,000.00; 20" - $24,000.00. Glass eyes: 20" - $28,000.00.

#112, #112X, #112A: Very rare. 15" - $9,800.00; 18" - $13,000.00; 23" - $18,000.00. Glass eyes: 18" - $18,000.00; 24" - $26,000.00. **#114:** Girl "Gretchen"; boy "Hans." 8" - $1,600.00; 10" - $2,800.00; 15" - $3,700.00; 17" - $5,400.00. Glass eyes: 18" - $7,000.00; 24" - $9,500.00. **#117:** Closed mouth. 15" - $3,700.00; 18" - $4,400.00; 22" - $5,400.00; 25" - $6,500.00; 28" - $7,200.00. **#117A:** Closed mouth. 15" - $4,100.00; 18" - $4,800.00; 22" - $5,800.00; 25" - $6,900.00; 28" - $7,600.00. **#117n:** Open mouth, flirty eyes (Take off $200.00 for just sleep eyes): 17" - $1,700.00; 21" - $2,300.00; 24" - $2,500.00; 27" - $2,900.00. **#123, #124 (Max & Moritz):** 17" - $25,000.00 up each. **#127:** Molded hair, open/closed mouth. Toddler or jointed body: 17" - $1,900.00; 21" - $2,500.00; 25" - $3,200.00.

Character Babies: Open/closed

28" Kammer & Reinhardt marked "K star R Simon Halbig 117N." Flirty, sleep eyes, open mouth and on teen type jointed wood and composition body. Courtesy Frasher Doll Auctions. 28" - $3,000.00.

mouth or closed mouth on five-piece bent limb baby body, solid dome or wigged. No damage and nicely dressed.

#100: Called "Kaiser Baby." Intaglio eyes, open/closed mouth. 10" - $550.00; 14" - $850.00; 17" - $1,000.00; 20" - $1,600.00. Glass eyes: 16" - $2,200.00; 18" - $2,800.00. Black: 16" - $5,300.00; 18" - $5,800.00. **#115 , #115a "Phillip":** 15" - $3,400.00; 18" - $4,600.00; 24" - $5,200.00; 26" - $5,600.00. Toddler: 16" - $3,900.00; 18" - $5,000.00; 24" - $5,700.00. **#116, #116a:** 16" - $2,500.00; 19" - $3,300.00; 23" - $4,700.00. Toddler: 16" - $2,900.00; 20" - $3,800.00; 25" - $5,200.00. Open Mouth: 16" - $1,700.00; 18" - $2,000.00. **#119:** 18" - $4,000.00 up; 26" - $4,800.00. **#127:** 13" - $1,100.00; 17" - $1,600.00; 21" - $2,000.00; 24" - $2,400.00. Toddler: 16" - $1,800.00; 20" - $2,100.00; 25" - $2,500.00. Child: 14" - $1,300.00; 17" - $1,500.00; 22" - $1,800.00; 25" - $2,300.00.

Babies with Open Mouth: Sleep eyes on five-piece bent limb baby body. Wigs, may have tremble tongues or "mama" cryer in body. No damage and nicely dressed. Allow more for flirty eyes. **#121:** 14" - $775.00; 18" - $1,050.00; 23" - $1,500.00. Toddler: 16"- $1,200.00; 19" - $1,600.00; 24" - $1,900.00. **#122, #128:** 14" - $800.00; 17" - $1,100.00; 21" - $1,500.00; 24" - $1,800.00. Toddler: 16" - $1,400.00; 19" - $1,900.00. **#126:** 12" - $550.00; 16" - $775.00; 20"- $950.00; 24" - $1,400.00; 28" - $2,000.00. Toddler: 9" - $650.00; 16" - $925.00; 21" - $1,400.00; 24" - $1,600.00; 29" - $2,000.00. **#118a:** 14" - $1,500.00; 17" - $1,900.00. 21" - $2,400.00. **#119:** 16" - $4,000.00; 20" - $4,900.00. **#135:** 15" - $1,200.00; 21" - $2,200.00.

Child Dolls: 1895-1930's. Open mouth, sleep or set eyes and on fully jointed body. No damage and nicely dressed. Most often found mold num-

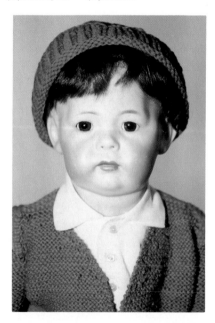

16" "Phillip" marked "K star R 115A." Glass eyes and closed mouth. On fully jointed body. Courtesy Barbara Earnshaw-Cain. 16" - $3,500.00.

26" marked "S&H/K star R." Open mouth with four teeth and on fully jointed body. Head by Simon and Halbig for Kammer & Reinhardt. Courtesy Frasher Doll Auctions. 26" - $1,200.00.

bers are: #400, #403, #109. Add more for flirty eyes. 8" - $485.00; 12" - $550.00; 15" - $695.00; 18" - $825.00; 21" - $900.00; 24" - $1,150.00; 29" - $1,500.00; 34" - $1,800.00; 39" - $2,400.00; 42" - $3,600.00. **#192:** Closed mouth, sleep eyes, fully jointed body. No damage. 16" - $1,600.00; 22"- $2,300.00; 25" - $2,600.00. Open mouth: 15" - $700.00; 21" - $950.00; 24" - $1,200.00.

Small Child Dolls: Open mouth, sleep eyes (some set) and on five-piece bodies. No damage. 5" - $385.00; 8" - $525.00. Jointed body: 8" - $550.00; 10" - $650.00.

Small Child Doll: Closed mouth: 7" - $500.00; 10" - $700.00.

Googly: See Googly section.

Celluloid: Babies will have kid, kidaleen or cloth bodies. Child will be on fully jointed body. Open mouth. Some mold numbers: **#225, 255, 321, 406, 717, 826, 828, etc.** Babies: 12" - $250.00; 15" - $550.00; 18" - $625.00; 22" - $775.00. Child: 14" - $350.00; 17" - $650.00; 21" - $950.00.

Infant: Molded hair and glass eyes, open mouth and cloth body with composition hands. 14" - $1,600.00; 17" - $2,200.00.

These 10" dolls, marked "K star R 126," are all original in their original box and have five-piece toddler bodies. Courtesy Shirley Bertrand. 10" - $1,300.00 pair; $1,500.00 in box.

These 10" dolls, marked "K star R 126," are all original in their original box. The boy has narrower eyes and a thinner face than the girl. Courtesy Shirley Bertrand. 10" - $1,300.00 pair; $1,500.00 in box.

Both of these dolls are marked "K star R 126 Simon & Halbig." They have five-piece toddler bodies and are both original in their original box. Courtesy Shirley Bertrand. 10" - $1,300.00 pair; 10" - $1,500.00 in box.

Left: One end of box that holds a boy and girl K star R 126. The AH/W is the symbol for Adolf Hulss, a dollmaker/distributor who operated in Germany from 1915 into the 1930's. Right: Another company name appears on the this end of the box. E.W. Matthers was also a maker/distributor of dolls and was located in Berlin into the 1930's. It is not known why three different companies were involved in making/selling of these doll sets.

KESTNER, J.D.

Johanne Daniel Kestner's firm was founded in 1802, and his name was carried through the 1920's. The Kestner Company was one of the few that made entire dolls, both body and heads. In 1895, Kestner started using the trademark of the crown and streams.

Child Doll: Ca. 1880. Closed mouth, some appear to be pouties, sleep or set eyes, jointed body with straight wrist. No damage and nicely dressed. **#X:** 15" - $2,600.00; 18" - $2,700.00; 22" - $3,000.00; 27" - $3,800.00. **#XI, XI, XII:** 15" - $2,600.00; 19" - $2,900.00; 23" -

Sample marks:

```
B   MADE IN   6
      GERMANY
       J.D.K.
        126


F   GERMANY   11


       J.D.K.
        208
      GERMANY
```

$3,400.00; 26" - $3,800.00. **#128x or 169:** 14" - $1,800.00; 18" - $2,400.00; 22" - $2,600.00; 26" - $3,100.00; 29" - $3,500.00.

Turned Shoulder Head: Ca. 1880's. Closed mouth. Set or sleep eyes, on kid body with bisque lower arms. No damage and nicely dressed. 18" - $1,000.00; 22" - $1,4000.00; 26" - $1,800.00. Open mouth: 18" - $525.00; 22" - $750.00; 26" - $900.00.

Early Child: Square cut porcelain teeth, jointed body and marked with number and letter. 14" - $900.00; 18" - $1,300.00; 22" - $1,700.00 up.

Bru Type: Open/closed mouth, modeled teeth. Composition lower arms: 18" - $5,900.00; 24" - $6,500.00. Bisque lower arms: 18" - $9,000.00; 24" - $1,400.00. On jointed composition body, straight wrists: 20" - $4,800.00; 26" - $5,600.00.

Character Child: 1910 and after. Closed mouth or open/closed unless noted. Glass or painted eyes, jointed body and no damage and nicely dressed. **#175, 176, 177, 178, 179, 180, 181, 182, 183, 184, 185, 187, 188, 189, 190, 208, 212, 241, 249:** These mold numbers can be found on the boxed set doll that has one body and interchangable four heads. Boxed set with four heads: 11-12" - $9,000.00 up. Larger size with painted eyes, closed or open/closed mouth: 12" - $2,200.00; 16" - $3,200.00; 18" - $4,500.00. Glass eyes, molded-on bonnet: 16" - $4,600.00; 18" - $5,600.00. **#151:** 16" - $2,600.00; 20" - $3,400.00. **#206:** 15" - $9,000.00 up; 19" - $16,000.00 up; 26" - $22,00.00 up. **#239:** Child or toddler (also see under "Babies"): 17" - $2,900.00; 21" - $3,900.00; 26" - $5,800.00. **#241:** Open mouth, glass

18" Kestner marked "XI." Closed mouth, set eyes, beautiful quality bisque. On jointed body with straight wrists. Courtesy Barbara Earnshaw-Cain. 18" - $2,700.00

19" marked "13." Kestner "Bru-type" with sleep eyes, open/closed mouth and molded teeth. Jointed body with straight wrists. These dolls always have a "bulge" around the back of the neck. Courtesy Frasher Doll Auctions. 19" - $6,100.00

KESTNER, J.D.

eyes: 15" - $3,400.00; 21"- $5,200.00.
#249: 22" - $2,000.00. **#260:** Jointed or
toddler body: 8" - $650.00; 12" - $850.00;
16" - $1,300.00; 22" - $1,800.00.

Child Doll: Late 1880's to 1930's.
Open mouth on fully jointed body, sleep
eyes, some set, with no damage and
nicely dressed. **#128, 129, 134, 136,
141, 142, 144, 145, 146, 152,
154,. 156, 159, 160, 161, 162,
164, 168, 174, 196, 211, 214,
215:** 10" - $450.00; 15" - $650.00; 18" -
$725.00; 21" - $800.00; 27" - $1,000.00;
32" - $1,500.00; 36" - $2,000.00; 40" -
$3,200.00. **#143, 189:** Character face,
open mouth. 9" - $650.00; 12" - $850.00;
18" - $1,000.00; 21" - $1,400.00. **#192:**
15" - $650.00; 18" - $775.00; 21" - $895.00.

Child Doll: "Dolly" face with open
mouth, sleep or set eyes, bisque shoulder head on kid with bisque lower arms.
No damage and nicely dressed. **#147,
148, 149, 166, 167, 195, etc.** (Add
more for fur eyebrows): 16" - $475.00;
19" - $550.00; 25" - $900.00; 29" -
$1,200.00. **#154, #171:** Most often
found mold numbers. "Daisy," jointed
body, open mouth. 16" - $600.00; 19" -
$800.00; 23" - $950.00; 26" - $1,200.00;
30" - $1,500.00; 39" - $2,200.00. Same
mold numbers, but with swivel bisque
head on bisque shoulder head. Open
mouth: 17" - $750.00; 21" - $950.00;
26" - $1,200.00. Same mold, numbers
on kid body: 17" - $525.00; 21" - $625.00;
26" - $750.000. Same mold numbers on
fully jointed bodies: 17" - $825.00; 21" -
$975.00; 26" - $1,350.00.

16" rare mold number made by
Kestner. Marked "H Made in Germany
12. J.D.K. 220." Open mouth, modeled
tongue and two upper teeth. On toddler
body. Courtesy Frasher Doll Auctions.
16" - $4,600.00.

Back: 28" marked "JDK 249." Sleep
eyes, open mouth character child. On
fully jointed body with "mama-papa" pull
strings. Front left: K star R mold number
116a that is 15", has open/closed mouth,
molded tongue and two upper teeth. On
bent limb baby body. Right: 20" Kestner
marked "JDK Made in Germany 15."
Painted hair, sleep eyes and open mouth
and two upper teeth and tongue. Courtesy
Frasher Doll Auctions. 28" - $2,800.00;
15" - $2,500.00; 20" - $1,400.00.

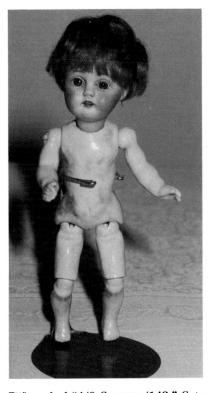

29" marked "J.D.K. 154-14." Socket head on fully jointed body. Open mouth. Courtesy Gloria Anderson. 29" - $1,200.00.

7¼" marked "4/0 Germany/143." Cute fully jointed tiny body. Sleep eyes, open mouth and original wig. Courtesy Joanna Brunkin. 7¼" - $550.00.

30" marked "L½ Made in Germany 15½/J.D.K. 241." Sleep eyes, open mouth character that is rare. On fully jointed body. Courtesy Frasher Doll Auctions. 30" - $9,000.00.

Character Babies: 1910 and later. On bent limb baby bodies, sleep or set eyes, open mouth, can be wigged or have solid dome with painted hair. No damage and nicely dressed. **#121, 142, 150, 151, 152:** 10" - $325.00; 14" - $525.00; 17" - $650.00; 20" - $725.00; 24" - $975.00. **#211, 226, 260:** 9" - $425.00; 14"- $525.00; 17" - $700.00; 21" - $1,000.00; 25" - $1,500.00. **#220:** (Add more for Toddler body) 15" - $4,000.00; 19" - $5,000.00. **#234, 235, 238:** 17" - $550.00; 21" - $950.00; 25" - $1,300.00. **#237, 245, 1070 (Hilda):** Wigged or solid dome. 12" - $2,600.00; 15" - $3,300.00; 21" - $4,700.00; 25" - $5,000.00. Kestner Toddler: 16" - $3,800.00; 21" - $4,200.00; 24" - $4,600.00. **#239:** 15" - $2,600.00; 17" - $2,900.00; 23" - $3,200.00. **#247:** 15" - $1,900.00; 17" - $2,400.00; 22" - $5,100.00; 26" - $5,500.00. **#249:** 17" - $1,600.00; 23" - $21,00.00. **#257:** 14" - $600.00; 18" - $825.00; 21" - $975.00; 25" - $1,600.00. **#262:** 16" - $675.00. **#257, 262 Tod-**

18" Kestner marked "J.D.K. 211." Five-piece bent limb baby body, sleep eyes and open mouth with two upper teeth. Courtesy Gloria Anderson. 18" - $800.00.

dler: 22" - $1,500.00; 27" - $2,000.00; **#279:** Century Doll. Molded hair with part, bangs, cloth body, composition hands. 16" - $1,000.00; 20" - $1,600.00. **#281:** Century Doll. Open mouth: 22" - $950.00.

J.D.K. Marked Baby: Solid dome, painted eyes and open mouth. 16" - $1,200.00; 21" - $1,900.00.

Adult Doll: #162. Sleep eyes, open mouth, adult jointed body (thin waist and molded breasts) with slender limbs. No damage and very nicely dressed. 15" - $1,400.00; 18" - $1,800.00; 23" - $2,400.00.

Adult #172: "Gibson Girl." Bisque shoulder head with closed mouth, kid body with bisque lower arms, glass eyes. No damage and beautifully dressed. 12" - $1,400.00; 18" - $2,900.00; 23" - $4,200.00.

Oriental #243: Olive fired-in color to bisque. Matching color five-

15" adorable Kestner baby marked "J.D.K. 220." Open mouth with two upper teeth and on jointed toddler body. Courtesy Patty Martin. 15" - $4,400.00.

piece bent limb baby body (or jointed toddler-style body), wig, sleep or set eyes. No damage and dressed in oriental style. 15" - $5,200.00; 19" - $7,400.00. Child: Same as above, but on jointed Kestner olive-toned body. 15" - $5,500.00; 19" - $8,000.00. Molded hair baby: 15" - $6,000.00.

Small Dolls: Open mouth, five-piece bodies or jointed bodies, wigs, sleep or set eyes. No damage and nicely dressed. 7" - $375.00; 9" - $465.00. **#133:** 8" - $625.00. **#155:** 8" - $625.00.

15" "Hilda" by Kestner marked "H Made in Germany 12/ 245 J.D.K. 245/1917 Hilda." Open mouth, two teeth and on bent limb baby body. 15" - $3,300.00.

All prices are for dolls that have no chips, hairlines or breaks. (See Modern section for composition and vinyl Kewpies.) Designed by Rose O'Neill and marketed from 1913.

Labels:

All Bisque: One-piece body and head, jointed. shoulders only. Blue wings, painted features with eyes to one side. 1½" - $95.00; 2½" - $125.00; 4½" - $165.00; 6" - $195.00; 7" - $250.00; 9" - $450.00; 12" - $1,400.00.

All Bisque: Jointed at hips and shoulders. 4" - $465.00; 9" - $875.00; 12" - $1,500.00.

Shoulder Head: Cloth body. 6-7" - $600.00.

Action Kewpie: Confederate Soldier: 4½" - $500.00. Farmer: 4" - $495.00. Gardener: 4" - $495.00. Governor: 4" - $450.00. Groom with Bride: 4" - $475.00. Guitar Player: 3½" - $365.00. Holding Pen: 3" - $385.00. Holding cat: 4" - $500.00; Holding butterfly: 4" - $475.00. Hugging: 3½" - $275.00. On stomach, called "Blunderboo": 4" - $450.00. Thinker: 4" - $425.00; 6" - $550.00. Traveler (tan or black suitcase): 3½" - $300.00. With broom: 4" - $450.00. With dog, Doodle: 3½" - $1,500.00. With helmet: 6" - $700.00. With outhouse: 2½" - $1,100.00. With Rabbit: 2½" - $365.00. With rose: 2" - $350.00. With Teddy Bear: 4" - $750.00. With turkey: 2" - $365.00. With umbrella and dog: 3½" - $1,400.00. Soldier: 4½" - $525.00.

7½", 7⅛", 6½", 6", 5¼" bisque Kewpies, jointed at shoulders only. These impish figures were designed by Rose O'Neill to have no gender and to be unaware of people in the world. They were designed with eyes painted to either side so they could be paired off looking at each other, as shown with the two tallest Kewpies. See listings for prices.

Kewpie Soldier & Nurse: 6" - $2,000.00.

Kewpie In Basket With Flowers: 3½" - $650.00.

Kewpie With Drawstring Bag: 4½" - $600.00.

Buttonhole Kewpie: $165.00.

Kewpie Doodle Dog: 1½" - $675.00; 3" - $1,400.00.

Hottentot Black Kewpie: 3½" - $345.00; 5" - $475.00; 9" - $875.00.

Kewpie Perfume Bottle: 3½" - $475.00 up.

Pincushion Kewpie: 2½" - $300.00.

Celluloid Kewpies: 2" - $45.00; 5" - $85.00; 9" - $165.00. Black: 5" - $125.00. Jointed shoulders: 3" - $60.00; 5" - $95.00; 9" - $175.00; 12" - $250.00; 16" - $600.00; 22" - $900.00.

Cloth Body Kewpie: With bisque head, painted eyes. 10" - $2,200.00.

Glass eyes: 12" - $2,200.00 up; 16" - $5,000.00 up.

Glass Eye Kewpie: On chubby toddler, jointed. Bisque head. Marks: "Ges. Gesch./O'Neill J.D.K." 10" - $4,200.00; 12" - $4,600.00; 16" - $6,500.00; 20" - $8,400.00.

All Cloth: (Made by Kreuger) All one-piece with body forming clothes, mask face. Mint condition: 12" - $185.00; 15" - $300.00; 21" - $485.00; 26" - $950.00. Fair condition: 12" - $90.00; 15" - $125.00; 21" - $200.00; 26" - $350.00.

All Cloth: Same as above, but with original dress and bonnet. Mint condition: 12" - $265.00; 15" - $385.00; 21"- $650.00; 26" - $1,200.00.

Kewpie Tin or Celluloid Talcum Container: Excellent condition: 7-8" - $195.00. Composition: See Modern section.

Very rare Kewpie Cowboy lamp of porcelain, 10¼" tall. The Kewpie is 4½" with gun and belt. Lamp is trimmed with lilac roses. Incised "Germany." Shown with bisque action Kewpies. Courtesy Glorya Woods. Lamp - $400.00 up; Action Kewpies - $365.00-450.00.

13½" Kewpie vase. Basketweave lower section and Kewpie in swing on front and back of vase. Made of chalk-like material and may have been a carnival item. Courtesy Frasher Doll Auctions. 13½" - $350.00 up.

KLEY & HAHN

Kley & Hahn operated in Ohrdruf, Germany from 1895 to 1929. They made general dolls as well as babies and fine character dolls.

Marks:

K & H $\geq$ KᢗH $\leq$

Character Child: Boy or girl. Painted eyes (some with glass eyes), closed or open/closed mouth; on jointed body. No damage and nicely dressed. #520, 523, 525, 526, 531, 536,

546, 549, 552: 17" - $3,500.00; 21" - $4,700.00; 23" - $5,000.00; 25" - $5,300.00.

Same Mold Numbers on Toddler Bodies: 15" - $1,500.00; 21" - $2,200.00; 23" - $2,600.00.

Same Mold Numbers on Bent Limb Baby Body: 14" - $900.00; 17" - $1,300.00; 21" - $2,000.00; 25" - $2,400.00.

Same Mold Numbers with Glass Eyes: 14" - $3,000.00; 17" - $3,800.00; 21" - $5,000.00; 25" - $5,700.00.

Character Baby: Molded hair or wig, glass sleep eyes or painted eyes. Can have open or open/closed mouth. On bent limb baby body, no damage

#680: 17" - $875.00. Toddler: 18" - $1,200.00.

#153, 154, 157, 169: Child, closed mouth: 15" - $2,800.00; 20" - $3,700.00. Open mouth: 15" - $1,200.00; 20" - $1,600.00.

#159 Two-faced Doll: 12" - $2,400.00; 15" - $3,000.00.

#166: With molded hair and open mouth. 18-19" - $1,600.00. Closed mouth: 17" - $2,600.00.

#119: Child, glass eyes, closed mouth. 21" - $4,600.00. Painted eyes: 21" - $3,200.00. Toddler: Glass eyes. 21" - $4,800.00.

Child Dolls: Walkure and/or 250 mold number. Sleep or set eyes, open mouth, jointed body. No damage and nicely dressed. 17" - $500.00; 21" - $675.00; 25" - $750.00; 29" - $925.00; 34" - $1,500.00.

21" Kley & Hahn mold number 160. Open/closed mouth, molded tongue and two upper painted teeth. Very large, chunky toddler jointed body. Sleep eyes and cheek dimples. Courtesy Barbara Earnshaw-Cain. 21" - $1,400.00.

and nicely dressed. **#130, 132, 138, 142, 150, 151, 158, 160, 162, 167, 176, 199, 522, 531, 585, 680:** 12" - $485.00; 15" - $600.00; 21" - $800.00; 25" - $1,100.00.

Same Mold Numbers on Toddler Bodies: 14" - $625.00; 17" - $800.00; 20" - $1,000.00; 25" - $1,500.00.

#548, #568: 15" - $725.00; 19" - $975.00; 22" - $1,250.00. Toddler: 19" - $1,400.00; 26" - $1,900.00.

#162 with Talker Mechanism in Head: 18" - $1,500.00; 24" - $2,500.00; 26" - $3,000.00.

#162 with Flirty Eyes and Clockworks in Head: 19" - $1,700.00; 26" - $3,300.00.

22" Kley & Hahn mold number 169 with closed mouth and sleep eyes. All original and on jointed toddler body. Courtesy Barbara Earnshaw-Cain. 22" - $4,200.00; 22" original - $6,000.00.

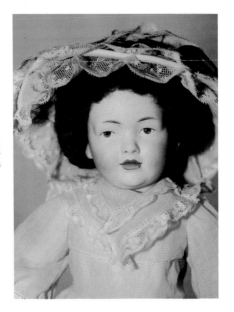

18" Kley & Hahn mold number 536. Open/closed mouth, intaglio eyes and on fully jointed body. Courtesy Barbara Earnshaw-Cain. 18" - $3,600.00.

KONIG & WERNICKE

15" made by Konig & Wernicke, marked "K&W 1070." Open mouth, two upper teeth, jointed toddler body. Courtesy Frasher Doll Auctions. 15" - $485.00; 19" - $700.00; 22" - $800.00; Flirty eyes: 18" - $750.00; 21" - $950.00.

Kathe Kruse began making dolls in 1910. In 1916, she obtained a patent for a wire coil doll and in 1923, she registered a trademark of a double K with the first one reversed, along with the name Kathe Kruse. The first heads were designed after her own children and copies of babies from the Renaissance period. The dolls have a molded muslin head that are handpainted in oils and a jointed cloth body. These early dolls will be marked "Kathe Kruse" on the foot and sometimes with a "Germany" and number.

Early Marked Dolls VII, I-H, I: In excellent condition and with original clothes: 16" - $3,100.00; 19" - $3,500.00. In fair condition, not original: 16" - $950.00; 19" - $1,200.00.

1920's Dolls: Molded hair, hips are wide. In excellent condition and original: 16" - $1,600.00; 21" - $1,900.00. In fair condition, not original: 16" - $500.00; 21" - $900.00.

U.S. Zone: Germany 1945-1951 (Turtle mark.) 17" - $1,000.00.

Plastic Dolls: With glued-on wigs, sleep or painted eyes. Marked with turtle mark and number on head and on back "Modell/Kathe Kruse/" and number. 15" - $500.00.

Baby: Painted closed or open eyes. 1922. 19" - $2,200.00. Plastic head: 22" - $3,600.00.

Celluloid: 15" - $500.00; 18" - $800.00.

1975 to date: 9" - $225.00; 13" - $375.00; 17" - $475.00.

12" all original Kathe Kruse with celluloid head, jointed cloth body, stitched fingers, and painted features. Ca. 1955. Courtesy Frasher Doll Auctions. 12" - $375.00.

Kathe Kruse dolls. Back: A#1 marked "908" on foot. 18" all cloth, oil painted, solemn expression. Front left to right: #IH marked "31301." 17" with wig over painted hair. 14" signed on foot. #VII with the DuMein head. 18" boy #1. All have wide hips, made of muslin cloth, oil-painted heads and features. All but girl may be original. Courtesy Frasher Doll Auctions. 14" - $1,300.00; 17" - $1,700.00; 18" - $1,800.00.

16" early plastic Kathe Kruse dolls made by Rheinische Gummi & Celluloid Fabrik Co. whose trademark is a turtle in a diamond (shown on tag.) Sleep eyes and lashes. Ca. 1953 "Hansel & Gretel." Courtesy Gloria Anderson. 16" - $450.00 each.

KUHNLENZ, GEBRUDER

Kuhnlenz made dolls from 1884 to 1930 and was located in Kronach, Bavaria. Marks from this company include the "G.K." plus numbers such as 56-38, 44-26, 41-28, 56-18, 44-15, 38-27, 44-26, etc. Other marks now attributed to this firm are:

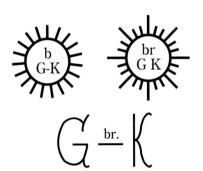

Child with Closed Mouth: Mold #32. Bisque head in perfect condition, jointed body and nicely dressed. 15" - $950.00; 19" - $1,450.00; 23" - $1,850.00. **Mold #34:** Bru type. 17" - $2,600.00. **Mold #38:** Kid body, bisque shoulder head. 15" - $650.00; 22" - $900.00.

Child with Open Mouth: Mold #41, 44, 56. Bisque head in perfect condition, jointed body and nicely dressed. 15" - $600.00; 19" - $850.00; 23" - $1,050.00. **Mold #165:** Bisque head in perfect condition, jointed body and nicely dressed. 17" - $450.00; 23" - $600.00.

Tiny Dolls: Bisque head in perfect condition, five-piece body with painted-on shoes and socks, open mouth. 8" - $200.00. Closed mouth: 8" - $685.00.

A. Lanternier & Cie of Limoges, France made dolls from about the 1890's on into the 1930's. Before making dolls, they produced porcelain pieces as early as 1855. Their doll heads will be fully marked and some carry a name such as "Favorite, Lorraine, Cherie," etc. They generally are found on papier maché bodies but can be on fully jointed composition bodies. Dolls from this firm may have nearly excellent quality bisque to very poor quality.

Marks:

FABRICATION FRANCAISE   **AL & CIE LIMOGES**

Child: Open mouth, set eyes on jointed body. No damage and nicely dressed. Good quality bisque with pretty face. 15" - $750.00; 21" - $950.00; 24" - $1,100.00; 27" $1,600.00. Poor quality

bisque with very high coloring or blotchy color bisque. 15" - $475.00; 21" - $595.00; 24" - $700.00; 27" - $800.00.

"Jumeau" Style Face: Has a striking Jumeau look. Good quality bisque: 19" - $1,000.00; 23" - $1,300.00. Poor quality bisque: 19" - $550.00; 23" - $650.00.

Character: Open/closed mouth with teeth, smiling fat face, glass eyes, on jointed body. No damage and nicely dressed. Marked "Toto." 17" - $850.00; 21" - $1,500.00.

Lady: Adult-looking face, set eyes, open/closed or closed mouth. Jointed adult body. No damage and nicely dressed. 15" - $950.00; 18" - $1,400.00.

22" child by Lanternier marked "Fabrication Francais Limoge France J.B." Open mouth with six teeth and on fully jointed body. Courtesy Frasher Doll Auctions. 22" - $600.00.

Right: 20" Lanternier marked "Fabrication Francaise A.L. & Co. Limoge. Cherie 8." Open mouth with six teeth and on fully jointed body. 24" Armand Marseille marked "A. 10M. Floradora." On fully jointed body, open mouth. Courtesy Frasher Doll Auctions. 20" - $925.00; 24" - $500.00.

29" marked "L - anchor mark - C13." Made by LeConte. Sleep eyes with lashes, open mouth and has French jointed body. Courtesy Frasher Doll Auctions. Open mouth: 16" - $765.00; 18" - $875.00; 23" - $1,000.00; 29" - $1,600.00.

LENCI

Lenci dolls are all felt with a few having cloth torsos. They are jointed at neck, shoulder and hips. The original clothes will be felt or organdy or a combination of both. Features are oil painted and generally eyes are painted to the side. Size can range from 5" - 45". Marks: On cloth or paper label "Lenci Torino Made in Italy." "Lenci" may be written on bottom of foot or underneath one arm. *Mint or rare dolls will bring higher prices.*

Children: No moth holes, very little dirt, doll as near mint as possible and all in excellent condition. 14" - $850.00 up; 16" - $975.00 up; 18" - $1,000.00 up; 20" - $1,400.00 up. Dirty, original clothes in poor condition or redressed: 14" - $185.00; 16" - $250.00; 18" - $325.00; 20" - $375.00.

Tiny Dolls (Called Mascottes): In excellent condition: 5" - $185.00; 9-10" - $325.00. Dirty, redressed or original clothes in poor condition: 5" - $60.00; 9-10" - $100.00.

Ladies with Adult Faces: "Flapper" or "Boudoir" style with long limbs. In excellent condition: 24" - $1,900.00 up; 27" - $2,000.00 up. Dirty or in poor condition: 24" - $500.00; 28" - $850.00.

Clowns: Excellent condition: 18" - $1,600.00; 27" - $2,000.00. Poor condition: 18" - $600.00; 27" - $950.00.

Indians or Orientals: Excellent condition: 17" - $3,700.00. Dirty and poor condition: 17" - $1,100.00.

Golfer: Excellent, perfect condition: 16" - $2,200.00. Poor condition: 16" - $700.00.

Shirley Temple Type: Excellent condition: 28" - $2,500.00. Dirty and poor condition: 28" - $1,000.00.

Bali Dancer: Excellent condition: 21" - $2,200.00. Poor condition: 22" - $650.00.

Smoking Doll: In excellent condition, painted eyes: 25" - $2,000.00 up. Poor condition: 25" - $950.00.

Glass Eyes: Excellent condition: 17" - $2,600.00; 22" - $3,300.00. Poor condition: 17" - $850.00; 22" - $1,000.00.

"Surprise Eyes" Doll: Very round painted eyes and "O"-shaped mouth. 15" - $1,900.00; 19" - $2,500.00. With glass eyes that are flirty: 15" - $2,500.00; 19" - $3,200.00.

Boys: Side part hairdo. Excellent condition: 18" - $1,900.00 up; 23" - $2,500.00. Poor condition: 18" - $600.00; 23" - $800.00.

Babies: Excellent condition: 15" - $1,400.00; 21" - $2,000.00. Poor condition: 16" - $500.00; 20" - $900.00.

11½" Lenci Mouse, all felt with applied felt features and original clothes. Tagged "Lenci Torino." 16" Kestner marked "J.D.K. 211." Open mouth with two lower teeth and on five-piece bent limb baby body. Courtesy Frasher Doll Auctions. 12" mouse - $400.00; 16" - $650.00.

7½" original Lenci "Mascotte" in mint condition. Organdy layered dress, felt shoes and hat. Doll is all felt with painted features. Courtesy Glorya Woods. 8" - $300.00.

21" Lenci Mermaid pajama bag made of all felt except back of head which is cloth. Heavy mohair wig, floss lashes, oil-painted features. Ca. early 1950's. 21" - $185.00.

Lower front: Rare 14½" Lenci "Aladdin" sitting on pillow. Brown felt, oil-painted features. Mint condition. Right: 24" very unusual lady Lenci with "surprised eyes." All felt and organdy, tapestry shoes with pointed toes and high heels. Left: 28" brown Simon & Halbig mold number 939 with slightly open mouth and four upper teeth. Factory clothes. Courtesy Frasher Doll Auctions. 14½" - $2,200.00; 24" - $1,300.00; 28" - $6,000.00.

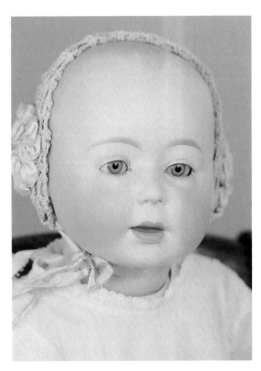

23" "Lori Baby" marked "D Lori 4/green stamp "Geschuz S & Co." Made by Swaine & Co. Lightly painted hair, sleep eyes and open/closed mouth. On five-piece bent limb baby body. Courtesy Frasher Doll Auctions. Glass eyes: 14" - $1,600.00; 20" - $2,500.00; 23" - $3,000.00; 26" - $3,700.00. Intaglio eyes: 20" - $1,900.00; 24" - $2,300.00. Flocked hair: 20" - $2,700.00; 25" - $3,400.00.

MASCOTTE

Mascotte Dolls were made by May Freres Cie. They operated from 1890 to 1897, then became part of Jules Steiner in 1898. This means the dolls were made from 1890 to about 1902, so the quality of the bisque can vary greatly, as well as the artist painting. Dolls will be marked "BÉBÉ MASCOTTE PARIS" and some incised with "M" and a number.

Child: Closed mouth and marked "Mascotte." Excellent condition and no damage. 17" - $4,200.00; 19" - $4,800.00; 23" - $5,700.00; 27" - $6,200.00.

Child: Same as above, but marked with "M" and a number. 17" - $3,800.00; 19" - $4,200.00; 23" - $5,200.00; 27" - $5,800.00.

A. Theroude mechanical walker patented in 1840 with papier maché head, bamboo teeth in open mouth and stands on three wheels (two large and one small), tin cart with mechanism attached to legs. 16" - $2,600.00.

Autoperipatetikos: Base is like clockworks and has tin feet and when key wound, the doll walks. Heads can be china, untinted bisque or papier maché. Early China Head: 11" - $1,800.00. Untinted Bisque: 11" - $1,100.00. Papier maché: 11" - $800.00.

Hawkins, George walker with pewter hands and feet, wood torso. Hands modeled to push a carriage, which should be a Goodwin, patented in 1867-1868. Carriage has two large wheels and one small one in front. Molded hair and dolls head will be marked "X.L.C.R./Doll head/Pat. Sept. 8, 1868." (China heads may not be marked.) 11" - $2,200.00.

Jumeau: Raises and lowers both arms and head moves. Holds items such as a hankie and bottle, book and fan, etc. - one in each hand. Key wound music box in base. Closed mouth and marked "Jumeau." 15" - $3,800.00 up; 20" - $4,700.00 up. Same with open mouth: 15" - $2,500.00 up; 20" - $3,600.00 up.

Jumeau: Marked "Jumeau." Standing or sitting on key wound music box and doll plays an instrument. 14" - $3,900.00 up; 18" - $5,300.00 up.

Jumeau: Marked "Jumeau" walker with one-piece legs, arms jointed at elbows. She raises her arm to an open mouth to throw kisses as head turns. 15" - $2,000.00 up; 21" - $2,900.00 up.

Jumeau: Marked "Jumeau" and stands on three-wheel cart and when cart is pulled, doll's head turns from side to side and arms go up and down. 15" - $3,600.00 up; 18" - $4,200.00 up.

Paris Bébé, R.D., E.D marked dolls standing on key wound music box and has closed mouth. Holds items in hands and arms move and head nods or moves from side to side. 21" - $5,200.00 up.

Jumeau: 18-20" doll stands at piano built to scale and hands attached to keyboard with rods. Key wound piano. $20,000.00 up.

Steiner, Jules: Bisque head, open mouth with two rows of teeth. Key wound, waltzes in circles, original clothes. Glass eyes, arms move as it dances. 17" - $9,400.00.

Steiner, Jules: Bisque head on composition upper and lower torso-chest, also lower legs and all the arms. Twill-covered sections between parts of body. Key wound, cries, moves head

15" bisque swivel head on bisque shoulder plate, open mouth with two rows of teeth, kid over wood upper arms, hinged elbows, bisque lower arms. When key is wound, she waltzes in circles, and raises and lowers arms. 16½" "A" series Steiner with closed mouth and on jointed Steiner body with straight wrists. Courtesy Frasher Doll Auctions. 15" - $9,000.00 up; 16½" - $4,600.00.

and kicks legs. Open mouth with two rows of teeth. 18" - $2,500.00; 23" - $3,100.00. Same as above, but Bisque Torso Sections: 18" - $7,000.00 up.

German Makers: One or two figures on music box, key wound, or pulling cart. Dolls have open mouths. Marked with name of maker: $1,400.00 up. 1960's, 1970's German-made reproductions of this style dolls: $300.00.

Overall 15½" tall musical automation (mechanical) with head incised "E.1D." and bisque lower limbs. Both dolls have closed mouths. Key wound music box. Shown with 22" Jumeau with open mouth and on Jumeau body. Courtesy Frasher Doll Auctions. 15½" - $3,800.00 up; 22" - $5,200.00.

9½" marked on platform "G. Vichy, Paris." Bisque head, closed mouth, all original costume. On three wheel metal platform with key wound mechanism. Doll's head turns and she raises and lowers one arm. Courtesy Frasher Doll Auctions. 9½" - $1,800.00.

The molded hair bisque dolls are just like any other flesh-toned dolls, but instead of having a wig, they have molded hair, glass set eyes or finely painted and detailed eyes, and generally they will have a closed mouth. They almost always are a shoulder head with one-piece shoulder and head. They can be on a kid body or cloth with bisque lower arms, with some having compostion lower legs. These dolls are generally very pretty. Many molded hair dolls are being attributed to A.B.G. (Alt, Beck & Gottschalck) mold numbers 890, 1000, 1008, 1028, 1064, 1142, 1256, 1288, etc.

Child: 10" - $175.00; 15" - $450.00; 20" - $750.00; 23" - $1,300.00; 26" - $1,500.00.

Boy: 17" - $650.00; 20" - $850.00; 23" - $1,200.00.

Decorated Shoulder Plate: With elaborate hairdo. 20" - $1,800.00.

19" beautiful molded hair bisque with large painted eyes, open/closed mouth with molded teeth. Shoulder head on cloth body with bisque lower arms. Courtesy Hagele Collection. 19" - $950.00.

Charles Motschmann has always been credited as the manufacturer of a certain style doll, but now his work is only being attributed to the making of the voice boxes in the dolls. Various German makers such as Heinrich Stier and others are being given the credit for making the dolls. They date from 1851 into the 1880's.

The early dolls were babies, children and Orientals. They have glass eyes, closed mouths, heads of papier maché, wax over papier maché or wax over composition. They can have lightly brush stroked painted hair or come with a wig. If the mouth is open, the doll will have bamboo teeth. The larger dolls will have arms and legs jointed at wrists and ankles. The torso (lower) body is composition or wooden, as are the arms and legs, except for the upper parts which will be twill-style cloth. The mid-section will also be cloth. If the doll is marked, it can be found on the upper cloth of the leg and will be stamped:

Baby: Motschmann marked or type. In extremely fine condition: 13" - $600.00; 16" - $725.00; 20" - $950.00; 25" - $1,500.00. In fair condition: 13" - $425.00; 16" - $525.00; 20" - $625.00; 25" - $750.00.

Child: In extremely fine condition: 15" - $700.00; 18" - $900.00; 23" - $1,300.00. In fair condition: 15" - $425.00; 18" - $625.00; 23" - $750.00.

ORIENTAL DOLLS

Bisque dolls were made in Germany by various firms with fired-in Oriental color and on jointed yellowish tinted bodies. They could be a child or baby and most were made after 1900. All must be in excellent condition in Oriental clothes and no damage to head.

Armand Marseille: Girl or boy marked only "A.M." 7" - $700.00; 11" - $900.00. Painted Bisque: 8" - $200.00; 12" - $425.00.

#353 Baby: 15" - $1,400.00; 19" - $2,100.00. Painted bisque: 15" - $550.00.

Bruno Schmidt (BSW) #220: Closed mouth. 16" - $3,600.00.

#500: 14" - $2,200.00; 18" - $3,200.00.

Kestner (J.D.K.) #243: Baby: 15" - $5,200.00; 19" - $7,400.00. Molded hair baby: 15" - $6,000.00. Child: 15" - $5,500.00; 19" - $8,000.00.

Schoenau & Hoffmeister: (S, PB in star H) #4900: 15" - $1,600.00; 19" - $1,900.00.

Pair of 13" Oriental babies made by Kestner. Both marked "243 J.D.K." Sleep eyes, open mouths, on five-piece bent limb baby bodies. Courtesy Frasher Doll Auctions. 13" - $5,000.00 each.

Orientals: 9" marked "Armand Marseille" with china legs and tiny painted feet, glass eyes and open mouth. 6" unmarked, closed mouth and very slanted eyes. 6" old man and lady with half modeled bisque body and head, molded-on clothes, stone bisque hands and lower legs with rest cloth. Both original. Courtesy Turn of Century Antiques. 9" - $695.00; 6" $400.00; mán/woman - $465.00 pair.

Simon & Halbig (S & H) #164: 15" - $2,400.00; 19" - $2,900.00.

#220: Solid dome or "Belton" type. Closed mouth. 18" - $3,000.00.

#1099, 1129, 1199: 15" - $2,500.00; 19" - $3,100.00.

#1329: 15" - $2,400.00; 19" - $2,900.00.

All Bisque: 7-8" - $1,200.00.

Unmarked: Open mouth: 15" - $1,300.00; 19" - $2,000.00. Closed mouth: 15" - $2,000.00; 19" - $3,000.00.

Nippon - Caucasian Dolls Made in Japan: 1918-1922. Most made during World War I. These dolls can be near excellent quality to very poor quality. Morimura Brothers mark is Ⓜ︎Ⓑ︎. Dolls marked 𝒴ℐ were made by Yamato. Others will just be marked with NIPPON along with other marks such as "J.W.", etc.

Nippon Marked Baby: Good to excellent bisque, well painted, nice body and no damage. 12" - $285.00; 16" - $375.00; 20" - $600.00; 25" - $825.00. Poor quality: 12" - $125.00; 16" - $175.00; 20" - $265.00; 25" - $365.00.

Nippon Child: Good to excellent quality bisque, no damage and nicely dressed. 15" - $325.00; 19" - $550.00; 23" - $700.00. Poor quality: 15" - $135.00; 19" - $225.00; 23" - $325.00.

Traditional Doll: Made in Japan. Papier maché swivel head on shoulder plate, cloth mid-section and upper arms and legs. Limbs and torso are papier maché, glass eyes, pierced nostrils. The early dolls will have jointed wrists and ankles and will be slightly sexed. **Early**

Left: 14½" Japanese baby with Morimura Brother mark. Open mouth and on five-piece baby body. Right: 11" German baby marked "P.M. 914." Open mouth, made by Otto Reinecke. Courtesy Frasher Doll Auctions. 14½" - $325.00; 11" $250.00.

fine quality: Original dress, 1890's. 14" - $325.00; 19" - $550.00; 26" - $1,000.00. **Early Boy:** With painted hair. 16" - $485.00; 21" - $800.00; 28" - $1,400.00. 1930's or later: 14" - $100.00; 17" - $185.00. **Lady:** All original and excellent quality. 1920's: 12" - $195.00; 16" - $300.00. Later Lady: 1940's-1950's. 12" - $100.00; 14" - $135.00. **Emperor or Empress in Sitting Position:** 1920's-1930's. 8" - $185.00 up; 12" - $350.00 up. **Warrior:** Early 1920's. 12" - $265.00 up. On horse: 12" - $675.00 up.

Japanese Baby: With bisque head. Sleep eyes, closed mouth and all white bisque. Papier maché body: Original and in excellent condition. Late 1920's. 8" - $65.00; 12" - $165.00. Glass Eyes: 8" - $80.00; 12" - $185.00.

Japanese Baby: Head made of crushed oyster shells painted flesh color, papier maché body, glass eyes and original. 8" - $85.00; 12" - $145.00; 16" - $200.00; 19" - $300.00.

Oriental Dolls: All composition, jointed at shoulder and hips. Painted features, painted hair or can have bald head with braid of yarn down back with rest covered by cap, such as "Ling Ling" or "Ming Ming" made by Quan Quan Co. in 1930's. Painted-on shoes. 10" - $145.00.

Chinese Traditional Dolls: Man or woman. Composition-type material with cloth-wound bodies or can have wooden carved arms and feet. In traditional costume and in excellent condition. 9" - $300.00; 12" - $500.00.

Door of Hope Dolls: Wooden head, cloth bodies and most have carved hands. Chinese costume. Adult: 11" - $365.00. Child: 7" - $450.00. Mother and Baby: 11" - $500.00. Man: 11" - $400.00.

24" all original Morimura Brothers with sleep eyes, open mouth and on fully jointed body. Courtesy Gloria Anderson. 24" - $800.00.

22" slant eyes with lashes. Oriental marked "S&H 1129." Made by Simon & Halbig. Olive tone bisque and jointed body. Courtesy Barbara Earnshaw-Cain. 22" - $3,900.00.

21" Simon & Halbig mold number 1329. Oriental with olive skin tones, pierced ears and on an olive tone jointed body. Belonged to Barbara Scott King, 1948 Olympic gold medalist. Courtesy Barbara Earnshaw-Cain. 21" - $3,400.00.

Left: 4½" all bisque "Baby Bud" marked "Nippon." Molded-on shirt. Center: 14" Japanese baby on five-piece baby body. Painted features, open mouth. Marked "3-3/0." 5" French child marked "Paris Unis France 301." Painted eyes, closed mouth and all original. Painted-on boots. Body is papier maché. Courtesy Frasher Doll Auctions. 4½" - $175.00; 14" - $325.00; 5" - $165.00.

14" traditional Japanese baby made of crushed oyster shell, then painted. Glass eyes and jointed at neck shoulder and hips. Original costume. Courtesy Frasher Doll Auctions. 14" - $185.00.

ORSINI

Jeanne I. Orsini of New York designed dolls from 1916 to the 1920's. It is not known who made the heads for her, but it is likely that all bisque dolls designed by her were made by J.D. Kestner in Germany. The initials of the designer are "J.I.O." and the dolls will be marked with those initials along with a year such as 1919, 1920, etc. Since the middle initial is "I," it may appear as a number 1. Dolls can also be marked "Copy. by J.I. Orsini/Germany."

Painted Bisque Character: Can be on a cloth body with cloth limbs or a bent limb baby body, a toddler body, have flirty eyes and an open smiling mouth. Can be wigged or have molded hair and be a boy or a girl. Head is painted or painted clay-like material. Prices are for excellent condition, no damage and nicely dressed. **#1429:** 15" - $1,900.00; 19" - $2,400.00.

Bisque Head Baby: Cloth body with bisque head with wide open screaming mouth, eye squinted and marked "JIO." 12" - $1,200.00; 14" - $1,500.00.

Bisque Head Baby: Fired-in color bisque head with sleep eyes (some may be set), open mouth and has cloth body and painted hair. Marked "KIDDIE JOY JIO. 1926." 15" - $1,700.00; 17" - $2,300.00.

All Bisque: See All Bisque section for Didi, Fifi, Dodo, Zizi, etc.

Pintal & Godchaux of Montreuil, France made dolls from 1890 to 1899. They held one trademark - "Bebe Charmount." The heads will be marked "P.G."

Child: 17" - $2,900.00; 22" - $3,500.00; 24" - $4,500.00.

Child, Open Mouth: 15" - $1,500.00; 20" - $2,000.00; 23" - $2,600.00.

22" marked "B/P 11 G." Made by Pintel & Godchaux. Closed mouth, pierced ears and on French fully jointed body. Courtesy Frasher Doll Auctions. 22" - $3,500.00.

8" marked "Germany 12/0." Sleep eyes, painted bisque head, open mouth. Five-piece body and all original. Courtesy Patty Martin. 8" - $145.00; 14" - $450.00.

6½" marked "A.M. 390 13/0." Made by Armand Marseille. Painted bisque head, set eyes, open mouth and on five-piece body. All original. Courtesy Patty Martin. 7" - $285.00; 12" - $375.00.

23" marked "A.M. Koppelsdorf Germany 1330 A.12.M." Open mouth and original wig. Five-piece bent limb baby body. Made by Armand Marseille. Courtesy Frasher Doll Auctions. 23" - $550.00.

Papier maché dolls were made in U.S., Germany, England, France and other countries. Paper pulp, wood and rag fibers containing paste, oil or glue is formed into a composition-like moldable material. Flour, clay and/or sand was added for stiffness. The hardness of papier maché depends on the amount of glue that was added.

Many so called papier maché parts were actually laminated paper with several thicknesses of molded paper bonded (glued) together or pressed after being glued.

"Papier maché" means "chewed paper" in French, and as early as 1810, dolls of papier maché were being mass produced by using molds.

Marked "M&S Superior": (Muller & Strassburger) Papier maché shoulder head with blonde or black molded hair, painted blue or brown eyes, old cloth body with kid or leather arms and boots. Nicely dressed and head not repainted, chipped or cracked. 17"- $565.00; 23" - $725.00. Glass eyes: 21" - $800.00. With wig: 19" - $725.00. Repainted nicely: 17" - $300.00; 23" - $500.00. Chips, Scuffs, or Not Repainted Well: 17" - $100.00; 23" - $135.00.

French or French Type: Painted black hair, some with brush marks, on solid dome. Some have nailed-on wigs. Open mouths have bamboo teeth. In-set glass eyes. In very good condition, nice old clothes. All leather/kid body. 16" - $1,300.00; 18" - $1,700.00; 21" - $1,900.00; 25" -$2,400.00; 29" - $3,300.00.

Early Papier Maché: With cloth body and wooden limbs. Early hairdo with top knots, buns, puff curls or braiding. Ca. 1840's. Not restored and in original or very well made clothes. In very good condition and may show a little wear. 10" - $500.00; 14" - $650.00; 18" - $800.00; 21" - $1,050.00; 25" - $1,400.00.

Marked "Greiner": Dolls of 1858 on: Blonde or black molded hair, brown or blue painted eyes, cloth body with leather arms, nicely dressed and with very little minor scuffs. See Greiner section.

Motschmann Types: With wood and twill bodies. Separate hip section, glass eyes, closed mouth and brush stroke hair on solid domes. Nicely dressed and ready to display. 15" - $700.00; 21" - $965.00; 25" - $1,500.00.

German Papier Maché: 1870-1900's. Molded various hairdos, painted eyes and closed mouth. May be blonde or black hair. Nicely dressed and not repainted: 17" - $500.00; 21" - $675.00; 25" - $1,400.00; 30" - $1,700.00. Glass eyes: 17" - $625.00; 21" - $800.00; 25" - $1,500.00; 30" - $1,800.00. Showing wear

16" French papier maché of the 1860's. All original. Kid and cloth body and limbs. Courtesy Barbara Earnshaw-Cain. 16" - $1,300.00.

and scuffs, but not touched up: 17" - $250.00; 21" - $300.00; 25" - $400.00; 30" - $600.00.

Turned Shoulder Head: Solid dome, glass eyes and closed mouth. Twill cloth body with composition lower arms. In very good condition and nicely dressed. 16" - $600.00; 21" - $850.00.

German Character Heads: These heads are molded just like the bisque ones. Glass eyes, closed mouth and on fully jointed body. In excellent condition and nicely dressed. 15" - $950.00; 21" - $1,300.00.

1920's on - Papier Maché: Head usually has bright coloring. Wigged, usually dressed as a child, or in provincial costumes. Stuffed cloth body and limbs or have papier maché arms. In excellent overall condition. 9" - $90.00; 13" - $150.00; 15" - $225.00.

Clowns: Papier maché head with painted clown features. Open or closed mouth, molded hair or wigged and on cloth body with some having composition or papier maché lower arms. In excellent condition. 12" - $385.00; 16" - $565.00.

16" papier maché styled with center part with comb marks and sausage curls around head. Kid body with wooden arms and legs. All original. Courtesy Frasher Doll Auctions. 16" - $650.00.

3" five-piece molded papier maché Palmer Cox "Brownie" Christmas tree ornament. Has painted-on clothes. Courtesy Jeannie Mauldin. 3" - $150.00.

27" wax over papier maché, cloth body with composition limbs, glass eyes, mohair wig. Courtesy Sally Freeman. 27" - $850.00.

PARIAN-TYPE (UNTINTED BISQUE)

"Parian-type" dolls were made from the 1850's to the 1880's, with the majority being made during the 1870's and 1880's. All seem to have been made in Germany and if marked, it will be found on the inside of the shoulder plate. There are hundreds of different heads, and it must be noted that the really rare and unique unglazed porcelain dolls are difficult to find and their prices will be high.

"Parian-type" dolls can be found with every imaginable thing applied to the head and shirt tops - flowers, snoods, ruffles, feathers, plumes, etc. Many have inset glass eyes, pierced ears and most are blonde, although some will have from light to medium brown hair, and a few will have glazed black hair.

Various Fancy Hairstyles: With molded combs, ribbons, flowers, head bands, or snoods. Cloth body with cloth/ "parian" limbs. Perfect condition and very nicely dressed. 18" - $1,500.00 up; 22" - $1,900.00 up. Painted eyes, unpierced ears: 18" - $900.00; 22" - $1,200.00.

Swivel Neck: 18" - $2,600.00; 22" - $3,300.00.

Molded Necklaces: Jewels or standing ruffles (undamaged). Glass eyes, pierced ears: 18" - $1,600.00; 22" - $2,000.00 up. Painted eyes, unpierced ears: 18" - $1,100.00; 22" - $1,500.00.

Bald Head: Solid dome, takes wigs, full ear detail. 1850's. Perfect condition and nicely dressed. 13" - $700.00; 17" - $950.00; 21" - $1,500.00.

Very Plain Style: With no decoration in hair or on shoulders. No damage and nicely dressed. 15" - $300.00; 18" - $500.00.

Men or Boys: Hairdos with center or side part, cloth body with cloth/ "parian" limbs. Decorated shirt and tie.

16" - $750.00; 19" - $1,050.00.

Undecorated Shirt Top: 16" - $350.00; 19" - $500.00; 25" - $800.00.

Molded Hat: 10" - $1,600.00; 15" - $2,500.00.

16" man and 20" woman, both "Parians." He has side part, molded brown hair and shirt top. Cloth body with leather arms. She has molded flowers in hairdo, bisque lower arms and cloth body. Maybe original clothes. Courtesy Turn of Century Antiques. 16" - $595.00. 20" - $685.00.

19" "Alice in Wonderland" hairdo "Parian" by Simon & Halbig. Marked "S 7 H" on front of shoulder plate. Band molded in hair, kid body with bisque lower arms. Courtesy Frasher Doll Auctions. 19" - $800.00.

23" "Parian" with brown molded hair with molded-on shirt top. Lacmann cloth body with sewn-on red corset, leather arms and sewn-on boots and stockings. Old clothes, painted features. Courtesy Barbara Earnshaw-Cain. 23" - $800.00.

25½" "Parian" untinted bisque shoulder head. Full exposed ears, full long hair molded hairdo. Cloth body, bisque lower arms and cloth body. Marked "0748." Courtesy Frasher Doll Auctions. 26" - $950.00.

These dolls were made by Danel
& Cie in France from 1889 to 1895.
The heads will be marked "Paris Bébé"
and the body's paper label is marked
with a drawing of the Eiffel Tower and
"Paris Bébé/Brevete."

Paris Bébé Child: Closed mouth,
no damage and nicely dressed. 17" -
$4,100.00; 21" - $4,300.00; 25" - $4,900.00;
27" - $5,400.00. High color to bisque,
closed mouth. 17" - $3,500.00; 21" -
$3,900.00; 25" - $4,300.00; 27" - $4,800.00.

**25" "Paris Bébé" by Danel & Cie. Closed
mouth and on fully jointed French body.
Courtesy Frasher Doll Auctions. 25" -
$4,900.00.**

**18" "Paris Bébé" with closed mouth,
paperweight eyes and on French jointed
body. Completely original. Courtesy
Frasher Doll Auctions. 18" - $3,500.00;
18" original - $4,800.00.**

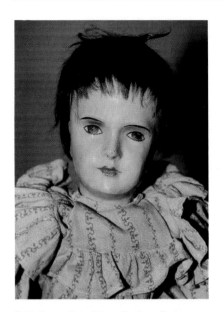

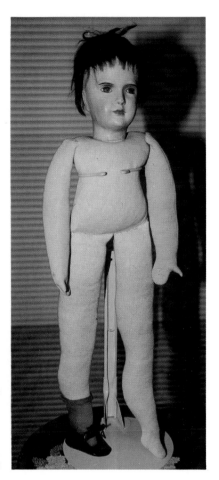

27" Dora Petzold - Berlin, Germany ca. 1920's. Head made of laminated pressed paper that is formed in two halfs and joined. Features are hand-painted in oils. The heavy stockenette body and legs are filled with sawdust. Legs have formed calfs; arms are stuffed with a soft material (most likely "wool dust"). Free-formed thumbs, stitched fingers. Shoulders and hips stitched to allow doll to "move" and all stitching is hand done. Right: Shows the short waisted, long limbed body, the form of the foot and calf, and freestanding thumbs and mitt hands. 20" - $825.00; 24" - $900.00; 27" - $975.00.

PHENIX

Phenix Bébé dolls were made by Henri Alexandre of Paris who made dolls from 1889 to 1900.

Mark:

Child - Closed Mouth: 17" - $3,600.00; 19" - $3,900.00; 23" - $4,400.00; 25" - $4,600.00.

Child - Open Mouth: 17" - $2,000.00; 19" - $2,300.00; 23" - $2,700.00; 25" - $2,900.00.

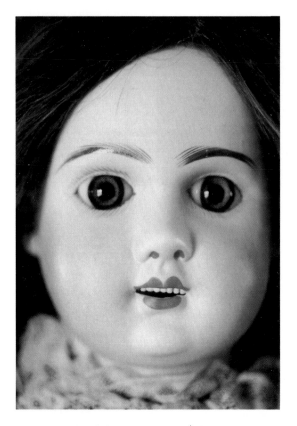

25" "Phenix Bébé" marked "9L☆." Open mouth, pierced ears and on French jointed body. Courtesy Frasher Doll Auctions. 25" - $4,600.00.

PIANO BABIES

Piano Babies were made in Germany from the 1880's into the 1930's and one of the finest quality makers was Gebruder Heubach. They were also made by Kestner, Dressel, Limbach, etc.

Piano Babies: All bisque, unjointed, molded hair and painted features. The clothes are molded on and they come in a great variety of positions. Excellent Quality: Extremely good artist workmanship and excellent detail to modeling. 4" - $185.00; 8" - $400.00 up; 12" - $725.00 up; 16" - $900.00 up. Medium Quality: May not have painting finished on back side of figure. 4" - $100.00; 8" - $250.00; 12" - $375.00; 16" - $500.00. **With Animal, Pot, On Chair, With Flowers or Other Items:** Excellent quality. 4" - $250.00; 8" - $450.00; 12" - $825.00 up; 16" - $1,200.00 up.

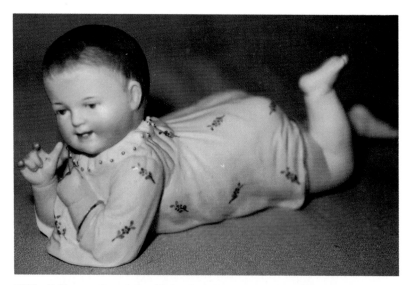

10½" all bisque piano baby. Unmarked, but excellent quality with open/closed mouth, ruffled neck and painted flowers. Courtesy Frasher Doll Auctions. 10½" - $375.00.

Center: Fantastic piano baby marked "942." 7½" tall, has pacifer in mouth and two rabbits attached. Left: 10" Belton type marked "123" on French body with straight wrists, closed mouth. Lower: Goebel (bee mark), 3½" all bisque. Right: Size #1 Jumeau, 10" tall, open mouth. Courtesy Frasher Doll Auctions. 7½" - $785.00; 10" - $965.00; 3½" - $75.00; #1 - $1,800.00.

Rabery & Delphieu began making dolls in 1856. The very first dolls have kid bodies and are extremely rare. The majority of their dolls are on French jointed bodies and are marked "R.D." A few may be marked "Bébé de Paris."

Child: With closed mouth, in excellent condition with no chips, breaks or hairlines in bisque. Body in overall good condition and nicely dressed. 15" - $2,700.00; 18" - $3,000.00; 21" - $3,500.00; 23" - $3,700.00; 26" - $4,300.00.

Child: With open mouth and same condition as above: 14" - $1,000.00; 18" - $1,600.00; 21" - $2,200.00; 23" - $2,600.00; 26" - $3,100.00.

Exceptional 29" marked "R.D." Excellent quality bisque, closed mouth and on jointed French body. Courtesy Barbara Earnshaw-Cain. 29" - $5,000.00.

This beautiful 20" doll is marked "R.D." and dressed in her original clothes. Has closed mouth. Below is the store label in her hat. "Au Nain Bleu" was a famous Paris toy store, from which this outfit was sold.

RECKNAGEL OF ALEXANDERINETHAL

Dolls marked with "R.A." were made by Recknagel of Alexanderinethal, Thur, Germany. The R.A. dolls date from 1886 to after World War I and can range from very poor workmanship to excellent quality bisque and artist work. Prices are for dolls with good artist workmanship, such as the lips and eyebrows painted straight, feathered or at least not off-center. Original or nicely dressed and no damage.

Child: Set or sleep eyes, open mouth with small dolls having painted-on shoes and socks. 8" - $165.00; 12" - $200.00; 16" - $300.00; 20" - $425.00; 23" - $600.00.

Baby: Ca. 1909-1910 on. Five-piece bent limb baby body or straight leg, curved arm toddler body and with sleep or set eyes. No damage and nicely dressed. 9" - $245.00; 12" - $300.00; 16" - $425.00; 20" - $550.00.

Character: With painted eyes, modeled bonnet and open/closed mouth, some smiling, some with painted-in teeth. No damage and nicely dressed. 8" - $600.00; 12" - $800.00.

Character: Glass eyes, closed mouth and composition bent limb baby body. 7" - $650.00; 10" - $750.00; 14" - $850.00.

16" doll marked "21 Germany R.A." Made by Recknagel of Alexanderinethal. Open mouth and on fully jointed body. 27½" marked "A.B.G. 1362. made in Germany 4½." Open mouth and on fully jointed body. Made by Alt, Beck & Gottschalk. Courtesy Frasher Doll Auctions. 16" - $300.00; 27½" - $900.00.

REINECKE

Dolls marked with "P.M." were made by Otto Reinecke of Hol-Moschendorf, Bavaria, Germany from 1909 into the 1930's. The mold number found most often is the #914 baby or toddler.

Child: Bisque head with open mouth and on five-piece papier maché body or fully jointed body. Can have sleep or set eyes. No damage and nicely dressed. 10" - $175.00; 14" - $300.00; 17" - $500.00; 21" - $650.00.

Baby: Open mouth, sleep eyes or set eyes. Bisque head on five-piece bent limb baby body. No damage and nicely dressed. 10" - $250.00; 12" - $350.00; 15" - $500.00; 21" - $625.00; 26" - $850.00.

13" marked "P.M. 23 Germany." Sleep eyes, open mouth and on fully jointed body. Made by Otto Reinecke. Courtesy Gloria Anderson. 13" - $300.00.

REVALO

The Revalo marked dolls were made by Gebruder Ohlhaver of Thur, Germany from 1921 to the 1930's. Bisque heads with jointed bodies, sleep or set eyes. No damage and nicely dressed.

Child: Open mouth. 15" - $425.00; 18" - $575.00; 21" - $675.00; 25" - $750.00.

Molded Hair Child: With or without molded ribbon and/or flower. Painted eyes and open/closed mouth. 12" - $685.00; 15" - $875.00.

Baby: Open mouth, sleep or set eyes on five-piece baby body. 14" - $475.00; 17" - $675.00.

Toddler: 16" - $625.00; 18" - $775.00.

21" Revalo marked "150 Germany 2." Open mouth, sleep eyes with lashes and on fully jointed body. Courtesy Frasher Doll Auctions. 21" - $675.00.

14" marked "Revalo." Deeply molded hair with head band and side bow. Open/closed mouth with painted upper teeth, painted eyes and on fully jointed body. Made by Gebruder Ohlhaver, Germany. Courtesy Elizabeth Burke. 14" - $800.00.

Bruno Schmidt's doll factory was located in Walterhausen, Germany and many of the heads used by this firm were made by Bahr & Proschild, Ohrdruf, Germany. They made dolls from 1898 on into the 1930's.

Marks:

2033-6

Child: Bisque head on jointed body, sleep eyes, open mouth, no damage and nicely dressed. 15" - $400.00; 21" - $600.00; 27" - $950.00. Flirty eyes: 21" - $700.00; 29" - $1,400.00.

Character Baby, Toddler or Child: Bisque head, glass eyes or painted eyes, jointed body, no damage and nicely dressed. **#2069*:** Closed mouth, glass eyes, sweet face, jointed body. 14" - $4,000.00; 18" - $6,500.00. **#2048, 2094, 2096** (called "Tommy Tucker"): Molded, painted hair, open mouth. 18" - $1,400.00; 23" - $1,800.00. **#2048, 2094, 2096:** "Tommy Tucker" with closed mouth. Otherwise, same as above. 18" - $2,500.00; 23" - $3,000.00. **#2072:** Closed mouth, wig. 19" - $3,500.00. **#2097:** Toddler. 15" - $475.00; 21" - $850.00.

Character Child: Closed mouth, painted eyes or glass eyes, jointed child body, no damage and nicely dressed. **Marked "BSW" in heart:** No mold number. 17" - $2,200.00; 21" - $2,600.00. **#2033 "Wendy":** 17" - $19,000.00 up; 21" - $22,000.00 up.

* *Estimated prices.*

Right: 19" marked "Eden Bébé Paris 8 Depose." Open mouth and on five-piece composition body. Left: 18" "Tommy Tucker" by Bruno Schmidt. Molded hair, glass eyes and on fully jointed German body. Courtesy Frasher Doll Auctions. 19" - $2,200.00; 18" - $1,400.00.

Franz Schmidt & Co. began in 1890 at Georgenethal, near Walterhausen, Germany. In 1902, they registered the cross hammers with a doll between and also the F.S.&C. mark.

Marks:

1310

F.S. & Co.

Made in
Germany

10

Baby: Bisque head on bent limb baby body, sleep or set eyes, open mouth and some may have pierced nostrils. No damage and nicely dressed. (Add more for toddler body.) **#1271, 1295, 1296, 1297, 1310:** 10" - $350.00; 16" - $625.00; 21" - $775.00; 25" - $1,000.00. Toddler: 16" - $765.00; 21" - $950.00; 25" - $1,100.00. **#1267:** Open/closed mouth, painted eyes. 15" - $2,000.00; 20" - $2,900.00. Glass eyes: 15" - $2,400.00; 20" - $3,400.00. **#1285:** 15" - $700.00; 21" - $950.00.

Child: Papier maché and composition body with walker mechanism with metal rollers on feet. Open mouth, sleep eyes. Working and no damage to head, nicely dressed. **#1250:** 15" - $550.00; 21" - $750.00. **#1262:** Closed mouth, almost smiling child. Painted eyes, wig, jointed body. 20" - $2,900.00; 24" - $3,500.00. **#1266, 1267:** Child with open mouth and sleep eyes. 21" - $2,500.00.

Right: 16" Franz Schmidt marked "1295 F.S. & C." Sleep eyes, open mouth and on five-piece baby body. Left: 13" Heubach Koppelsdorf 320 baby with sleep eyes and open mouth. Center: 10" "Bye-lo" with sleep eyes and cloth body with celluloid hands. Courtesy Frasher Doll Auctions. 16" - $625.00; 13" - $325.00; 10" - $475.00.

Schmitt & Fils produced dolls from 1870's to 1891 in Paris, France. The dolls have French jointed bodies and came with closed mouths or open/closed ones.

Marks:

Child: Bisque head on jointed body with closed mouth or open/closed mouth. No damage and nicely dressed. Marked on head and body. 16" - $12,000.00 up; 19" - $17,000.00 up; 23" - $22,000.00 up; 26" - $27,000.00 up; 29" - $32,000.00.

19½" marked "Schmitt" with crossed hammer and "SCH" in shield/3. Closed mouth, jointed body with straight wrists and is marked on the buttocks with the Schmitt shield. Courtesy Frasher Doll Auctions. 20" - $18,000.00.

SCHOENAU & HOFFMEISTER

Schoenau & Hoffmeister began making dolls in 1901 and were located in Bavaria. The factory was called "Porzellanfabrik Burgrubb" and this mark will be found on many of their doll heads. Some of their mold numbers are 21, 169, 170, 769, 900, 914, 1800, 1906, 1909, 1923, 4000, 4900, 5000, 5300, 5500, 5700, 5800 and also Hanna.

Marks:

Princess Elizabeth: Smiling open mouth, set eyes, bisque head on jointed five-piece body and marked with name on head or body. 15" - $2,000.00; 21" - $2,600.00; 24" - $3,200.00.

Hanna: Child with black or brown fired-in color to bisque head. Sleep or set eyes, five-piece body or jointed body. Marked with name on head. 8" - $325.00; 14" - $425.00.

Hanna Baby: Bisque head, open mouth, sleep eyes and on five-piece bent limb baby body. 10" - $400.00; 13" - $600.00; 16" - $700.00; 23" - $1,200.00.

Character Baby: #169, 769, etc. Bisque head on five-piece bent limb baby body. 12" - $345.00; 16" - $575.00; 19" - $650.00; 23" - $750.00. Toddler Body: 18" - $750.00; 21" - $900.00.

Child: #1909, 5500, 5900, 5800, etc. Bisque head with open mouth, sleep or set eyes, jointed body. No damage and nicely dressed. 10" - $165.00; 16" - $385.00; 19" - $485.00; 22" - $600.00; 27" - $850.00; 30" - $1,000.00; 34" - $1,400.00.

Painted Bisque: Painted head on five-piece body or jointed body. 10" - $145.00; 13" - $225.00.

Das Lachende Baby (My Laughing Baby): 20" - $2,000.00; 25" - $2,500.00.

Right: 24" marked "5500 S, pb in star, H DEP. 8." Made in Germany by Schoenau & Hoffmeister. Open mouth, set eyes and on fully jointed body. Left: 27" marked "119-13 Handwerck 5 Germany." Made by Heinrich Handwerck. Open mouth and on fully jointed body. Courtesy Frasher Doll Auctions. 24" - $700.00; 27" - $950.00.

28" marked "Carmencita. S, pb in star H. 1919." Made by Schoenau & Hoffmeister. Sleep eyes, open mouth and on fully jointed body. Courtesy Frasher Doll Auctions. 28" - $950.00.

25" marked "S. pb in star H." Made by Schoenau & Hoffmeister. Sleep eyes, open mouth and on fully jointed toddler body. Courtesy Frasher Doll Auctions. 25" - $1,200.00.

17" all original in original box. Head marked "S pb in star H. 1800" and box is marked "My Little Beauty." Made by Schoenau & Hoffmeister. Courtesy Gloria Anderson. 17" - $400.00; 17" original - $750.00.

SCHOENHUT

The Albert Schoenhut & Co. was located in Philadephia, PA from 1872 until the 1930's. The dolls are all wood with spring joints, have holes in bottom of feet to fit in a metal stand.

Marks:

(1911-1913)

(1913-1930)

SCHOENHUT DOLL
PAT. JAN. 17, '11, USA
& FOREIGN COUNTRIES
(Incised - 1911 on)

Child With Carved Hair: May have comb marks, molded ribbon, comb or bow. Closed mouth. Original or nice clothes. Excellent condition: 14" - $2,000.00; 21" - $2,500.00. Very good condition with some wear: 14" - $1,200.00; 21" - $1,800.00. Poor condition with chips and dents: 14" - $500.00; 21" - $600.00.

Man With Carved Hair: 19", mint - $2,800.00; some wear - $1,600.00; chips, dirty - $650.00.

Baby Head: Can be on regular body or bent limb baby body. Bald spray painted hair or wig, painted decal eyes. Nicely dressed or original. Excellent condition: 12" - $550.00; 16" - $700.00; 18" - $775.00. Good condition: 16" - $450.00; 18" - $550.00. Poor condition: 16" - $200.00; 18" - $250.00.

Toddler: Excellent condition. 15" - $850.00; 17" - $900.00.

15" Schoenhut, never played with and original clothes. Courtesy Turn of Century Antiques. 15" - $800.00; 15", in this original condition - $2,400.00.

21" Schoenhut that is extremely mint and original. Open/closed mouth with painted teeth. Holes in shoes to fit stand. Painted eyes and hair in original set. Courtesy Barbara Earnshaw-Cain. 21" - $1,000.00; 21" in this original condition - $1,500.00 up.

16" character Schoenhut girl with open/closed mouth with painted teeth. Original sailor suit. 19" Schoenhut with decal sleep eyes, open mouth. All wood Schoenhut "Felix the Cat"; cemented wood body. Courtesy Frasher Doll Auctions. 16" - $725.00; 19" - $1,400.00; 8" cat - $425.00.

Cap Molded To Head: 14" - $2,900.00 up.

Tootsie Wootsie: Molded, painted hair, toddler or regular body. 12" - $2,200.00; 17" - $3,000.00.

"Dolly" Face: Common doll, wigged, open/closed mouth with painted teeth, decal painted eyes. Original or nicely dressed. Excellent condition: 14" - $665.00; 21" - $885.00. Good condition: 14" - $450.00; 21" - $650.00. Poor condition: 14" - $150.00; 16" - $200.00.

Sleep Eyes: Has lids that lower down over the eyes and has an open mouth with teeth or just slightly cut open mouth with carved teeth. Original or nicely dressed. Excellent condition: 17" - $1,300.00; 22" - $1,500.00. Good condition: 16" - $650.00; 21" - $800.00. Poor condition: 17" - $200.00; 22" - $275.00.

Walker: One-piece legs with "Walker" joints in center of legs and torso. Painted eyes, open/closed or closed mouth. Original or nicely dressed. Excellent condition: 15" - $875.00; 18" - $1,000.00; 21" - $1,300.00. Good condition: 15" - $400.00; 18" - $500.00; 21" - $700.00. Poor condition: 15" - $125.00; 18" - $185.00; 21" - $250.00.

All Composition: Molded curly hair, "Patsy"-style body, paper label on back, 1924. 14" - $550.00.

Schoenhut circus includes "Sparkplug" horse with original burlap blanket, oriental clown, ringmaster, donkey and accessories. Courtesy Turn of Century Antiques. Horse - $550.00; Oriental Clown - $190.00; Clown - $130.00; Elephant - $95.00; Ringmaster - $150.00; Large Ringmaster - $190.00; Donkey - $125.00; Small Donkey - $95.00; Accessories - $30.00-40.00 each.

Schuetzmeister & Quendt made dolls from 1893 to 1898. This short term factory was located in Boilstat, Germany.

Marks:

Child: Mold numbers #251, 252, etc. Can have cut pate or be a bald head with two string holes. No damage and nicely dressed, open mouth. 15" - $465.00; 21" - $600.00; 25" - $750.00.

Baby: Includes mold #201 & 301. Five-piece bent limb baby body. Not damaged and nicely dressed. Open mouth. 12" - $365.00; 15" - $500.00; 18" - $600.00; 23" - $800.00. Toddler: 15" - $1,000.00; 19" - $1,500.00; 23" - $1,900.00.

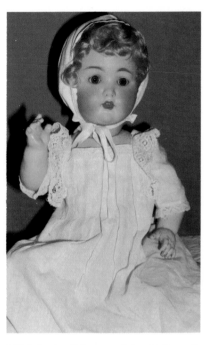

21" baby by Schuetzmeister & Quendt. Marked "201 S.Q. Germany." Sleep eyes, open mouth with two upper teeth. Five-piece bent limb baby body. Courtesy Frasher Doll Auctions. 21" - $700.00.

SIMON & HALBIG

Simon & Halbig began making dolls in the late 1860's or early 1870's and continued until the 1930's. Simon & Halbig made many heads for other companies and they also supplied some doll heads from the French makers. They made entire dolls, all bisque, flange neck dolls, turned shoulder heads and socket heads.

All prices are for dolls with no damage to the bisque and only minor scuffs to the bodies, well dressed, wigged and have shoes. Dolls should be ready to place into a collection.

Marks:

S $''$ H
729

1279-3
DEP

SH
GERMANY

Child: 1889 to 1930's. Open mouth and jointed body. **#600, 719, 739, 749, 939, 949, 979, 1019, etc.:** 17" - $1,200.00; 21" - $2,100.00; 26" - $2,500.00; 29" - $2,900.00.

#130, 530, 540, 550, 1039, 1040, 1078, etc: Open mouth. (More for flirty eyes.) 12" - $475.00; 16" - $550.00; 19" - $650.00; 23" - $750.00; 27" - $1,000.00; 32" - $1,800.00; 35" - $2,000.00; 40" - $2,800.00.

#1009, 1049, 1079, 1099: Open mouth. 15" - $550.00; 21" - $785.00; 26" - $1,000.00; 32" - $1,500.00.

#1009: With fashion kid body. 19" - $800.00; 24" - $1,000.00; 26" - $1,350.00.

#1010, 1029, 1040, 1080, etc: Open mouth and kid body. 15" - $465.00; 22" - $650.00; 26" - $800.00; 29" - $1,000.00.

#1250, 1260: Open mouth, kid body. 16" - $550.00; 19" - $650.00; 25" - $950.00.

Left to right: 18" "Gretchen" by Kammer & Reinhardt marked "K star R 114." Closed mouth, painted eyes and expressive face. 16½" very rare character by Simon & Halbig marked "150 S&H 0½." Closed mouth, molded eyelids over painted eyes. Both on fully jointed bodies. Courtesy Frasher Doll Auctions. 18" - $5,500.00; 16½" - $8,600.00.

Characters: 1910 and after. Wig or molded hair, glass or painted eyes, with open/closed, closed, or open mouth. On jointed child bodies. **#IV:** 20" - $16,000.00 up. **#120:** 15" - $1,800.00; 23" - $2,900.00; **#150:** 16" - $8,500.00; 19" - $10,000.00; 23" - $16,000.00. **#151:** 15" - $5,500.00; 23" - $13,000.00. **#153 "Little Duke":** 15" - $19,000.00 up. **#600:** 15" - $675.00; 19" - $1,100.00; 23" - $1,500.00. **#718, 719:** 15" - $1,800.00; 21" - $2,400.00. **#720, 740:** Kid body, closed mouth. 10" - $575.00; 16" - $1,300.00; 18" - $1,600.00. **#740:** Jointed body. 10" - $675.00; 17" - $1,500.00; 21" - $2,200.00. **#729:** 16" - $2,400.00; 20" - $3,000.00. **#739:**

24" Simon & Halbig mold number 151. Open/closed mouth with molded teeth, painted eyes and on fully jointed body. Courtesy Frasher Doll Auctions. 24" - $13,000.00.

17" - $2,600.00. **#749:** Closed mouth, jointed body. 17" - $2,400.00; 21" - $3,100.00. **#905, 908, 929:** Closed mouth. 15" - $1,800.00; 18" - $2,900.00. **#905, 908, 929:** Open mouth. 15" - $1,700.00; 21" - $2,100.00; 29" - $2,900.00. **#919:** 16" - $2,600.00; 20" - $3,400.00. **#939:** Closed mouth: 18" - $2,800.00; 21" - $3,100.00; 26" - $3,500.00. Jointed body. 18" - $1,800.00; 21" - $3,100.00; 26" - $3,700.00. Kid body. 18" - $1,900.00; 21" - $2,500.00; 26" - $2,500.00. **Black, closed mouth:** 18"- $3,200.00; 21" - $4,300.00; 26" - $5,000.00. Open mouth: 18" - $1,800.00; 21" - $2,300.00; 26" - $2,900.00. **#940:** 21" - $2,000.00. **#949:** Closed mouth. 18" - $2,500.00; 21" - $2,900.00; 26" - $3,300.00. Open mouth.

20" marked "S 9 H/940." Closed mouth, solid dome head, kid body with bisque lower arms, original factory dress. Courtesy Frasher Doll Auctions. 20" - $2,000.00.

18" - $1,400.00; 21" - $1,700.00; 26" - $2,300.00. Black, closed mouth. 18" - $2,600.00; 21" - $3,100.00. Open mouth: 18" - $1,500.00; 21" - $2,000.00. Kid body. 18" - $1,600.00; 21" - $2,100.00; 26" - $2,600.00. Jointed body. 18" - $1,900.00; 21" - $2,500.00; 26" - $3,100.00. **#969, 979:** Black. 16" - $3,600.00. **#1248, 1249 Santa:** 17" - $900.00; 21" - $1,200.00; 25" - $1,700.00. **#1279:** 10" - $850.00; 15" - $1,800.00; 20" - $2,700.00; 26" - $3,400.00; 30" - $5,000.00. **#1299:** 18" - $1,100.00; 22" - $1,400.00. **#1302:** See Black Dolls. **#1304:** 15" - $2,800.00; 18" - $4,000.00. **#1308:** 18" - $5,000.00. **#1338:** Open mouth, jointed body. 19" - $1,500.00; 25" - $2,700.00; 29" - $3,500.00. **#1339:** Character face, open mouth. 19" - $1,600.00; 25" - $2,900.00. **#1345:** 16" - $3,000.00; 18" - $4,800.00. **#1358:** Black. 18" - $5,700.00; 21" - $6,400.00; 25" - $7,000.00. **#1388, 1398:** Lady Doll. 22" - $12,000.00 up;

Left: 17" marked "908 S 10 H." Made by Simon & Halbig and a rare mold number. Small closed mouth, glass eyes and on early jointed body with straight wrists. Right: An open mouth version of this same doll with square cut teeth. Marked "S 7 H/908" and is 15½" tall. On fully jointed body. Courtesy Frasher Doll Auctions. 17" - $2,900.00; 15½" - $1,700.00.

32" marked "SH 949 17." Made by Simon & Halbig. Open mouth, set eyes and on fully jointed body. Courtesy Frasher Doll Auctions. 32" - $3,400.00.

30" marked "Simon & Halbig 1079. Sleep eyes, open mouth and on fully jointed body. Courtesy Frasher Doll Auctions. 30" - $1,300.00 up.

11½" marked "850." Made by Simon & Halbig. Bisque shoulder head, cloth body with bisque lower arms. Closed mouth and all original provincial costume. Courtesy Frasher Doll Auctions. 11½" - $650.00.

33" marked "1339 S&H/L.L. & S. 15." Open mouth and on fully jointed body. Courtesy Frasher Doll Auctions. 33" - $3,700.00.

27" - $18,000.00 up. **#1428:** 21" - $2,000.00. **#1478:** 17" - $7,000.00 up. **#1488:** 17" - $3,000.00; 21" - $3,800.00. **Character Babies:** 1909 to 1930's. Wigs or molded hair, painted or sleep eyes, open or open/closed mouth and on five-piece bent limb baby bodies. (Allow more for toddler body.) **#1294:** 16" - $600.00; 19" - $750.00; 23" - $1,100.00; 26" - $1,700.00. With clockwork in head to move eyes. 25-26" - $2,800.00. **#1299:** With open mouth. 10" - $365.00; 16" - $800.00. Toddler: 16" - $900.00; 18" - $1,100.00. **#1428 Toddler:** 12" - $1,400.00; 16" - $1,700.00; 20" - $2,000.00; 26" - $2,600.00. **#1428 Baby:** 12" - $950.00; 16" - $1,400.00; 20" - $1,900.00. **#1488 Toddler:** 18" - $3,500.00; 22" - $4,000.00. Baby: 18" - $2,300.00; 22" - $2,600.00; 26" - $3,200.00. **#1489: Erika** Baby. 20" - $3,100.00; 22" - $3,800.00; 26" - $4,500.00. **#1498 Toddler:** 17" - $3,300.00; 21" - $4,000.00. Baby: 17" - $2,600.00; 21" - $3,400.00. **#1039 Walker:** Key wound. 17" - $1,500.00; 19" - $2,000.00; 21" - $2,400.00.

Walking/Kissing: 19" - $1,000.00; 23" - $1,300.00.

Miniature Dolls: Tiny dolls with open mouth on jointed body or five-piece body with some having painted-on shoes and socks. Fully jointed: 8" - $585.00; 10-12" - $650.00. Five-piece Body: 8" - $425.00; 10-12" - $500.00. **#1160:** "Little Women" type. Closed mouth and fancy wig. 6" - $385.00; 10" - $500.00.

Ladies: Ca. 1910. Open mouth, molded lady-style slim body with slim arms and legs. **#1159, 1179:** 15" - $1,300.00; 19" - $1,900.00; 26" - $2,900.00.

Ladies: Closed mouth. Ca. 1910. Adult slim limb body. **#1303:** 16" - $7,500.00; 19" - $9,200.00. **#1305:** Lady. Open/closed mouth, long nose. 18" - $8,000.00 up; 22" - $10,000.00 up. **#1307:** Lady, long face. 18" - $9,000.00 up; 24" - $12,000.00 up. **#1398:** 18" - $10,000.00. **#1468, 1469:** 16" - $2,900.00; 19" - $4,200.00. **#1527:** 20" - $8,000.00 up; 24" - $10,000.00 up.

#152 Lady: 17" - $14,000.00 up.

11½" Simon & Halbig mold number 1428 character toddler with glass eyes, open/closed mouth. Courtesy Barbara Earnshaw-Cain. 11½" - $950.00.

Left: Fantastic all original 25" man and woman with Simon & Halbig mold number 1159 heads and on marked Jumeau composition lady's bodies. Dressed in French Court era outfits. Both have glass eyes, open mouths and wear original clothes right down to the gloves. Left: Back view of Simon & Halbig head mold and shows the Jumeau body sticker. Courtesy Barbara Earnshaw-Cain. 25" - $2,200.00 each; 25" Jumeau body and original - $3,700.00 up each.

21" marked "Erika 1489 Simon & Halbig." Sleep eyes, open mouth and on five-piece toddler body. A rare mold number and named doll. Courtesy Frasher Doll Auctions. 21" - $3,200.00.

17½" marked "DEP. Germany Santa 7." Made by Simon & Halbig. Sleep eyes, open mouth, shaded lower lip and on fully jointed body. Courtesy Frasher Doll Auctions. 17½" - $950.00.

23" marked "Made in Germany C/ S&H Simon Halbig." Sleep eyes, open mouth and on fully jointed body. Original in original box. Box marked "Kringle Society Dolls." Courtesy Frasher Doll Auctions. 23" - $750.00; 23" original in box - $1,400.00.

S.F.B.J.

The Societe Française de Fabrication de Bébé St. Jouets (S.F.B.J.) was formed in 1899 and known members were Jumeau, Bru, Fleischmann & Blodel, Rabery & Delphieu, Pintel & Godchaux, P.H. Schmitz, A. Bouchet, Jullien and Danel & Cie. By 1922, S.F.B.J. employed 2,800 people. The Society was dissolved in the mid-1950's. There are a vast amount of "dolly-faced" S.F.B.J. dolls, but some are extremely rare and are character molds. Most of the characters are in the 200 mold number series.

Marks:

S.F.B.J.
239
PARIS

$_D E P O S_E$
S.F.B.J.
301

S	F
B	J

Child: Sleep or set eyes, open mouth and on jointed French body. No damage and nicely dressed. **#60:** 15" - $600.00; 21" - $800.00; 25" - $950.00. **#301:** 8" - $325.00; 14" - $675.00; 18" - $875.00; 21" - $1,100.00; 29" - $1,700.00.

Jumeau Type: Open mouth. 17" - $1,400.00; 21" - $1,800.00; 25" - $2,300.00. Closed mouth: 17" - $2,500.00; 21" - $3,100.00; 25" - $3,500.00.

Lady #1159: Open mouth, adult body. 22" - $2,200.00.

Character: Sleep or set eyes, wigged, flocked, molded hair, jointed body. No damage and nicely dressed. **#211:** 17" - $5,500.00. **#226:** 15" - $1,800.00; 20" - $2,500.00. **Painted eyes:** 15" - $1,300.00. **#227:** 17" - $2,500.00; 22" - $3,000.00. **#229:** 17" - $3,200.00. **#230:** 24" - $2,000.00. **#233:** 15" - $3,400.00; 18" - $4,500.00. **#234:** 17" - $3,200.00; 22" - $3,700.00. **#235:** 15" - $2,300.00; 22" - $3,000.00. Painted eyes:

14" S.F.B.J. 237. Glass eyes, original flocked hair with open/closed mouth and molded teeth. Old and maybe original sailor suit. Courtesy Barbara Earnshaw-Cain. 14" - $3,200.00; 14" open mouth - $1,600.00.

21" walking doll marked "S.F.B.J. 60 Paris." Sleep eyes with lashes, open mouth, walker body (legs move). Courtesy Frasher Doll Auctions. 21" - $1,900.00.

15" - $1,500.00; 19" - $1,900.00. **#236 Toddler:** 12" - $1,200.00; 17" - $2,000.00; 21" - $2,400.00; 26" - $2,800.00; 28" - $3,200.00. **Baby:** 15" - $1,500.00; 20" - $1,900.00; 24" - $2,400.00. **#237:** 17" - $2,300.00; 22" - $2,600.00. **#238:** 15" - $3,000.00; 22" - $3,400.00. **Lady:** 21" - $4,200.00. **#239 Poubout:** 15" - $15,000.00 up; 18" - $20,000.00 up. **#242:** 18" - $4,800.00. **#247:** 15" - $2,900.00; 18" - $4,700.00. **#248:** Very pouty, glass eyes. 15" - $4,000.00; 18" - $5,000.00. **#251 Toddler:** 17" - $1,800.00; 21" - $2,300.00; 25" - $2,800.00. **Baby:** 15" - $1,500.00; 21" - $2,300.00; 25" - $2,900.00. **#252 Toddler:** 15" - $5,400.00; 19" - $7,600.00; 25" - $8,900.00. **Baby:** 10" - $2,000.00; 15" - $5,100.00; 21" - $7,600.00; 25" - $8,600.00. **#257:** 17" - $2,500.00. **#266:** 21" - $3,800.00.

Googly: See Googly section.

Kiss Throwing, Walking Doll: Composition body with straight legs, walking mechanism and when walks, arms goes up to throw kiss. Head moves from side to side. Flirty eyes and open mouth. In working condition, no damage to bisque head and nicely dressed. 21-22" - $1,900.00.

19½" lady marked "SFBJ 238 Paris." Excellent pale bisque, "jewel eyes," open mouth and on adult lady body. Courtesy Frasher Doll Auctions. 19½" - $4,000.00.

20" S.F.B.J. 251. Open mouth with two upper teeth. Glass eyes and on jointed toddler body. Courtesy Barbara Earnshaw-Cain. 20" - $2,400.00.

12" S.F.B.J. 252. Very pouty, glass eyes and on jointed body. Courtesy Barbara Earnshaw-Cain. 12" - $3,400.00.

26" S.F.B.J. Jumeau marked "21 R S.F.B.J. Paris 11" and red artist's check marks. Fully jointed body marked "#11" and red/white/blue paper label of S.F.B.J. Open mouth, sleep eyes with lashes. Courtesy Frasher Doll Auctions. 26" - $2,400.00.

22" marked "France. S.F.B.J. 301 Paris." Open mouth and on fully jointed body. Courtesy Frasher Doll Auctions. 22" - $1,100.00.

SNOW BABIES

Snow Babies were made in Germany and Japan and they can be excellent to poor in quality from both countries. Snow Babies have fired-on "pebble-textured" clothing. Many are unmarked and the features are painted. Prices are for good quality painted features, rareness of pose and no damage to the piece.

Single Figure: 1½" - $45.00; 3" - $85.00-125.00.

Two Figures: Together. 1½" - $100-125.00; 3" - $150-195.00.

Three Figures: Together. 1½" - $145.00-185.00; 3" - $195.00-245.00.

One Figure On Sled: 2-2½" - $165.00.

Two Figures On Sled: 2-2½" - $185.00.

Three Figures On Sled: 2-2½" - $245.00.

Jointed: Shoulders and hips. 3¼" - $165.00 up; 5" - $365.00 up; 7" - $450.00 up.

Shoulder head: Cloth body with china limbs. 9" - $385.00; 12" - $450.00.

On Sled in Glass: "Snow" scene - $185.00 up.

With Bear: $185.00.

With Snowman: $175.00.

With Musical Base: $185.00 up.
Laughing Child: $125.00 up.
Snow Bear with Santa: $275.00.

With Reindeer: $150.00
Snow Baby Riding Polar Bear:
$175.00.

STEIFF

Steiff started business in 1894 and this German maker is better known for their plush/stuffed animals than for dolls.

Steiff Dolls: Felts, velvet or plush with seam down middle of face. Button-style eyes, painted features and sewn on ears. The dolls generally have large feet so they stand alone. Prices are for dolls in excellent condition and with original clothes. Second price is for dolls that are soiled and may not be original.

Adults: 16-17" - $1,800.00 up; 21-22" - $2,300.00 up.

Military Men: 17" - $3,500.00 up; 21" - $4,600.00 up.

Children: 12" - $950.00 up; 15-16" - $1,500.00; 18-19" - $1,800.00 up.

Made is U.S. Zone Germany: Has glass eyes. 12" - $700.00 up; 16" - $900.00 up.

Comic Characters: Such as chef, elf, musician, etc. 14" - $2,400.00 up; 16" - $3,200.00 up.

12½" Steiff Elf dolls. Soft felt bodies, wire jointed inside body to permit posing. Felt arms with stitched fingers, felt face with center seam. Shoe button eyes and mohair beard and brows. Original, ca. 1950's. Courtesy Frasher Doll Auctions. 13" - $700.00.

17" Steiff military man or officer (customs, railroad, etc.). All original and all felt with seam line down middle of face. Courtesy Barbara Earnshaw-Cain. 17" - $3,500.00.

17" Steiff felt man with seam line down middle of face. Original clothes, hand-carved shovel, blue glass eyes. Courtesy Barbara Earnshaw-Cain. 17" - $1,800.00.

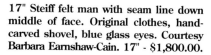

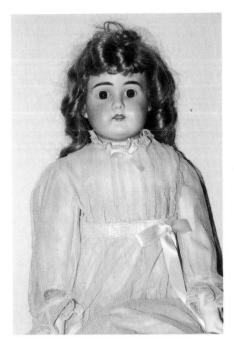

26" Herm Steiner girl. Bisque shoulder head and bisque lower arms, kid body and open mouth. Courtesy Gloria Anderson. 8" - $125.00; 14" - $275.00; 17" - $365.00; 22" - $475.00; 26" - $595.00.

7" clown marked "Germany Herm Steiner 16/0." White bisque with fired-in color. Painted eyes, closed mouth and five-piece body with painted-on shoes and socks. Courtesy Frasher Doll Auctions. 7" clown - $175.00.

Jules Nichols Steiner operated from 1855 to 1892 when the firm was taken over by Amedee LaFosse. In 1895, this firm merged with Henri Alexander, the maker of Phenix Bébé and a partner, May Freres Cie, the maker of Bébé Mascotte. In 1899, Jules Mettais took over the firm and in 1906, the company was sold to Edmond Daspres.

In 1889, the firm registered the girl with a banner and the words "Le Petite Parisien" and in 1892, LaFosse registered "Le Parisien."

Marks:

> J. STEINER
> STE. S.G.D.G.
> FIRE A12
> PARIS
>
> STE C3
> J. STEINER
> B. S.G.D.G.

Burned-in mark found on some Jules Steiner bodies.

"A" Series Child: 1885. Closed mouth, paperweight eyes, jointed body and cardboard pate. No damage and nicely dressed. 14" - $3,500.00; 20" - $5,500.00; 24" - $6,800.00; 27" - $8,000.00.

"A" Series Child: Open mouth, otherwise same as above. 14" - $1,800.00; 20" - $2,800.00; 26" - $3,800.00.

"C" Series Child: Ca. 1880. Closed mouth, round face, paperweight eyes, no damage and nicely dressed. 17" - $4,800.00; 21" - $6,400.00; 26" - $7,400.00; 29" - $8,800.00.

Bourgoin Steiner: 1870's. With "Bourgoin" incised or in red stamp on head along with the rest of the Steiner mark. Closed mouth. No damage and nicely dressed. 16" - $4,800.00; 20" - $6,200.00; 25" - $7,400.00.

Wire Eye Steiner: Closed mouth, flat glass eyes that open and close by moving wire that comes out the back of the head. Jointed body, no damage and nicely dressed. **Bourgoin:** 17" - $4,900.00; 21" - $5,900.00; 26" - $7,000.00. **"A" Series:** 17" - $5,000.00; 21" - $6,100.00; 26" - $7,400.00. **"C" Series:** 17" - $4,900.00; 21" - $5,900.00; 26" - $7,200.00.

Paper label found on Steiner bodies.

"Le Parisien" - "A" Series: 1892.
17" - $4,000.00; 21" - $5,600.00; 26" -
$7,500.00.

Mechanical: See that section.

Bisque Hip Steiner: Motsch-
mann-style body with bisque head,
shoulders, lower arms and legs and
bisque torso sections. No damage any-
where. 18" - $5,400.00.

Early White Bisque Steiner:
With round face, open mouth with two
rows of teeth. Unmarked. On jointed
Steiner body, pink wash over eyes. No
damage and nicely dressed. 14" -
$4,200.00; 18" - $5,900.00.

**25" marked "J. Steiner Bte. S.G.D.G. Paris
Fre A17." Closed mouth and on jointed
Steiner body with straight wrists and has
paper label of child with flag. 25" -
$7,000.00.**

16" "C" Series Steiner with wire
eyes that has a lever to open and
close the eyes located by ear. Closed
mouth and on Steiner body impressed
with "J. ST" emblem. Eyes also
marked "Steiner." Courtesy Frasher
Doll Auctions. 16" - $4,600.00.

23" marked "Sie C 4 Steiner Cie SGDG
Bourgoin." Marked Steiner body with
straight wrists. Sleep eyes operate by
lever in back of head. Shown with 22"
Tete Jumeau with closed mouth and on
fully jointed marked Jumeau body.
Courtesy Frasher Doll Auctions. 23" -
$6,400.00; 22" - $5,200.00.

"Tynie Baby" made for Horsman Doll Co. in 1924. Sleep eyes, closed pouty mouth and frown between eyes. Cloth body with celluloid or composition hands. Marked "1924/E.I. Horsman/ Made in Germany." Some will be incised "Tynie Baby" also. No damage and nicely dressed. Bisque head: 11" - $425.00; 16" - $800.00. Composition head: 14" - $285.00. All bisque: 6" - $1,000.00; 9" - $1,700.00.

UNIS

"Unis, France" was a type of trade association or a "seal of approval" for trade goods to consumers from the manufacturers. This group of business-men, who were to watch the quality of French exports, often overlooked guide-lines and some poor quality dolls were exported. Many fine quality Unis marked dolls were also produced.

Unis began right after World War I and is still in business. Two doll companies are still members, "Poupee Bella" and "Petit Colin." There are other type manufacturers in this group and they include makers of toys, sewing machines, tile, pens, etc.

#60, 70, 71, 301: Bisque head with papier maché or composition body. Sleep or set eyes, open mouth. No damage and nicely dressed. 15" - $1,300.00; 18" - $1,600.00; 22" - $1,900.00; 25" - $2,200.00. Closed mouth: 16" -

Marks:

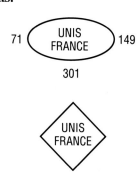

71 UNIS FRANCE 149

301

UNIS FRANCE

$2,400.00; 20" - $3,000.00. Black or brown: 15" - $600.00; 18" - $800.00.

Provincial Costume Doll: Bisque head, painted, set or sleep eyes, open mouth (or closed on smaller dolls.) Five-piece body. Original costume, no damage. 6" - $185.00; 12" - $325.00; 14" - $400.00.

Baby #272: Glass eyes, open mouth, cloth body, celluloid hands. 15" - $575.00; 18" - $975.00. Painted eyes, composition hands: 15" - $325.00; 18" - $500.00.
#251 Toddler: 16" - $1,800.00 up. Princess Elizabeth: 1938. Jointed body, closed mouth. (Allow more for flirty eyes.) 18" - $1,800.00; 23" - $2,500.00; 31" - $3,700.00.

15½" marked "Unis France 301. E.R.T." Sleep eyes with lashes, open mouth and fully jointed body. Courtesy Frasher Doll Auctions. 16" - $550.00.

8" dolls marked "Unis 60 France." Both have original dresses and wigs. Open mouths and on five-piece bodies. Ca. 1950. 8" - $135.00 each.

Right: 21" turned head with closed mouth. Eyelid area is very flat underneath painted eyebrows. Made by Wagner & Zetzsche. Left: 18" open mouth turned head with arched eyebrows and attributed to Alt, Beck & Gottschalck. Both have kid bodies with bisque lower arms. Courtesy Frasher Doll Auctions. 21" - $950.00; 18" - $525.00.

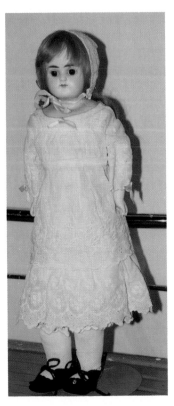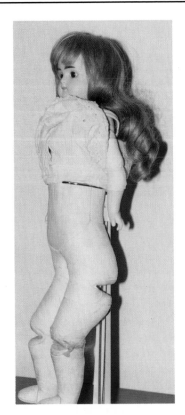

Left: Made by Wagner & Zeztsche, this closed mouth, turned shoulder head doll has a very flat eyelid area beneath eyebrow. Right: Typical Wagner & Zeztsche kid body with bisque lower arms. It will have an interwoven "WZ" on paper label under shoulder head. Courtesy Gloria Anderson. Closed mouth: 16" - $800.00; 21" - $950.00; 24" - $1,350.00; 27" - $1,550.00. Open mouth: 16" - $485.00; 21" - $650.00; 24" - $800.00; 27" - $1,000.00.

WAX

Poured Wax: Cloth body with wax head, limbs and inset glass eyes. Hair is embedded into wax. Nicely dressed or in original clothes, no damage to wax, but wax may be slightly discolored (evenly all over.) Not rewaxed. 16" - $1,400.00; 19" - $1,700.00; 22" - $1,900.00; 25" - $2,300.00. Lady or Man: 20" - $2,200.00 up.

Wax Over Papier Maché or Composition: Cloth body with wax over papier maché or composition head and with wax over composition or wood limbs. Only minor scuffs with no chipped out places, good color and nicely dressed. **Early Dolls:** 12" - $450.00; 16" - $725.00. **Later Dolls:** 12" - $250.00; 16" - $450.00. **Bonnet or Cap:** (Baby) 16" - $1,200.00.

Lady: 17" - $1,900.00 up.

Slit Head Wax: (English) 1830-1860's. Glass eyes, some open and closed by an attached wire. 14" - $400.00 up.

Center: 12" doll with wax head and arms doll. Open/closed mouth with painted teeth, pull strings move arms. This is acutally a candy container and all original. Left: 25" toddler marked "K star R" (Kammer & Reinhardt)/Simon & Halbig 122." Sleep eyes and open mouth. Right: Large Kestner child with closed mouth and on fully jointed body. Courtesy Frasher Doll Auctions. 12" - $1,600.00; 25" - $2,600.00; Kestner - $3,000.00.

Left: 22" poured wax shoulder head with molded eyelids. Shoulder head on muslin body and poured wax limbs. Hair inserted into wax. All original clothes. Right: 21" poured wax child with brown hair inserted into wax, muslin body and poured wax limbs. May be original. Center: 13" wax over papier maché lady with painted boots, muslin body and lower limbs are wood. In original costume. All have glass eyes. Courtesy Frasher Doll Auctions. 22" - $2,200.00; 21" - $1,900.00; 13" - $450.00.

25" poured wax with glass eyes and cloth body. Excellent condition. Rear: 18" Kammer & Reinhardt (K star R) 127 boy on toddler body. 18" Jules Steiner with open mouth, key wound, head moves and raises arms and kicks legs. 8½" Parian "Alice in Wonderland." Courtesy Turn of Century Antiques. 25" - $2,300.00; 18" toddler - $1,700.00; 18" - $2,500.00; 8½" - $495.00.

WELLINGS, NORAH

Norah Welling's designs were made for her by Victoria Toy Works in Wellington, Shopshire, England. These dolls were made from 1926 into the 1960's. The dolls are velvet as well as other fabrics, especially felt and velour. They will have a tag on the foot "Made in England by Norah Wellings."

Child: All fabric with stitch jointed hips and shoulders and have a molded fabric face with oil painted features. Some faces are papier maché with a stockenette covering. All original felt and cloth clothes, clean condition. Painted eyes: 14" - $425.00; 17" - $650.00;

21" - $950.00; 23" - $1,300.00. Glass eyes: 14" - $565.00; 17" - $785.00; 21" - $1,100.00.

Mounties, Black Islanders, Scots, and Other Characters: These are most commonly found. Must be in same condition as child. 8" - $95.00; 12" - $145.00; 14" - $185.00.

Glass Eyes: White: 14" - $265.00; 17" - $400.00. Black: 14" - $200.00; 20" - $350.00; 26" - $600.00.

Babies: Same description as child and same condition. 15" - $425.00; 22" - $850.00.

15" Norah Wellings-type child. Fabric body jointed at hips and shoulders. Original felt clothing. 10" Norah Wellings, tagged on foot. All velvet, glass eyes, oil-painted features. Called "Black Islander." Courtesy Frasher Doll Auctions. 15" - $500.00; 10" - $135.00.

WISLIZENUS, ADOLF

The Adolf Wislizenus doll factory was located at Walterhausen, Germany and the heads he used were made by Bahr & Proschild, Ernst Heubach of Kopplesdorf and Simon & Halbig. The company was in business starting in 1851, but it is not known when they began to make dolls.

Marks:

GERMANY
A.W.

Child: 1890's into 1900's. Bisque head on jointed body, sleep eyes, open mouth. No damage and nicely dressed. 12" - $185.00; 14" - $325.00; 17" - $450.00; 22" - $500.00; 25" - $600.00.

Baby: Bisque head in perfect condition and on five-piece bent limb baby body. No damage and nicely dressed. 17" - $465.00; 21" - $625.00; 26" - $950.00.

#115: 16" - $1,000.00.
#110: 17" - $1,100.00.

32" marked "A.W. Germany." Made by Adolf Wislizenus. Open mouth and fully jointed body. Courtesy Frasher Doll Auctions. 32" - $1,100.00.

MODERN DOLLS

1953-1954: 7½-8" straight leg, non-walker, heavy hard plastic. **Party Dress:** Mint and all correct - $525.00 up. Soiled, dirty hair mussed or parts of clothing missing - $125.00. **Ballgown:** Mint and correct - $850.00 up. Soiled, dirty, bad face color, not original - $200.00. **Nude:** Clean and good face color. $175.00. Dirty and bad face color - $50.00.

1955: 8" straight leg walker. **Party Dress:** Mint and all correct. $475.00. Soiled, dirty, parts of clothes missing - $85.00. **Ballgown:** Mint and all correct - $950.00. Dirty, part of clothing missing, etc. - $100.00. **Basic sleeveless dress:** Mint - $235.00. Dirty - $50.00. **Nude:** Clean and good face color - $140.00. Dirty, not original, faded face color - $45.00.

1956-1965: Bend Knee Walker. **Party Dress:** Mint and all correct - $300.00. Dirty, part of clothes missing, etc. - $70.00. **Ballgown:** Mint and correct - $1,200.00. Soiled, dirty, parts missing, etc. - $200.00. **Nude:** Clean, good face color - $120.00. Dirty, faded face color - $35.00. **Basic sleeveless dress:** Mint - $185.00. Dirty, faded face color - $50.00. **Internationals:** $275.00. Dirty, parts missing - $45.00.

8" Alexander-kins. From top to bottom: Greek Boy, Wendy Ann, Nurse with Baby, Hawaii, Cowboy, and Maggie Mixup Skater. All are original. Courtesy Turn of Century Antiques. Greek Boy - $475.00; Wendy Ann - $300.00; Nurse - $600.00; Hawaii - $500.00; Cowboy - $575.00; Maggie Mixup - $650.00.

1965-1972: Bend Knee, Non-Walkers: **Party Dress:** Mint and original - $300.00. Dirty, parts missing, etc. - $65.00. **Internationals:** Clean and mint - $125.00. Dirty or soiled - $45.00. **Nude:** Clean, good face color - $85.00. Dirty, faded face color - $25.00.
1973-1976: "Rosies." Straight leg, non-walker, rosy cheeks and marked "Alex." **Bride or Ballerina:** Bend knee walker - $275.00. Bend knee only - $150.00. Straight leg - $50.00-60.00. **Internationals:** $85.00. **Storybook:** $100.00.
1977-1981: Straight leg, non-walker marked "Alexander." **Bride or Ballerina:** $50.00-60.00. **International:** $50.00-60.00. **Storybook:** $50.00-60.00.
1982-1987: Straight leg, non-walker with deep indentation over upper lip that casts a shadow and makes the doll look as if it has a mustache. **Bride or ballerina:** $50.00-60.00. **International:** $50.00-60.00. **Storybook:** $50.00-60.00.
1988-1989: Straight leg, non-walker with new face that is more like the older dolls than others and still marked with full name "Alexander." **Bride or ballerina:** $50.00-60.00. **International:** $50.00-60.00. **Storybook:** $55.00-65.00.

8" "Agatha" made in 1953 and 1954 only. "Baby Clown" made in 1955. Both are rare dolls. Courtesy Frasher Doll Auctions. Agatha - $1,000.00 up; Clown - $1,400.00 up.

8" Bridesmaid, Bride and Groom from 1957. They are all bend knee walkers and all original. Courtesy Patty Martin. Bride - $350.00; Bridesmaid - $800.00 up; Groom - $450.00.

MADAME ALEXANDER - BABIES

Prices are for mint condition dolls.
Baby McGuffey: Composition. 22" - $250.00. Soiled - $85.00.
Bonnie: Vinyl. 19" - $125.00. Soiled - $40.00.
Cookie: Composition. 19" - $300.00. Soiled - $95.00.
Genius, Little: Composition. 18" - $185.00. Soiled - $60.00.
Genius, Little: Vinyl, may have flirty eyes. 19" - $150.00. Soiled - $45.00.
Genius, Little: 8" - $150.00. Soiled - $45.00.
Happy: Vinyl. 20" - $350.00. Soiled - $100.00.
Honeybun: Vinyl. 23" - $200.00. Soiled - $55.00.
Kathy: Vinyl. 19" - $150.00; 26" - $195.00. Soiled: 19" - $40.00; 26" - $55.00.
Kitten, Littlest: Vinyl. 8" - $185.00. Soiled - $65.00.

Mary Mine: 14" - $145.00. Soiled - $40.00.
Pinky: Composition. 23" - $125.00. Soiled - $40.00.
Precious: Composition. 12" - $100.00. Soiled - $40.00.
Princess Alexandria: Composition. 24" - $200.00. Soiled - $55.00.
Pussy Cat: Vinyl. 14" - $95.00. Black: 14" - $165.00. Soiled: $10.00-30.00.
Rusty: Vinyl. 20" - $465.00. Soiled - $100.00.
Slumbermate: Composition. 21" - $650.00. Soiled - $200.00.
Sunbeam: Vinyl. 16" - $165.00. Soiled - $40.00.
Sweet Tears: 9" - $85.00. With layette - $200.00. Soiled - $65.00.
Victoria: 20" - $65.00. Soiled - $25.00.

8" "Fischer Quints" with hard plastic heads and vinyl bodies and limbs. Uses the "Little Genius" doll and was made as "Quints" in 1964 only. Courtesy Frasher Doll Auctions. 8" set - $400.00 up.

20" "Victoria" with spray painted hair and "Puddin" with rooted hair. Both are original. Also shown is an all celluloid baby. Courtesy Frasher Doll Auctions. 20" - $75.00 up.

Right: 13" "Baby Genius" of 1950. Hard plastic head and limbs, cloth body, all original. Courtesy Gloria Anderson. 13" - $165.00 up.

This 10-11" high heel doll named "Cissette" was made from 1957 to 1963, but it was used for other dolls later. She is made of hard plastic, and clothes will be tagged "Cissette."

First prices are for mint condition dolls; second prices are for soiled, dirty or faded clothes, tags missing and hair messy.

Street Dresses: $245.00, $65.00.
Ballgowns: $450.00 up, $100.00.
Ballerina: $185.00, $55.00.
Gibson Girl: $1,300.00, $300.00.
Jacqueline: $475.00, $150.00.
Margot: $400.00, $100.00.
Portrette: $600.00, $185.00.
Wigged in case: $650.00, $200.00.

10" "Cissette" (1955-1959). All hard plastic, jointed knees, all original. Replaced shoes. Courtesy Frasher Doll Auctions. 10" - $225.00 up.

MADAME ALEXANDER - CISSY

"Cissy" was made 1955-1959 and had hard plastic with vinyl over the arms, jointed at elbows, and high heel feet. Clothes are tagged "Cissy."

First prices are for mint condition dolls; second prices for dirty, not original, bad face color, and played with dolls.

Street Dress: $375.00, $125.00.

Ballgown: $900.00, $165.00.
Bride: $450.00, $150.00.
Queen: $625.00, $165.00.
Portrait: "Godey," etc. 21" - $650.00, $175.00.
Scarlett: $800.00, $300.00.
Flora McFlimsey: Vinyl head, inset eyes. 15" - $500.00, $185.00.

20" "Cissy" (1955-1959). Hard plastic, jointed knees. Arms are vinyl and jointed at elbows. Original except replaced shoes. Courtesy Frasher Doll Auctions. 20" - $350.00 up.

MADAME ALEXANDER - CLOTH DOLLS

The Alexander Company made cloth and plush dolls and animals and also oil cloth baby animals in the 1930's, 1940's and early 1950's. In the 1960's, a few were made.

First prices are for mint condition dolls; second prices are for ones in poor condition, dirty, not original, played with or untagged.

Animals: $200.00 up, $75.00.

Dogs: $300.00, $100.00.

Alice in Wonderland: $650.00, $175.00.

Clarabelle, The Clown: 19" - $225.00, $85.00.

David Copperfield or Other Boys: $650.00, $200.00.

Eva Lovelace: $600.00, $165.00.

Funny: $100.00, $20.00.

Little Shaver: 7" - $350.00; 10" - $325.00.

Little Women: $600.00 each, $200.00.

Muffin: 14" - $135.00, $35.00.

So Lite Baby or Toddler: 20" - $350.00, $100.00.

Susie Q: $650.00, $200.00.

Tiny Tim: $650.00, $200.00.

Teeny Twinkle: Has disc floating eyes. $600.00, $185.00.

17" "Dottie Dumbunnie" with white muslin body with black flannel feet. White velvet head with yellow inside ears. Black button eyes. Original from 1938. Tagged "Madame Alexander/ New York." Courtesy Bonnie Chichura. 17" - $500.00.

MADAME ALEXANDER - COMPOSITION

First prices are for mint condition dolls; second prices are for dolls that are crazed, cracked, dirty, soiled clothes or not original.

Alice in Wonderland: 9" - $185.00, $60.00; 14" - $425.00, $100.00; 20" - $685.00, $160.00.

Baby Jane: 16" - $900.00, $300.00.

Brides or Bridesmaids: 7" - $175.00, $50.00; 9" - $200.00, $80.00; 15" - $300.00, $95.00; 21" - $575.00, $125.00.

Dionne Quints: 8" - $150.00, $50.00; Set of five - $1,000.00. 11" - $300.00, $125.00; Set of five - $1,800.00. Cloth Baby: 14" - $425.00, $140.00; Set of five - $2,500.00. Cloth Baby: 16" - $650.00, $150.00. 19-20" - $600.00, $200.00; Set of five - $3,200.00.

Dr. DeFoe: 14-15" - $900.00, $350.00.

Flora McFlimsey: (Marked Princess Elizabeth) Freckles: 15" - $625.00, $200.00; 22" - $750.00, $225.00.

Internationals/Storybook: 7" - $150.00, $50.00; 11" - $175.00, $65.00.

Jane Withers: 13" - $800.00, $300.00; 18" - $950.00, $425.00.

18" "Kate Greenaway." All composition and head with yellow-gold mohair wig will be marked "Princess Elizabeth." Original dress tagged "Kate Greenaway." Courtesy Frasher Doll Auctions. 18" - $500.00 up.

Jeannie Walker: 13" - $475.00, $150.00; 18" - $650.00, $250.00.

Kate Greenaway: (Marked Princess Elizabeth) Very yellow blonde wig. 14" - $500.00, $165.00; 18" - $675.00, $225.00.

Little Colonel: 9" - $350.00, $125.00; 13" - $550.00, $225.00; 23" - $800.00, $400.00.

Margaret O'Brien: 15" - $525.00, $225.00; 18" - $700.00, $250.00; 21" - $900.00, $350.00.

Marionettes: Tony Sarg: 12" Disney - $465.00, $165.00. Others: 12" - $325.00, $100.00.

McGuffey Ana: (Marked Princess Elizabeth) 13" - $450.00, $165.00; 20" - $700.00, $300.00.

Portrait Dolls: 1939-1941, 1946: 21" - $1,600.00, $600.00.

Princess Elizabeth: Closed mouth. 13" - $425.00, $150.00; 18" - $600.00, $250.00; 24" - $700.00, $350.00.

Scarlett: 9" - $350.00, $125.00; 14" - $600.00, $200.00; 18" - $800.00, $300.00; 21" - $1,000.00, $450.00.

Sonja Henie: 17" - $625.00, $250.00; 20" - $750.00, $300.00. Jointed waist: 14" - $475.00, $185.00.

Wendy Ann: 11" - $350.00, $125.00; 15" - $500.00, $175.00; 18" - $600.00, $200.00.

7" "Tiny Betty" as Bridesmaid (top), Nurse, Scotch, and Red Riding Hood (lower). All are original and came in original floral print boxes. The Red Riding Hood has a misprinted tag "Fletion Doll" rather than "Fiction Doll" along with name and "Madame Alexander/New York." Courtesy Glorya Woods. 7" - $175.00-195.00.

18" "Sonja Henie" - 1939. All original with tagged outfit. All composition, open mouth, dimples and brown sleep eyes. Head marked with name. Courtesy Glorya Woods. 18" - $550.00 up.

16" "Princess Elizabeth" dolls (1937-1940), marked with name on head. All composition, human hair wigs, open mouth and both are all original. The "Princess Elizabeth" marked doll was used as several different "personalities." Courtesy Frasher Doll Auctions. 16" - $500.00 up.

15" "Scarlett" using the "Wendy Ann" doll (1937-1941). All composition and original. Frasher Doll Auctions. 15" - $600.00.

First prices are for mint condition dolls; second prices are for dolls that are dirty, played with, soiled clothes or not original.

Alice in Wonderland: 14" - $425.00, $165.00; 17" - $565.00, $200.00; 23" - $750.00, $300.00.

Annabelle: 15" - $500.00, $200.00; 18" - $600.00, $200.00; 23" - $750.00, $300.00.

Babs: 20" - $525.00, $185.00.

Babs Skater: 18" - $575.00, $200.00; 21" - $625.00, $300.00.

Binnie Walker: 15" - $185.00, $90.00; 25" - $375.00, $125.00.

Ballerina: 14" - $375.00, $165.00.

Cinderella: 14" - $600.00, $250.00; 18" - $700.00, $300.00.

Cynthia: Black doll. 15" - $700.00, $300.00; 18" - $775.00, $365.00; 23" - $850.00, $425.00.

Elise: Street dress. 16½" - $350.00, $175.00. Ballgown: $450.00, $200.00.

Bride: 16" - $325.00, $165.00.

Fairy Queen: 14½" - $450.00, $200.00.

Glamour Gals: 18" - $950.00, $400.00.

Godey Lady: 14" - $900.00, $350.00.

Man/Groom: 14" - $800.00, $400.00.

Kathy: 15" - $500.00, $200.00; 18" - $600.00, $265.00.

Kelly: 12" - $500.00, $175.00; 16" (MaryBel): $325.00, $160.00.

Lady Churchill: 18" - $950.00, $325.00.

Lissy: Street dress: 12" - $365.00, $185.00. Bride: $325.00, $185.00. Ballerina: $365.00, $195.00.

Little Women: 8" - $125.00, $60.00; Set of five (bend knee) - $700.00; Set of five (straight leg) - $400.00. 12" Lissy: $350.00, $135.00; Set of five - $1,500.00. 14" - $450.00; Set of five - $1,800.00.

Laurie: 8" - $75.00 up, $30.00; 12" - $475.00, $195.00.

Maggie: 15" - $425.00, $185.00;

17" - $600.00, $250.00; 23" - $850.00, $300.00.

Maggie Mixup: 8" - $475.00, $200.00; 16½" - $425.00, $175.00. 8" Angel: $1,200.00, $450.00.

Margaret O'Brien: 14½" - $650.00, $250.00; 18" - $865.00, $350.00; 21" - $900.00, $400.00.

Mary Martin: Sailor suit or ballgown. 14" - $600.00, $185.00; 17" - $900.00, $400.00.

Peter Pan: 15" - $500.00, $200.00.

Polly Pigtails: 14" - $450.00, $200.00; 17" - $575.00, $250.00.

Prince Charming: 14" - $625.00, $300.00; 18" - $850.00, $375.00.

15" original "Binnie Walker." Hard plastic and vinyl arms, jointed at elbows and knees, flat feet. 8" "Maggie Mixup" skater (1961). All hard plastic. Courtesy Turn of Century Antiques. 15" - $450.00 up; 8" - $650.00.

Prince Phillip: 17" - $850.00, $300.00; 21" - $900.00, $400.00.

Queen: 18" - $900.00, $400.00.

Shari Lewis: 14" - $450.00, $165.00; 21" - $500.00, $225.00.

Sleeping Beauty: 16½" - $550.00, $200.00; 21" - $900.00, $400.00.

Story Princess: 15" - $500.00, $250.00.

Violet, Sweet: 18" - $700.00, $250.00.

Wendy (Peter Pan Set): 14" - $600.00, $185.00.

Wendy Ann: 14½" - $500.00, $185.00; 17" - $700.00, $250.00; 22" - $850.00, $350.00.

Winnie Walker: 15" - $275.00, $100.00; 18" - $350.00, $150.00; 23" - $400.00, $185.00.

17" "Rosamund Bridesmaid" of 1951. Uses the "Maggie" face doll. All hard plastic and original. Courtesy Gloria Anderson. 17" - $600.00 up.

12" "Marme" from the Little Women series. Uses the "Lissy" doll. All hard plastic and original. Courtesy Frasher Doll Auctions. 12" - $350.00.

First prices are for mint condition dolls; second prices are for dolls that are played with, soiled, dirty and missing original clothes.

Barbara Jane: 29" - $400.00, $100.00.

Caroline: 15" - $350.00, $125.00.

First Ladies: First set of six - $1,000.00. Second set of six - $800.00. Third set of six - $900.00. Fourth set of six - $900.00. Fifth set of six - $900.00. Sixth set of six - $900.00.

Fischer Quints: Hard plastic with vinyl heads, set of five - $500.00.

Gidget: 14" - $400.00, $100.00.

Granny, Little: 14" - $375.00, $100.00.

Jacqueline: Street Dress. 21" - $650.00, $250.00. Ballgown: $750.00, $350.00. Riding Habit: $650.00, $275.00.

Janie: 12" - $385.00, $150.00.

12" "Cleopatra" and "Mark Antony" (1980-1985). All vinyl with rooted hair and all original. Courtesy Frasher Doll Auctions. 12" - $75.00 up each.

Top row: "Lissy" as "McGuffey Ana"; composition "Margaret O'Brien." Lower row: FAO Schwarz special dolls "Katie" and "Tommy" made of plastic and vinyl. Courtesy Frasher Doll Auctions. "Lissy" - $1,200.00 up; "Margaret" - $800.00; "Katie" - $1,200.00; "Tommy" - $1,200.00.

Joanie: 36" - $450.00, $185.00.

Jenny Lind & Cat: 14" - $465.00, $150.00.

Leslie: Black doll. Ballgown: 17" - $500.00, $175.00. Ballerina: $400.00, $125.00. Street Dress: $400.00, $150.00.

Madame Doll: 14" - $475.00, $175.00.

Madelaine: 18", jointed knees, elbows and wrists. $700.00, $285.00.

Marlo Thomas: 17" - $525.00, $200.00.

Marybel: 16" - $265.00, $95.00; In case - $350.00; $185.00.

Mary Ellen: 31" - $600.00, $200.00.

Melinda: 14" - $365.00, $150.00; 16" - $450.00, $200.00.

Michael with Bear: Peter Pan set. 11" - $475.00, $175.00.

Mimi: 30" - $850.00, $350.00.

Peter Pan: 14" - $350.00, $150.00.

Polly: 17" - $425.00, $165.00.

Rozy: 12" - $465.00, $165.00.

Smarty: 12" - $385.00, $165.00.

14" plastic and vinyl "Mary Ann" dolls shown (back row) "Cinderella," "Scarlett," "McGuffey Ana," "Madame Doll," "Poor Cinderella," (front row) "Alice in Wonderland" and "Degas." Courtesy Turn of Century Antiques. 14" - $65.00 up each.

Sound of Music: Liesl: 10" - $275.00, $95.00; 14" - $250.00, $85.00. **Louisa:** 10" - $350.00, $100.00; 14" - $250.00, $90.00. **Brigitta:** 12" - $225.00, $75.00; 14" - $250.00, $75.00. **Maria:** 12" - $300.00, $80.00; 17" - $350.00, $85.00; **Marta:** 8" - $225.00, $75.00; 11" - $225.00, $75.00. **Gretl:** 8" - $225.00, $75.00; 11" - $225.00, $75.00. **Freidrich:** 8" - $225.00, $75.00; 11" - $250.00, $80.00.

Sound of Music: Small set: $1,400.00. Large set: $1,600.00.

Timmie Toddler: 23" - $225.00, $95.00; 30" - $275.00, $100.00.

Wendy: Peter Pan set. 14" - $300.00, $125.00.

17" "Formal Elise" made in 1968-1969. Vinyl and plastic, all original. Courtesy Frasher Doll Auctions. 17" - $200.00.

Prices are for mint condition dolls. The 21" Portrait dolls are many and all use the Jacqueline face with the early ones having jointed elbows and then all having one-piece arms. All will be marked "1961" on head.

21" Portrait: Depending upon individual doll. $400.00-$1,300.00.

Coco: 1966. 21" Portrait: $2,500.00. Street Dress: $2,500.00. Ballgown (other than portrait series): $2,500.00.

21" Portraits. Background, "Melanie" (1979-1981); left, "Manet" (1982) and right, "Scarlett" in green velvet (1979-1985). Courtesy Frasher Doll Auctions. "Melanie" - $425.00; "Manet" - $400.00; "Scarlett" - $475.00.

AMERICAN CHARACTER DOLL COMPANY

All American Character dolls are very collectible and all are above average in quality of doll material and clothes. Dolls marked "American Doll and Toy Co." are also made by American Character, and this name was used from 1959 until 1968 when the firm went out of business. Early dolls will be marked "Petite." Many will be marked "A.C."

First prices are for mint dolls; second prices are for dolls that have been played with, dirty, with soiled clothes or not original.

Annie Oakley: 17" hard plastic. $325.00, $95.00.

Betsy McCall: See Betsy McCall section.

Butterball: 19" - $185.00, $75.00.

Cartwright: Ben, Joe or Hoss. 8" - $70.00, $30.00.

Chuckles: 23" - $165.00, $85.00. Baby: 18" - $125.00, $50.00.

Composition Babies: Cloth bodies, marked "A.C." 14" - $85.00, $25.00. 22" - $125.00, $60.00. Marked "Petite": 14" - $145.00, $70.00; 22" - $200.00, $85.00.

Cricket: 9" - $25.00, $9.00. Growing hair: $30.00, $12.00.

Freckles: Face changes. 13" - $40.00, $15.00.

Hedda-Get-Betta: 21" - $95.00, $40.00.

Miss Echo, Little: 30" Talker: $165.00, $70.00.

"Petite" marked child: Composition. 14" - $165.00, $70.00; 20" - $225.00, $100.00; 23" - $265.00, $100.00.

"A.C." marked child: Composition. 14" - $145.00, $50.00; 20" - $200.00, $75.00.

Popi: 12" - $20.00, $6.00.

Puggy: All composition, painted eyes, frown, marked "Petite." 13" - $450.00, $130.00.

Ricky, Jr.: 13" - $75.00, $30.00; 20" - $125.00, $50.00.

Sally: Composition, molded hair in "Patsy" style: 12" - $160.00, $50.00; 14" - $175.00, $60.00; 16" - $225.00, $70.00; 18" - $250.00, $90.00.

Sally Says: Talker, plastic/vinyl. 19" - $85.00, $35.00.

Sweet Sue/Toni: Hard plastic, some walkers, some with extra joints at knees, elbows and/or ankles, some combination hard plastic and vinyl. Marked "A.C. Amer.Char.Doll," or "American Character" in circle. **Ballgown:** 15" - $225.00, $75.00; 18" - $300.00, $125.00. **Street dress:** 15" - $175.00, $50.00; 18" - $300.00, $125.00;

30" "Sweet Sue" with hard plastic body and legs, vinyl head and arms. Arms jointed at elbows. All original in original box. This same "face" also used as "Toni." Courtesy Frasher Doll Auctions. 30" - **$525.00 up.**

22" - $350.00, $145.00; 24" - $400.00, $165.00; 30" - $500.00, $200.00. **Vinyl:** 10½" - $100.00, $40.00; 17" - $200.00, $50.00; 21" - $300.00, $90.00; 25" - $400.00, $150.00; 30" - $525.00, $200.00. **Groom:** 20" - $400.00, $150.00.

Tiny Tears: Hard plastic/vinyl. 8" - $45.00, $15.00; 13" - $125.00, $45.00; 17" - $165.00, $85.00. All vinyl: 8" - $35.00, $10.00; 12" - $65.00, $30.00; 16" - $100.00, $45.00.

Toodles: Baby: 14" - $100.00, $40.00. Tiny: 10½" - $100.00, $40.00. Toddler with "follow me eyes": 22" - $200.00, $80.00; 28" - $300.00, $125.00; 30" - $375.00, $165.00.

Toodle-Loo: 18" - $185.00, $55.00. **Tressy:** 12½" - $40.00, $12.00. **Whimette/Little People:** 7½" - $30.00, $10.00. **Whimsey:** 19" - $110.00, $45.00.

10½" "Toni" by American Character (1958-1959). Wears gown called "Romance with Mink." All vinyl, sleep eyes, rooted hair. Courtesy Sandy Johnson-Barts. 10½" - **$100.00 up.**

19½" "Pittie Pat" using the "Butterball" doll of 1961. "Pittie Pat" was on market in 1962 and 1963. Rooted hair, smile mouth and all vinyl. The child could hear the doll's heart beat (key wound). All original. Courtesy Jeannie Mauldin. 19½" - $225.00.

20" "Sweet Sue Sophisticate" with vinyl head, rooted hair, rigid vinyl body, sleep eyes, and high heel feet. Pale toe and nail polish. Has bra, panties and hose. All original. Original price tag: $10.98. 20" - $300.00 up.

15" "Tiny Tears" has hard plastic head, all rubber body, sleep eyes, molded hair. All original. Courtesy Gloria Anderson. 15" - $145.00.

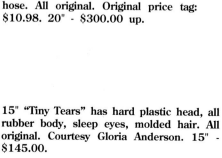

13" "Freckles" made by American Character in 1966. Rooted hair, painted eyes. Face changes by moving left arm. Shown with 1950's "Lassie." Courtesy Jeannie Mauldin. 13" - $40.00; Lassie - $100.00.

ANNALEE MOBILITEE DOLLS

The following information courtesy Joan Amundsen.

Tag: First were red woven lettering on white rayon tape. Second tags (around 1969) were red printing on white satin tape. Third tags (around 1976) were red printing on gauze-type cloth.

Hair: From 1934 to 1963, the hair was made of yarn. From 1960-1963, the hair was made of feathers (chicken), hair of yellow or orange. From 1963 to date, the hair is made of synthetic fur in various colors.

8½" Monk with ski from 1970; 9" Monk with ceramic jug from 1971. Courtesy Glorya Woods. 8½", 9" - $75.00 up.

Animals: First introduced into the line in 1964. Fabrics are changed each year and often date can be determined by this feature.

Tails: The oldest were made of same felt as the body. From the mid to late 1970's, cotton bias tape was used; the ones of the 1980's are made of cotton flannel.

Annalee all felt "Little Baby" with oil-painted features and flannel blanket. From 1980's. Courtesy Jeannie Mauldin. $75.00 up.

1970's Annalee Angel. All felt with oil-painted features. Original on cotton "cloud." Courtesy Jeannie Mauldin. 6" - $90.00 up.

Annalee "Mice" dressed in diapers. One has boxing gloves; the other has a baby bottle. Both from late 1970's. Courtesy Jeannie Mauldin. Mice - $80.00 up each.

The Arranbee Doll Company began making dolls in 1922 and was purchased by the Vogue Doll Company in 1959. Vogue used the Arranbee marked molds until 1961. Arranbee used the initials "R & B."

First prices are for mint condition dolls; second prices are for dolls that have been played with, are cracked, crazed, dirty or do not have original clothes.

Babies: Bisque heads. See Armand Marseille section.

Babies: Composition/cloth bodies. 16" - $85.00, $40.00; 22" - $145.00, $60.00.

Bottletot: Has celluloid bottle molded to celluloid hand. 18" - $185.00, $75.00.

18" all original Arranbee boy. All composition with sleep eyes and glued-on wig. Courtesy Gloria Anderson. 18" - $300.00.

Debu-Teen: Composition girl with cloth body. 14" - $165.00, $60.00; 18" - $225.00, $80.00; 21" - $300.00, $125.00.

Dream Baby, My: See Armand Marseille section for bisque heads. Composition: 14" - $200.00, $85.00. Vinyl/cloth: 16" - $75.00, $35.00; 26" - $175.00, $75.00.

Kewty: Composition "Patsy" style molded hair. 10" - $125.00, $45.00.

Littlest Angel: All hard plastic. 10" - $50.00, $15.00. Vinyl head: 10" - $45.00, $15.00. Red hair/freckles: 10" - $95.00, $40.00.

Miss Coty: Vinyl. 10" - $90.00, $30.00.

My Angel: Plastic/vinyl. 17" - $55.00, $20.00; 22" - $75.00, $35.00; 36" - $165.00, $70.00.

Nancy: Composition. Molded hair or wig. 12" - $165.00, $50.00; 17" - $300.00, $100.00; 19" - $350.00, $125.00; 23" - $400.00, $150.00.

Nancy Lee: Composition. 14" - $185.00, $70.00. Hard plastic: 14" - $200.00, $85.00; 20" - $400.00, $125.00.

Nancy Lee: Unusual eyebrows/vinyl. 15" - $125.00, $50.00.

Nancy Lee: Baby, painted eyes and looks as if crying. 15" - $80.00, $40.00.

Nancy Lee: Baby with composition head and limbs, open mouth with upper and lower teeth. 25" - $265.00, $85.00.

Nanette: Hard plastic. 14" - $185.00, $75.00; 17" - $265.00, $90.00; 21" - $325.00, $100.00; 23" - $400.00, $150.00.

Sonja Skater: Composition. 14" - $185.00, $80.00; 18" - $225.00, $90.00; 21" - $325.00, $125.00.

Storybook Dolls: All composition. Molded hair, painted eyes. 10" - $165.00, $45.00.

Taffy: Looks like Alexander's "Cissy." 23" - $85.00, $45.00.

18" "Nanette" with floss hair in elaborate hairdo. Original and all hard plastic. Courtesy Bonnie Stewart. 18" - $285.00.

20" "Nancy Lee." All hard plastic, sleep eyes, mohair wig and marked "R & B" on head. Original box marked "Nancy Lee by Arranbee Doll Co." 20" - $400.00 up.

25" "Baby Nancy" was made from early 1930's to 1939. Later ones have deeper stroke hair and thinner opening in mouth. Cloth body and composition head and limbs. Courtesy Glorya Woods. 25" - $265.00.

18" "Nanette" by Arranbee. All hard plastic and original clothes and skates. Walker, head turns from side to side. Marked on head "R & B." Original price tag: $10.98. 18" - $265.00 up.

20" "Nanette Walker." All hard plastic and original with tag and curlers. Marked on head "R & B." Courtesy June Schultz. 20" - $325.00.

20" all hard plastic walker with no cryer box and one-piece legs. Slightly curled arms, sleep eyes and open mouth. Ca. 1952-1955. Box marked "Astor Corp." Courtesy Marjorie Uhl. 20" - $85.00.

19" "Captain Kangaroo." Cloth stuffed with vinyl head and painted features. Marked "1961 Robt. Keeshan/Assoc. Inc." Modeled-on hat and hair. Made by Baby Berry. Courtesy Shirley Puertzer. 19" - $150.00.

First prices are for mint condition dolls; second prices are for played with, dirty, soiled or not original dolls.

8": All hard plastic, jointed knees. Made by American Character Doll Co. Street Dress: $145.00, $60.00; Ballgown: $175.00, $75.00; Bathing Suit or Romper: $125.00, $40.00.

11½": Brown sleep eyes, reddish rooted hair, vinyl/plastic and made by Uneeda, but unmarked. $100.00, $40.00.

13": Made by Horsman in 1975, although doll is marked "Horsman Dolls, Inc. 1967" on head. $55.00, $25.00.

14": Vinyl with rooted hair, medium high heels, round sleep eyes and made by American Character Doll Company and will be marked "McCall 1958. $225.00, $90.00.

14": Vinyl head, rooted hair, rest hard plastic marked "P-90 body." Made by Ideal Doll Company. $200.00, $75.00.

22": Unmarked. Has extra joints at waist, ankles, wrists and above knees. Made by American Character. $250.00, $85.00.

20": Vinyl with rooted hair, slender limbs and made by American Character Doll Company. $250.00, $95.00.

22": Vinyl/plastic with extra joints and made by Ideal Doll Company. $250.00, $85.00.

All "Betsy McCall" dolls. Left to right: 29" (all blue) Horsman, 1974; 36" American Character (redressed), 1959; 29" American Character, 1961; 22" multi-jointed, original, (red/white), Uneeda, 1959; 14" original (in pink), multi-jointed, American Character, 1960; 20" (blue), not original, 1958; 14" by Ideal, 1952 (red/white stitching on bodice); 11½" Uneeda teen, original; 8" American Characters, original. Courtesy Jeannie Mauldin. For all sizes, see listing.

29-30": All vinyl, rooted hair and made by American Character Doll Company. $400.00, $150.00.

29": Marked "McCall 1961." Has extra joints at ankles, knees, waist and wrists. Made by American Character. $475.00, $150.00.

29": Marked "B.M.C. Horsman 1971." $250.00, $80.00.

36": All vinyl with rooted hair and made by American Character Doll Company. $500.00, $200.00.

36": Marked "McCall 1959." Made by Ideal Doll Company. $400.00, $185.00.

39": Boy called "Sandy McCall." Marked same as above girl. Made by Ideal Doll Company. $425.00, $200.00.

14" and 8" "Betsy McCall." Both are original. 8" is all hard plastic with jointed knees and 14" is all vinyl. Courtesy Frasher Doll Auctions. 8" - $150.00 up; 14" - $225.00 up.

20" American Character "Betsy McCall" wearing "Sugar & Spice" outfit. Vinyl, rooted hair and flirty eyes. Courtesy Sandy Johnson-Barts. 20" - $250.00 up.

Wooden rocker for the 8" size "Betsy McCall." Courtesy Sandy Johnson-Barts. $65.00.

Left: 14" American Character "Betsy McCall" wearing birthday dress. The 8" has a matching dress. Right: 29" American Character multi-jointed "Betsy McCall" in original box. Has been attributed to Ideal Doll Co. Courtesy Sandy Johnson-Barts. 14" - $225.00; 14" in box - $350.00; 29" - $475.00 up.

11½" "Betsy McCall" made by Uneeda with sleep eyes and made of plastic and vinyl with rooted hair. Original clothes. Courtesy Marie Ernst. 11½" - $100.00 up.

The following information is courtesy of Pat Sebastian.

"Buddy Lee" dolls were made in composition to 1949, then changed to hard plastic and discontinued in 1962-1963. "Buddy Lee" came dressed in two "Coca-Cola" uniforms. The tan with green stripe outfit matched the uniforms worn by delivery drivers while the white with green stripe uniforms matched those of plant workers. (Among Coca-Cola employees the white uniform became more popular and in warmer regions of the country, the white outfit was also worn by outside workers.)

"Buddy Lee" came in many different outfits.

Engineer: $250.00 up.
Gas Station attendant: $250.00 up.
Cowboy: $300.00 up.
Coca-Cola uniform: White with green stripe - $300.00 up. Tan with green stripe - $350.00 up.
Other soft drink companies uniforms: $300.00 up.

"Buddy Lee" Engineer and Cowboy. Both are all composition. The "Lassie" is fully jointed, including swivel head and was made in 1976 by Gabriel, Ind. Inc. Courtesy Shirley Bertrand. Engineer - $250.00 up; Cowboy - $300.00 up.

CABBAGE PATCH

The following was written by Betty Chapman, editor of "Patchwork" (Rt. 1, Box 184; Dekalb Jct., NY 13630.)

Values of Coleco's vinyl face Cabbage Patch Kids vary due to availability, rareness, popularity of certain models and the general economy of the doll market. It should be noted that along with Coleco, the American manufacturer, there were also four foreign licensed producers, so to help explain the Cabbage Patch Kids, the dolls discussed will be mint in box (M.I.B.) COLECOS and then a few words regarding the foreign made ones. Another point of interest to the collector is the fact that there are 21 different faces, many different hairstyles and great many different outfits. It would not be possible to discuss them all here, but we will cover the most desirable.

1983: First year on market. #1: No dimples. #2: Two dimples, large eyes and no freckles. #3: One dimple, large eyes. #4: Two dimples and pacifier. Values from $50.00-75.00.

Red Shag Hairdo Boys: In any face mold. $250.00-600.00.

Freckles #2: With small eyes are regular. #2: Doll with large eyes reduced, has freckles and except for the tan/champagne loop hairdo and Baldie dolls, can bring high second market prices. The highest priced dolls here are the red shag boy, Black dolls with freckles, with the Black girl being the rarest, and the Black shag hair boy, second rarest. The red shag hair boy or Black girl with freckles can bring as high as $800.00. The Black shag hair boy with freckles would be $600.00 and the Black Baldie with freckles is valued at $500.00. When the market is down, these prices will drop to $350.00-$450.00.

More Freckles: Girls with single auburn ponytail, two blonde (lemon) ponytails, two red ponytails, red braids, gold braids or loop hairdo: $175.00-$300.00.

Tan poodle with loop hairdo and two ponytails, brunette braids, brunette poodle hairdo, blonde loop hairdo: $150.00.

Tan poodle with loop hairdo and two ponytails, brunette braids, brunette poodle hairdo, blonde loop hairdo: $150.00.

Tan loop braids, Baldie: $100.00-125.00.

Auburn loop hairdo boy, brunette shag hair boy: $200.00-300.00.

Tan shag hair boy: $150.00 (has been as high as $200.00-225.00.)

1983 - #1: Black with shag hairdo: $125.00-150.00. Black Baldie: $100.00-125.00. Black girl with two ponytails: $75.00-100.00.

1983 black shag boy with freckles, #2 small eyes. Made by Coleco. Courtesy Betty Chapman. $600.00.

1983 - #4 with Pacifiers: Red shag hair boys: $400.00-500.00. Blacks: $175.00-225.00. Auburn single ponytail girl: $150.00. Tan poodle hair girl: $125.00. Remainder of 1983 #4 pacifier dolls range from $50.00-100.00.

1984-1985: Only a few Cabbage Patch Kids of these years are worth more than retail prices. 1985 single tooth brunette with ponytail: $150.00-200.00 up. Rare popcorn hairdos: $100.00-125.00. Gray eye girls, 1985: $50.00-75.00. Gray eye girls, 1983: Very few made. $150.00-275.00. 1985 freckled gold hair girl: $75.00.

Valued from $150.00 up: Baldies with eye colors other than blue, 1985 single tooth with brunette side ponytail and blue eyes, popcorn curl with pacifier, red popcorn with single tooth, double gold or double auburn hairdo, 1985 gray eye girls, 1985 gold braided, freckled girls, UT marked tag (body tag indicating the factory where it was made) with high cheek color, pacifiers and/or 1984 dates.

The 16 other molds are not discussed, nor the various types, such as Cornsilk Kids, Splash Kids, preemies, talking Kids, babies, twins, travelers, astronauts, baseball Kids, clowns and ringmasters, as the values have not risen enough to warrant it. These dolls are collectible due to personal preference. The 1983 dolls with Hong Kong on the body tag or with embroidered tag, with footed terrycloth sleeper or blue flowered corduroy overalls bring slightly higher prices. The powder scent 1983 Colecos are valued $10.00-25.00 above the others of this year.

As for the foreign Cabbage Patch Kids, the rarest seem to be those with freckles made in Mexico by Lili Ledi. Also rare are those made in Spain by Jesmar in 1983, with well-placed eyes and the freckle/pacifier combination (notably the red hair boys again.) Rarer ones from the South Africa Triang Pedi-

Standing left: 1983 Coleco rare small eyed #2, freckles and single auburn ponytail. Right: 1985 Coleco rare #1 freckled with gold braids. Sitting: 1983 #2 small eyes, freckles, bald in rare blue stripe sleeper. Courtesy Betty Chapman. 1983 - $175.00-200.00; 1985 - $75.00; 1983 bald - $150.00.

gree firm are the ones with gaudy yellow hair or freckles and pacifier together. From Japan's Tsukuda firm are ones from 1983 with red or lemon hair and brown eyes or with specialty outfits such as kimonos, Elegance dresses, Samuri outfits, baseball uniforms, Karate outfits and happy coats. Most of these foreign dolls sell for $100.00-$150.00. The Japanese powder scent dolls are valued at $200.00-250.00 up. Also the pacifier/freckle, red hair dolls from Jesmar, Spain are worth $150.00-200.00.

The dolls are stamped on the left buttock with Xavier Roberts's signature. Sometimes a year appears also. There are six signature colors to date, seven Coleco factories and four foreign licensed makers, 21 face molds thus far, seven hair colors, five eye colors and 13 basic hairstyles, plus additional hairstyles variations, eye shades and hair color shades. If one considers the large variation in these dolls as compared to any other modern dolls, it becomes obvious why they are an established collector's item only five years after they were introduced. The accompanying photographs, although a good cross section, are a relatively small sampling of the many unique combinations.

Xavier Roberts Cabbage Patch "Irish Edition" boy and girl. Green eyes and red curly hair. Courtesy Frasher Doll Auctions. $400.00 up.

Left: Xavier Roberts original girl, "Kay Merry," Coral Edition, has red curly hair and freckles. Right: Coral Edition, "Pansy Edith" with auburn hair in two braids. Courtesy Frasher Doll Auctions. $400.00 up.

Xavier Roberts Cabbage Patch Ivory Edition, 1985. "Wanda Valonia" has brown eyes and black hair in twin ponytails. Courtesy Frasher Doll Auctions. $400.00 up.

1983 Coleco #4's. Red shag boy and Black shag boy. Courtesy Betty Chapman. Red head - $400.00. Black: $200.00.

Rear: 1983 powder scent red loopy hair, brown eye made in Japan and in rare made in Japan outfit. Black shag hair boy made in Mexico and is #4 with freckles, pacifier and made in Mexico outfit. Front: 1984 South African #4, freckles, bald in green sleeper with lace, which is rare (not doll's own outfit.) 1983 made in Spain #2 red shag hair, freckles in rare mint green duck romper (not doll's own outfit.) Courtesy Betty Chapman. 1983 Japan - $350.00. Mexico - $150.00. South African - $125.00; Sleeper - $50.00. Spain - $200.00; Romper $25.00.

Standing: 1984 made in Canada Coleco Couture Kid (fur coat) with rare red corduroy snowsuit. Sitting: 1986 #5 single tooth with rare burgundy twin outfit. Courtesy Betty Chapman. 1984 - $100.00. 1986 - $40.00.

16" limited edition porcelain Cabbage Patch "Jessica Louise" with painted green eyes and long dark tosca blonde hair (1984). Courtesy Frasher Doll Auctions. 16" - $300.00 up.

16" limited edition porcelain Cabbage Patch "Georgia Dee" with green painted eyes and long yellow hair (1985). Courtesy Frasher Doll Auctions. 16" - $300.00 up.

Coleco Cabbage Patch doll with rigid vinyl head dressed in cowgirl outfit. Shown with official Cabbage Patch horse. Courtesy Sally Bethscheider. Doll - $85.00 up; Horse - $65.00 up.

Annie Rooney, Little: All composition, legs painted black, molded shoes. 16" - $700.00.

Baby Bo Kaye: Bisque head, open mouth. 17-18" - $2,800.00. Celluloid head: 15-16" - $825.00. Composition head, mint: 18" - $700.00. Light craze and not original: 18" - $375.00.

Baby Mine: Vinyl/cloth, sleep eyes. Mint: 16" - $125.00; 19" - $175.00. Slightly soiled and not original: 16" - $60.00; 19" - $70.00.

Betty Boop: Composition head, wood jointed body. Mint: 12" - $600.00. Light craze and a few paint chips: 12" - $275.00.

Champ: Composition/freckles. Mint: 16" - $600.00. Light craze, not original: 16" - $300.00.

Giggles: Composition, molded loop for ribbon. Mint: 11" - $285.00; 14" - $525.00. Light craze: 11" - $165.00; 14" - $325.00.

Ho-Ho: Plaster in excellent condition. 4" - $50.00. Vinyl in excellent condition: 4" - $15.00.

Joy: Composition, wood jointed body. Mint: 10" - $285.00; 15" - $380.00. Slight craze: 10" - $160.00; 15" - $285.00.

Kewpie: See Kewpie section.

Margie: Composition. Mint: 6" - $185.00; 10" - $245.00. Slight craze and not original: 6" - $80.00; 10" - $125.00.

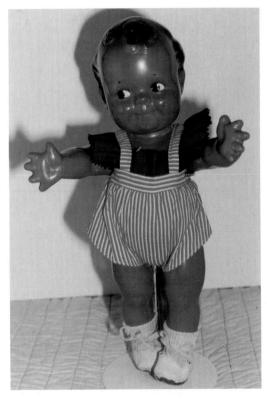

14" black "Scootles," ca. 1925. Designed by Rose O'Neill. All composition with jointed shoulders, hips and neck, original. Courtesy Frasher Doll Auctions. 14" - $700.00.

Miss Peep: Pin jointed shoulders and hips. Vinyl. Mint and original: 1960's. 18" - $60.00. Black: 18" - $95.00. Slightly soiled and not original: 18" - $28.00. Black: 18" - $35.00.

Miss Peep, Newborn: Plastic and vinyl. Mint and original: 18" - $50.00. Slight soil and not original: 18" - $20.00.

Peanut, Affectionately: Vinyl. Mint and original: 18½" - $90.00. Slight soil and not original: 18½" - $40.00.

Pete the Pup: Composition, wood jointed body. Mint: 8" - $200.00. Slight craze and few paint chips: 8" - $100.00.

Pinkie: Composition, 1930's. Mint and original: 10" - $285.00. Slight craze: 10" - $125.00. Wood jointed body: 10" - $300.00. Vinyl/plastic: 1950's. Mint: $185.00. Slight soil and not original: 10" - $125.00.

Scootles: Composition. Mint and original: 8" - $350.00 up; 12" - $385.00 up; 15" - $500.00 up. Light craze and not original: 8" - $100.00; 12" - $225.00; 15" - $285.00. Composition with sleep eyes: Mint: 15" - $550.00; 21" - $750.00. Slight craze: 15" - $300.00; 21" - $400.00. Black, composition: Mint: 15" - $700.00. Slight craze: 15" - $300.00. Vinyl: Mint and original: 14" - $150.00 up; 19" - $285.00 up; 27" - $400.00 up. Lightly soiled and not original: 14" - $45.00; 19" - $85.00; 27" - $125.00.

21" and 12" "Scootles" by Cameo. All composition and original except 12" doll is missing shoes and socks. Courtesy Turn of Century Antiques. 12" - $385.00 up; 21" - $750.00.

18" all oil cloth doll and clothes made during World War II. Has painted features and yarn hair. Courtesy Gloria Anderson. 18" - $65.00.

17" Anili toddlers. Left is "Bienchina" and on the right is "Pastorello." Pressed felt faces, arms, and legs. Cloth body. Signed "Anili" on sole of foot. Eyes defined and painted to side. Courtesy Glorya Woods. 17" - $500.00 up.

20" all cloth "Eloise" doll from the 1950's. "Eloise" is the fictional character from the books authored by Kay Thompson. The stories centered around a little girl who lived in New York's Plaza Hotel. (A large painting of "Eloise" still exists at the Plaza Hotel's entry.) The doll was designed by Bette Gould and made by American Character Doll Co. Courtesy Jeannie Mauldin. 20" - $300.00.

Left: 17" black cloth "Mammy"-style doll from World War II era. All original. Right: 13" mask face doll with painted features, stuffed red and white polka dot body and limbs, and sewn-on shoes. Courtesy Gloria Anderson. 17" - $80.00; 13" - $55.00.

"Ginger" in Activity Series, #556 "Toreador." Courtesy Maureen Fukushima. $145.00 up.

Hard plastic "Ginger" as "Cha-cha-cha Senorita" - #1007 of the Adventureland of Disneyland Series. Courtesy Maureen Fukushima. $150.00 up.

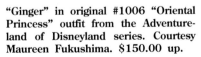

"Ginger" in original #1006 "Oriental Princess" outfit from the Adventureland of Disneyland series. Courtesy Maureen Fukushima. $150.00 up.

"Ginger" in "Gay Nineties" Series - #884 gown. Courtesy Maureen Fukushima. $135.00 up.

8" "Ginger" with hard plastic body and vinyl head marked "Ginger." "Character Series" #662. Courtesy Maureen Fukushima. $65.00 up.

Vinyl head "Ginger" visits Tomorrowland of Disneyland as "Space Girl" #1005. Courtesy Maureen Fukushima. $85.00.

8" "Ginger." All hard plastic and original and original box. Courtesy Sandy Johnson-Barts. 8" - $65.00; In box - $100.00.

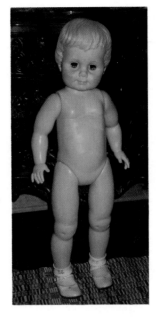

32" "Debbie Ann" with vinyl head and molded hair. Plastic body and limbs. Marked "D" on head. Original tag reads "Debbie Doll Co." Courtesy Shirley Bertrand. 32" nude - $100.00; original - $165.00.

DELUXE TOPPER

19" battery-operated "Baby Catch A Ball. She has metal rings around arms and when child throws the metal ball, the doll "catches" it and also returns the throw. Her molded tongue is stuck out of corner of mouth. Marked "2871/17 Eye/PB2/75/Deluxe Topper/196." Courtesy Jeannie Mauldin. 19" - $75.00; Other 19-20" battery-operated dolls from this company - $65.00.

DELUXE TOPPER

"Dawn" on her floral stand. She came in pink, yellow, green, and blue. Stand will hold up to three dolls. One doll came with each stand. Doll has bendable knees and is marked "K11A" on her head. Doll alone - $12.00; With stand - $18.00; Boys of series - $20.00 each; Black dolls of series - $20.00 each; Models - $35.00 each.

DOLL ARTIST

27" "Sarah" modeled in wax with glass eyes and hair lashes. Very few have been made. Cloth body with wax limbs. Artist is Nicholas Bramble. A beautiful doll that will be remembered in history. Courtesy Barbara Earnshaw-Cain. 27" - $3,000.00 up.

"Babes in Wonderland" Series by Dunham Arts of Oregon was limited to 25 numbered and signed editions for each doll. Dolls are 15" tall and all jointed bisque. Left to right: "Little Bo Peep," "Little Miss Muffet," "Little Red Riding Hood," "Little Boy Blue," and "Lucy Locket."

10" all metal doll made from railroad spikes. This original is called "Gandy Dance Ghost." The term comes from the name given to the workers who repaired and made safe the millions of miles of railroad track during the "romantic" era of the steam engines. The artist is "Dutch" Voss. 10" - $95.00 up.

Pair of 14" artist dolls incised "Little Big Chief 1981 by Barbara Peterson Comley/Souvenir 1983 Tulsa." Tall 18" doll is incised "Bicentennial 1976 Clay Eagle by Ernestine Hargis." Courtesy Frasher Doll Auctions. 14" - $265.00; 18" - $300.00.

"Time To Eat Yet?" is hand carved from wood and made by Paul Spencer, who is an artist with a true style of his own. Paul Spencer also makes dolls and babies, some with glass sleep eyes. $350.00 up.

"Crystal" is a hand-carved wooden girl with painted features made by Paul Spencer. His inspiration came from the abused children that he and his mother work with in a Waco, Texas center. Anyone that owns one of Paul Spencer's dolls/figures has a great investment for the future. $1,200.00 up.

17" "Mary Lu" made by Doll Bodies, Inc.. All hard plastic walker with open mouth, sleep eyes and all original in original box. Doll is unmarked. Courtesy Gloria Anderson. 17" - $70.00 up

EEGEE DOLL COMPANY

The name of this company was made up from the name of the founder E.G. Goldberger. Founded in 1917, the early dolls were marked "E.G.", then E. Goldberger" and now the marks of "Eegee" and "Goldberger" are used.

Andy: Teen type. 12" - $30.00.

Annette: Teen type. 11½" - $35.00.

Annette: Plastic and vinyl walker. 25" - $45.00; 28" - $60.00; 36" - $85.00.

Baby Luv: Cloth/vinyl, marked "B.T. Eegee." 14" - $45.00.

Baby Susan: Name marked on head. 8½" - $15.00.

Baby Tandy Talks: Foam body, rest vinyl, pull string talker. $50.00.

Ballerina: Foam body and limbs, vinyl head. 1967. 18" - $40.00.

Ballerina: Hard plastic/vinyl head. 20" - $45.00.

Boy Dolls: Molded hair, rest vinyl. 13" - $35.00; 21" - $45.00.

Composition: Sleep eyes, open mouth girls. 14" - $145.00 up; 18" - $200.00 up. Babies: Cloth and composition. 16" - $100.00 up; 20" - $160.00 up.

Debutante: Vinyl head, rest hard plastic, jointed knees. 28" - $95.00.

Dolly Parton: 1980. 12" - $25.00; 18" - $65.00.

Flowerkins: Plastic/vinyl, marked "F-2" on head. 16" - $75.00 in box.

Gemmette: Teen type. 14" - $30.00.

Georgie or Georgette: Redhead twins. Cloth and vinyl. 22-23" - $55.00.

Gigi Perreaux: Hard plastic, early vinyl head. 17" - $250.00 up.

Granny: from "Beverly Hillbillies." Old lady modeling, grey rooted hair, painted or sleep eyes. 14" - $85.00.

Miss Charming: All composition Shirley Temple look-alike. 19" - $300.00 up. Pin - $18.00.

Miss Sunbeam: Plastic/vinyl, dimples. 17" - $50.00.

Musical Baby: Has key wind music box in cloth body. 17" - $22.00.

My Fair Lady: All vinyl, jointed waist, adult type. 10½" - $45.00; 19" - $85.00.

Posey Playmate: Foam and vinyl. 18" - $22.00.

Susan Stroller: Hard plastic/vinyl head. 20" - $50.00; 23" - $65.00; 26" - $75.00.

Tandy Talks: Plastic/vinyl head, freckles, pull string talker. 20" - $75.00.

Left: 19" vinyl, fully jointed and high heel feet, sleep eyes, streaked gray hair (long to waist), curled at nape of neck. All original, unmarked. Right: 14½" "Ma Brown" advertisement for "Ma Brown Pickles." Vinyl and plastic, painted eyes/no lashes, rooted long gray hair pulled up to roll at crown. Original clothes but replaced shawl. Marked "Eegee Co." on head. Courtesy Marie Ernst. 19" - $85.00; 14½" - $60.00.

15" stands on music box and is marked on head and back "Eegee Co. 1963." Tag on dress: "EG Musical Doll on windup turntable." Vinyl head and arms, plastic body and legs. Sleep eyes/lashes and blue eyeshadow. Original. Courtesy Lee Crane. 15" - $75.00.

"Dolly Parton" is made of vinyl and plastic and has painted features with open/closed mouth and rooted hair. All original, 1987 only. 18" - $65.00.

First prices are for mint condition dolls; second prices for dolls that are played with, soiled, dirty, cracked or crazed or not original. Dolls marked with full name or "F & B."

American Children: Marked with that name, some have "Anne Shirley" marked bodies, others are unmarked. All composition, painted or sleep eyes. Closed Mouth Girls: 18-19" - $1,400.00. Closed Mouth Boy: 15" - $1,200.00; 17" - $1,300.00. Open Mouth Girl: 15" (Barbara Joan) - $750.00; 18" (Barbara Ann) - $900.00; 21" (Barbara Lou) - $1,100.00.

Anne Shirley: Marked with name. All composition. 15" - $250.00; 21" - $350.00; 27" - $475.00.

Babyette: Cloth/composition. Sleeping. 12" - $300.00, $150.00.

Babykin: All composition. 9-12" - $185.00, $85.00. All vinyl: 10" - $50.00.

Baby Cuddleup: 1953, vinyl coated cloth body, rest vinyl. Two lower teeth. 20" - $60.00, $30.00.

12" marked "F&B Babyette." Ca. 1937. Sleeping baby with composition head and gauntlet hands. Cloth body and legs. All original. Eyes painted asleep. Courtesy Gloria Anderson. 12" - $300.00.

Baby Dainty: Marked with name. Composition/cloth. 17" - $200.00, $95.00.

Baby Evelyn: Marked with name. Composition/cloth. 17" - $200.00, $95.00.

Baby Grumpy: See Grumpy.

Baby Tinyette: Composition. 8-9" - $175.00, $70.00. Toddler: 8-9" - $175.00; $70.00.

Betty Brite: Marked with name. All composition, fur wig, sleep eyes. 16-17" - $250.00, $100.00.

Bicentennial Boy & Girl: (Pun'kin) 11" - $145.00.

Bridal Sets: 1970's. 4 dolls. White: $250.00, $100.00. Black: $350.00, $165.00.

Bright Eyes: Same doll as Tommy Tucker and Mickey. Composition/cloth, flirty eyes. 18" - $300.00; 22-23" $350.00.

Brother or Sister: Composition head and hands, rest cloth, yarn hair, painted eyes. 12" - $165.00, $65.00; 16" - $185.00, $70.00.

Bubbles: Marked with name. Composition/cloth. 1924. 16" - $250.00, $95.00; 20" - $325.00, $125.00; 26" - $450.00, $165.00. Black: 16" - $400.00; 20" - $650.00.

Button Nose: Composition. 8-9" - $175.00, $60.00. Vinyl/cloth: 18" - $50.00, $20.00.

Candy Kid: All composition. White: 12" - $250.00, $70.00. Black: 12" - $300.00, $85.00.

Carolina: Made for Smithsonian, 1980. 12" - $65.00, $30.00.

Charlie McCarthy: Composition/cloth. 19-20" - $325.00, $125.00.

Composition Dolls: Molded hair, all composition, jointed neck, shoulders and hips. Painted or sleep eyes. Open or closed mouth. Original clothes. All composition in perfect condition. Marked "Effanbee." 1930's. 9" - $165.00, $50.00; 15" - $200.00, $90.00; 18" - $265.00, $100.00; 21" - $350.00, $150.00.

Composition Dolls: 1920's. Cloth body, composition head and limbs, open or closed mouth, sleep eyes. Original clothes and in perfect condition. Marked

"Effanbee." 18" - $200.00, $90.00; 22" - $250.00, $125.00; 25" - $350.00, $125.00; 27-28" - $400.00, $150.00.

Currier & Ives: Plastic/vinyl. 12" - $50.00, $25.00.

Disney Dolls: Cinderella, Snow White, Alice in Wonderland and Sleeping Beauty. 1977-1978. 14" - $200.00, $80.00.

Emily Ann: 13" puppet, composition. $145.00, $50.00.

Dydee Baby: Hard rubber head, rubber body. Perfect condition. 14" - $125.00, $40.00. Hard plastic/vinyl: 15" - $150.00, $50.00; 20" - $225.00, $150.00.

Fluffy: All vinyl. 10" - $45.00, $15.00. Girl Scout: 10" - $50.00, $15.00. Black: 10" - $50.00, $15.00.

Grumpy: Frown, painted features, cloth and composition. 12" - $185.00, $70.00; 14" - $200.00, $90.00; 18" - $300.00, $150.00. Black: 12" - $245.00, $95.00; 14-15" - $325.00, $100.00.

Historical Dolls: All composition and original. 14" - $500.00, $150.00; 21" - $1,250.00, $500.00.

Honey: All composition. 14" - $200.00, $95.00; 20" - $350.00, $150.00; 27" - $500.00, $200.00.

Honey: All hard plastic, closed mouth. 14" - $175.00, $70.00; 18" - $300.00, $125.00; 21" - $350.00, $150.00.

Ice Queen: Skater outfit, composition, open mouth. 17" - $800.00, $250.00.

Limited Edition Club: 1975: Precious Baby - $500.00. **1976:** Patsy - $365.00. **1977:** Dewees Cochran - $225.00. **1978**: Crowning Glory - $200.00. **1979:** Skippy - $350.00. **1980:** Susan B. Anthony - $200.00. **1981:** Girl with watering can - $200.00. **1982:** Princess Diana - $165.00. **1983:** Sherlock Holmes - $185.00. **1984:** Bubbles - $100.00. **1985:** Red Boy - $145.00.

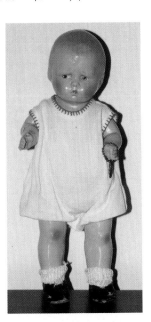

"Baby Grumpy" dolls had a cloth body, composition head and limbs, and painted features. Both are all original. The doll on the left has metal bracelet. The black version on the right has three tuffs of yarn hair. Courtesy Gloria Anderson. 14" - $200.00 up; 14" black: $325.00 up.

Little Lady: All composition. 15" - $225.00, $80.00; 18" - $325.00, $100.00; 21" - $400.00, $150.00; 27" - $600.00, $225.00. Cloth body, yarn hair: 21" - $300.00 up. Pink cloth body, wig: 17" - $225.00 up.

Lovums: Marked with name. Composition/cloth, open mouth smiling. 15-16" - $275.00, $90.00. 22" - $350.00, $150.00.

Mae Starr: Marked with name. Composition/cloth. Record player in torso. 30" - $450.00, $200.00.

Marionettes: Composition/wood. 14" - $145.00, $50.00.

Martha and George Washington: 1976. 11" - $200.00.

Mary Ann or Lee: Marked with name. Open smile mouth, composition and cloth and all composition. 16" - $200.00, $70.00; 18" - $300.00, $100.00;

20" - $350.00, $125.00; 24" - $400.00, $150.00.

Marilee: 1920's. Marked with name. Composition/cloth, open mouth. 14" - $185.00, $90.00; 22" - $300.00, $125.00.

Mary Jane: Plastic/vinyl, walker and freckles. 31" - $200.00, $90.00.

Mary Jane: 1920's. Composition, jointed body or cloth, "Mama" type. 20-22" - $275.00.

Mickey: (Also Tommy Tucker and Bright Eyes.) Composition/cloth, flirty eyes. 18" - $300.00, $100.00; 22-23" - $350.00, $125.00.

Mickey: All vinyl. Some with molded on hats. 11" - $95.00, $30.00.

Pat-O-Pat: Composition/cloth, painted eyes. Press stomach and pats hands together. 13-14" - $145.00, $50.00.

14" Effanbee Historical Doll "Covered Wagon Days." All composition and original. Uses the "Little Lady-Anne Shirley" mold. Painted eyes. Courtesy Frasher Doll Auctions. 14" - $500.00.

Right: 19" "Honey Walker" by Effanbee. All hard plastic and original. Original price tag marked $9.98. Sleep eyes, saran wig and closed mouth. Original wrist tag with curlers. Marked "Effanbee" on head. 19" - $325.00 up.

Patricia: All composition. 14" - $325.00, $125.00.

Patricia-kin: 11" - $265.00, $80.00.

Patsy: All composition. 14" - $300.00, $100.00. Composition/cloth: 14" - $300.00, $125.00.

Patsy Babyette: 9-10" - $185.00, $90.00.

Patsyette: 9" - $200.00, $80.00.

Patsy Ann: 19" - $400.00, $150.00. Vinyl: 15" - $145.00, $50.00.

Patsy Joan: 16" - $450.00, $175.00. Black: 16" - $525.00 up, $225.00.

Patsy, Jr.: 11" - $265.00, $95.00.

Patsy Lou: 22" - $485.00, $175.00.

Patsy Mae: 30" - $650.00, $250.00.

Patsy Ruth: 26-27" - $625.00, $225.00.

Patsy, Wee: 5-6" - $300.00, $100.00.

Polka Dottie: 21" - $200.00, $80.00.

Portrait Dolls: All composition. 12" - $200.00, $80.00.

Prince Charming: All hard plastic. 16" - $350.00 up, $145.00.

Rootie Kazootie: 21" - $200.00, $80.00.

14" "Mickey" from 1948. Cloth body with composition head, gauntlet hands, large flirty eyes and all original. Courtesy Gloria Anderson. 14" - $225.00.

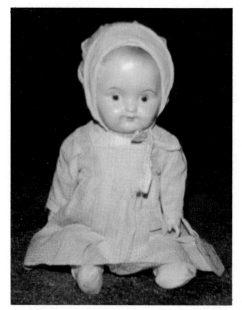

14" "Little Girl" from 1918 and all original. Composition shoulder head, arms, and legs with stuffed cloth body, painted eyes and hair. Closed mouth. Courtesy Jeannie Mauldin. 14" - $165.00 up.

14" "Patsy" made of all composition and original with original box. Painted features and hair. Courtesy Gloria Anderson. 14" - $300.00; In box and original - $500.00.

16" "Patsy," an 1987 exclusive limited edition made by Effanbee for Shirley's Doll House in Wheeling, IL. All vinyl with painted features. Courtesy Gloria Anderson. 16" - $200.00 up.

16" "Patsy Joan" dolls. Both are all composition and original and have sleep eyes and molded hair. Courtesy Gloria Anderson. 16" original - $450.00.

9" "Little Bo Peep" and "Patsyette Dutch Boy and Girl" are made of all composition with painted features. Fully jointed and all original. Smallest doll shown has molded hair. Courtesy Frasher Doll Auctions. 9" - $250.00 each.

Rosemary: Marked with name. Composition/cloth. 14" - $200.00, $85.00; 22" - $300.00, $125.00; 28" - $400.00, $150.00.

Skippy: All composition. 14" - $350.00, $125.00.

Sugar Baby: Composition/cloth, sleep eyes, molded hair or wig. 16-17" - $225.00, $90.00.

Sunny Toddler: Plastic/vinyl. 18" - $65.00, $30.00.

Suzanne: Marked with name. All composition. 14" - $275.00, $125.00.

Suzette: Marked with name. All composition. 12" - $185.00, $80.00.

Sweetie Pie: Composition/cloth. 14" - $175.00, $50.00; 19" - $250.00, $90.00; 24" - $350.00, $125.00.

Tommy Tucker: (Also Mickey and Bright Eyes.) Composition/cloth, flirty eyes. 22-23" - $350.00, $125.00.

W.C. Fields: Composition/cloth. 22" - $695.00, $200.00. Plastic/vinyl: 15" - $265.00.

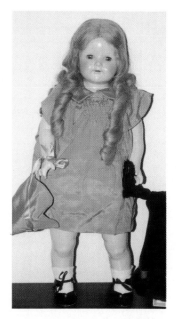

25" "Rosemary" with cloth body and the rest is composition. Sleep eyes and all original clothes and wig. Courtesy Gloria Anderson. 25" - $400.00.

12" "Suzette" dressed as George Washington. All composition with painted features. Shown with all wood early "Popeye." Courtesy Gloria Anderson. 12" - $200.00. Popeye - price not available.

ELVIS PRESLEY

16" "Elvis Presley" with vinyl head and magic skin body, ca. 1950's. Original clothes. Shown with all original 14" "Sweet Sue" made by American Character Doll Co. She is an all hard plastic walker made in 1950's. 16" (mint) - $1,200.00 up; 14" - $225.00 up.

These vinyl and plastic "Elvis Presley" figures with molded hair and painted features came in various costumes. They are original in boxes and from 1984. Courtesy Gloria Anderson. $35.00 up each.

EVERGREEN

12" "Miss Teenage USA" made by Evergreen, British Colony, Hong Kong. Plastic and vinyl with painted eyes, rooted hair and no nail polish. Extra dress came in box and is tagged "Miss American Pageant Dolls." (Doll dress belongs on doll made by Sayco.) Ca. 1962-1964. Courtesy Gloria Anderson. 12" mint in box - $35.00 up.

14" doll made in England by Rosebud. All composition and original, ca. 1949. Large sleep eyes/lashes and molded hair. Courtesy Gloria Anderson. 14" - $70.00.

14" toddler made in England by Rosebud. All hard plastic with cryer box. All original except shoes. Sleep eyes/lashes and unpainted molded hair. Holds all celluloid girl. Courtesy Gloria Anderson. 14" - $70.00; Celluloid girl - $35.00.

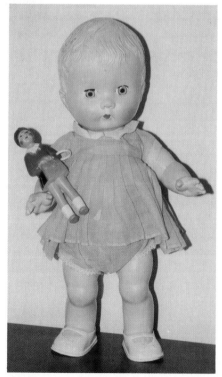

New "Munich Art Doll" made by Elizabeth Pongratz and purchased in Munich, Germany in 1985. All wooden, hand carved and spring jointed. Human hair wig and original clothes. Courtesy Diane Kornhauser. 15" - $225.00.

Top right: 11" "Trine" is all vinyl with rooted red hair. Painted green eyes and one molded tooth. Marked "V/bee mark/W. Goebel/1957/Charlot Byj/ 2901 Made in Germany," inside ear - "10", back of left leg - "02", back of right leg - "01." Charlot Byj is the designer. Made in Germany by Goebel Company. 11" - $55.00.

Bottom right: This 16" Germany-made doll is tagged "Mulli's Liebling" (Darling) and was made during the 1950's. Has sleep eyes/lashes, all early vinyl and all original. Courtesy Gloria Anderson. 16" - $65.00.

15" Furga made of all vinyl and all original except shoes. Made in Italy. Sleep, long lashes. Courtesy Gloria Anderson. 15" - $50.00.

22" "Milady" made in Italy 1949-1952. Made of all hard plastic and has flirty sleep eyes. All original with cryer box in torso. Courtesy Gloria Anderson. 22" - $100.00.

18" all original Furga made in Italy, ca. 1970's. All vinyl with rooted hair and sleep eyes. 18" - $75.00.

GIBBS, RUTH

Ruth Gibbs of Flemington, New Jersey made china dolls with china glazed heads and limbs and pink cloth bodied dolls during the 1940's to 1952. Most will be 7-8" tall with a few being 8-13" tall. A paper label and box will be marked "Ruth Gibbs Godey Little Lady Dolls" and the dolls will be marked "R.G." on back of shoulder plate. The doll designer was Herbert Johnson. Not all dolls were "Godeys"; many had other names.

7-8": $80.00. In box - $125.00.
10-12": $165.00. In box - $200.00.

7" Ruth Gibbs "Godey's Little Lady Doll" named "Susann" and name can be seen on lower part of doll in original box. Courtesy Gloria Anderson. 7" - $125.00 up.

HALCO

34" "Lady Lee" is made of all hard plastic with sleep eyes and open mouth by the Halco Doll Co. Original with original box. Excellent quality doll and clothes. Courtesy Jeannie Mauldin. 34" - $100.00; 34" original - $200.00; 34" original in box - $300.00.

HASBRO

18" "Aimee" made by Hasbro in extra packaged outfit of gold satin with velveteen coat vest and earrings. Courtesy Marie Ernst. 18" - $55.00.

All prices are for mint condition dolls.

Adam: Boy for World of Love series. 9" - $15.00.

Aimee: 1972. Plastic/vinyl. 18" - $55.00.

Defender: One-piece arms and legs. 1974. 11½" - $35.00.

Dolly Darling: 1965. 4½" - $7.00.

Flying Nun: Plastic/vinyl, 1967. 5" - $30.00.

G.I. Joe: 1964, Flocked or molded hair, no beard. Original. 12" - $50.00 up. **1965:** Black. 12" - $75.00 up. **1966:** Green Beret. $70.00 up. **Foreign:** $125.00 up each. **Nurse:** 11" - $500.00 up. **1969:** Negro Adverturer from G.I. Joe Adventure Series. No beard. Origi-nal, in box: $300.00. Played with: $125.00. Box only: $100.00. **1974:** Kung Fu grip. $50.00 up. Eagle eyes: $45.00 up. Talking: $45.00 up.

Leggy: 10" - $12.00.

Little Miss No Name: 1965. 15" - $85.00.

Mamas and Papas: 1967. $35.00 each.

Monkees: Set of four. 4" - $75.00.

Show Biz Babies: 1967. $25.00 each. Mama Cass: $35.00.

Storybooks: 1967. 3" - $25.00-35.00 in boxes.

Sweet Cookie: 1972. 18" - $30.00.

That Kid: 1967. 21" - $85.00.

World of Love Dolls: 9", 1968. White: $9.00. Black: $12.00.

Foreign G.I Joe figures. Left is a German in original German uniform. On the right is a Japanese with oriental face modeling, original uniform and accessories. Each - $125.00 up.

First prices are for mint condition dolls; second prices for ones that have been played with, are dirty and soiled or not original. Marked "Horsman" or "E.I.H."

Answer Doll: Button in back moves head. 1966. 10" - $18.00, $8.00.

Billiken: Composition head, slant eyes, plush or velvet body. 1909. 12" - $365.00, $125.00; 16" - $450.00.

Baby Bumps: Composition/cloth. 1910. 11" - $185.00, $75.00; 16" - $245.00, $85.00. Black: 11" - $275.00, $90.00; 16" - $300.00, $125.00.

Baby First Tooth: Cloth/vinyl, cry mouth with one tooth, tears on cheeks. 16" - $50.00, $20.00.

Baby Tweaks: Cloth/vinyl, inset eyes. 1967. 20" - $40.00, $18.00.

Bedknobs and Broomsticks: Came with plastic and tin bed. Doll has jointed waist, painted eyes. 6½" - $30.00 (complete).

Betty: All composition. 16" - $200.00, $80.00. Plastic/vinyl: 16" - $30.00, $15.00.

Betty Jo: All composition. 16" - $200.00, $80.00. Plastic/vinyl: 16" - $30.00, $15.00.

Betty Ann: All composition. 19" - $265.00, $100.00. Plastic/vinyl: 19" - $45.00, $20.00.

Betty Jane: All composition. 25" - $325.00, $150.00. Plastic/vinyl: 25" - $55.00, $30.00.

Betty Bedtime: All composition. 16" - $200.00, $90.00; 20" - $300.00, $100.00.

Body Twist: All composition. Top of body fits down into torso. 11" - $175.00, $65.00.

Bright Star: All composition. 18-19" - $300.00, $100.00. All hard plastic, 1952: 15" - $200.00, $85.00.

Brother: Composition/cloth. 22" - $200.00 up, $90.00. Vinyl: 13" - $35.00, $15.00.

Campbell Kids: Marked "E.I.H." Ca. 1911. Composition/cloth, painted features. 13" - $550.00 up. 12": 1930-1940's. "Dolly Dingle" style face. All composition. $400.00 up.

Celeste Portrait Doll: In frame. Eyes painted to side. 12" - $35.00, $10.00.

Christopher Robin: 11" - $45.00, $10.00.

Child Dolls: All composition: 15" - $175.00, $60.00; 19" - $285.00, $90.00. All composition, very chubby toddler: 16" - $175.00, $70.00. All hard plastic: 14" - $100.00, $45.00; 18" - $200.00 up, $90.00.

Cindy: All hard plastic. 1950's. 15" - $100.00 up, $40.00; 17" - $165.00 up, $70.00. All early vinyl: 18" - $65.00, $15.00. Lady type, jointed waist: 19" - $75.00, $35.00.

Very large 20" "Billikin" made of all soft felt-like stuffed body and limbs with wide spread legs. Necklace is metal; head is composition. Ca. 1909. The other is a 16" "Billikin" is a newer copy. This one may not have been made by Horsman for the Billikin Company as theirs generally had plush Teddy bear-type bodies. Steiff did make a "Billikin" but it is not certain that this is one. Courtesy Anne Grauls. 20" - $600.00; 16" - $450.00.

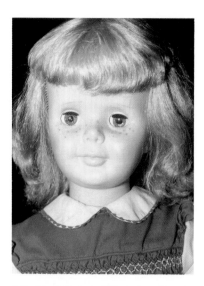

36" "Buffy" from TV series "Family Affair" (1966-1971). Vinyl and rigid plastic, sleep eyes, freckles and rooted hair. Made by Horsman Dolls. Courtesy Lee Crane. 36" - $600.00.

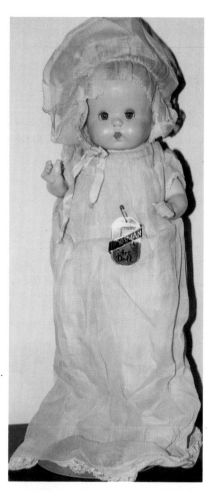

15" "Baby Horsman." Clothes are 22" inches long. Cloth and composition, round sleep eyes and all original. Courtesy Gloria Anderson. 15" - $150.00; 15" all original - $245.00.

18" "Cindy" is made of rigid vinyl and has a jointed body with high heel feet and jointed knees. Swivel waist, vinyl head with rooted hair, sleep eyes. Head marked "Horsman/83." Some bodies unmarked; others will be marked "B-18." All original. Courtesy Marie Ernst. 18" - $175.00 up.

Cinderella: Plastic/vinyl. Painted eyes to side. 11½" - $35.00, $12.00.

Composition Dolls: 1910's to 1920's "Can't Break Em" composition/cloth body, marked "E.I.H." 12" - $165.00, $60.00; 16" - $195.00, $100.00. 1930's: 16" - $160.00, $70.00; 18" - $225.00, $90.00; 22" - $285.00, $125.00.

Country Girl: 9" - $15.00, $6.00.

Crawling Baby: Vinyl, 1967. 14" - $40.00, $18.00.

Dimples: Composition/cloth. 14" - $165.00, $70.00; 20" - $265.00, $100.00; 24" - $300.00, $125.00. Toddler: 20" - $300.00, $125.00; 24" - $365.00, $150.00. Laughing, painted teeth: 22" - $325.00, $150.00.

Gold Medal Doll: Composition/cloth, upper & lower teeth. 21" - $185.00, $60.00. Vinyl/molded hair: 26" - $175.00, $85.00. Vinyl Boy: 15" - $65.00, $25.00.

Ella Cinders: Comic character. Composition/cloth. 14" - $375.00; 18" - $650.00.

Elizabeth Taylor: 1976. 11½" - $75.00, $40.00.

Flying Nun: (Sally Field) 1965. 12" - $65.00, $30.00.

Hebee-Shebee: All composition. 10½" - $525.00, $225.00

Jackie Coogan: 1921. Composition/cloth, painted eyes. 14" - $500.00, $200.00.

Jackie Kennedy: Marked "Horsman J.K." Adult body. Plastic/vinyl, 1961. 25" - $165.00, $60.00.

Jeanie Horsman: All composition. 14" - $225.00, $90.00. Composition/cloth: 16" - $185.00, $80.00.

Jojo: All composition. 12" - $200.00, $90.00.

Life-size Baby: Plastic/vinyl. 26" - $225.00, $95.00.

15" "Hansel & Gretel" of 1963. Both are all original. All soft vinyl with rooted hair implanted into scalp, sleep eyes and unmarked. Tagged "Horsman's Hansel Doll." These dolls were designed to represent Hansel and Gretel from the movie by the same name produced by Michael Meyerberg, Inc. Courtesy Jeannie Mauldin. 15" - $165.00 each.

Lullabye Baby: Cloth/vinyl. Music box in body. 12" - $20.00, $8.00. All vinyl: 12" - $15.00, $5.00.

Mary Poppins: 12" - $35.00, $10.00; 16" - $65.00, $20.00; 26" - $185.00, $90.00; 36" - $350.00, $150.00.

Mama Style Babies: Composition/cloth. Marked "E.I.H" or "Horsman." 16" - $175.00, $85.00; 22" - $245.00, $100.00. Hard plastic/cloth: 16" - $75.00; $35.00; 22" - $90.00, $40.00. Vinyl/cloth: 16" - $20.00, $8.00; 22" - $30.00, $15.00.

Peggy Pen Pal: Multi-jointed arms. Plastic/vinyl. 18" - $45.00, $15.00.

Pippi Longstockings: Vinyl/cloth. 1972. 18" - $45.00, $20.00.

Pipsqueaks: Four in set. 1967. 12" - $20.00 each, $9.00.

Polly & Pete: Black dolls, molded hair. All vinyl. 13" - $225.00, $60.00.

Poor Pitiful Pearl: 12" - $45.00, $20.00; 17" - $95.00, $40.00.

Peterkin: All composition, painted googly-style eyes. 12" - $350.00, $125.00.

Roberta: All composition. Molded hair or wigs, 1937. 14" - $225.00, $90.00; 20" - $325.00, $125.00.

Rosebud: Composition/cloth. Marked with name, dimples and smile. Sleep eyes, wig. 18" - $265.00, $100.00.

Ruthie: All vinyl or plastic/vinyl. 14" - $22.00, $8.00; 20" - $38.00, $12.00.

Ruthie's Sister: Plastic/vinyl. 1960. 26" - $95.00, $40.00.

Sleepy Baby: Vinyl/cloth, eyes molded closed. 24" - $50.00, $25.00.

Tuffie: All vinyl. Upper lip molded over lower. 16" - $85.00, $30.00.

16" hard-to-find size "Mary Poppins." Both are original. Plastic and vinyl, rooted hair and sleep eyes. Marked "Horsman Doll, Inc./1964/216" on head. Courtesy Marie Ernst. 16" - $65.00 each.

22" "Rosette" with composition head, arms and legs. Tin sleep eyes, open mouth and cloth body. 1928. Marked on shoulder plate "E.I.H. A.D.C." (American Doll Company). Courtesy Jeannie Mauldin. 22" - $285.00.

The Mary Hoyer Doll Mfg. Co. operated in Reading, Pa. from 1925. The dolls were made in all composition, all hard plastic, and last ones produced were in plastic and vinyl. Older dolls are marked in a circle on back "Original Mary Hoyer Doll" or "The Mary Hoyer Doll" embossed on lower back.

First price is for perfect doll in tagged factory clothes. Second price for perfect doll in outfits made from Mary Hoyer patterns and third price is for redressed doll in good condition with only light craze to composition or slight soil to others.

Composition: 14" - $500.00, $400.00 up, $165.00.

Hard Plastic: 14" - $500.00, $400.00 up, $185.00; 17" - $575.00 up, $450.00 up, $325.00.

Plastic and Vinyl: 14-15" (Margie) Marked "AE23." 12" - $125.00, $60.00, $15.00; 14" - $185.00, $85.00; $30.00.

14" "Mary Hoyer" is made of all hard plastic with long saran wig that makes her look like an Ideal "Toni." Outfit made from Mary Hoyer pattern of 1950's. Sleep eyes and marked with name in circle on back. Courtesy Jeannie Mauldin. 14" - $400.00.

14" bride that is direct from the Mary Hoyer factory. White box with company name and address and is all orginal. The long train snaps around waist of sheath gown. Design is finished in seed pearls. Doll is in mint condition. Courtesy Shirley Bertrand. $1,000.00 up.

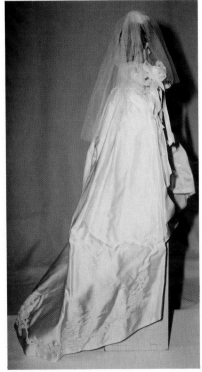

Photo shows the extreme length of the bridal train that snaps around the waist of the bridal gown.

First prices are for mint condition dolls. Second prices are for cracked, crazed, dirty, soiled or not original dolls.

Baby Belly Button: 9″ plastic/vinyl. White: $12.00, $5.00; Black: $20.00, $10.00.

Baby Crissy: 24″. White: $75.00, $25.00. Black: $95.00, $30.00.

Baby Snooks and Other Flexies: Wire and composition. 12″ - $275.00, $100.00.

Bam-Bam: Plastic/vinyl or all vinyl. 12″ - $20.00, $8.00; 16″ - $30.00, $10.00.

Batgirl and Other Super Women: Vinyl. 12″ - $95.00, $30.00.

Betsy McCall: See that section.

Betsy Wetsy: Composition head, excellent rubber body. 16″ - $125.00, $20.00. Hard plastic/vinyl: 12″ - $75.00, $20.00; 14″ - $90.00, $35.00. All vinyl: 12″ - $25.00, $9.00; 18″ - $75.00, $30.00.

Betty Big Girl: Plastic/vinyl. 30″ - $200.00, $95.00.

Betty Jane: Shirley Temple type. All composition, sleep eyes, open mouth. 1941-1943. 14″ - $175.00, $70.00; 18″ - $285.00, $125.00; 26″ - $350.00, $165.00.

Bizzy Lizzy: Plastic/vinyl. 17″ - $35.00, $20.00.

Blessed Event: Called "Kiss Me." Cloth body with plunger in back to make doll cry or pout. Vinyl head with eyes almost squinted closed. 21″ - $125.00, $50.00.

Bonnie Braids: Hard plastic/vinyl head. 13″ - $60.00, $25.00. Baby: 13″ - $50.00; $10.00.

Bonnie Walker: Hard plastic, pin jointed hips, open mouth, flirty eyes. Marked "Ideal W-25." 23″ - $95.00, $40.00.

Brandi: Of Crissy family. 18″ - $80.00, $40.00.

Brother/Baby Coos: Composition/cloth with hard plastic head. 25″ - $125.00, $70.00. Composition head/latex: 24″ - $35.00, $10.00. Hard plastic head/vinyl: 24″ - $50.00, $15.00.

Bye Bye Baby: Lifelike modeling. 12″ - $145.00, $50.00, 25″ - $325.00, $135.00.

14″ "April Showers" has a plastic body and vinyl head and limbs. Battery-operated, she splashes the water and turns head. Has holes in bottom of her feet for water drainage. Courtesy Jeannie Mauldin. 14″ doll - $35.00; 14″ doll and tub - $45.00.

Cinnamon: Of Crissy family. 12″ - $70.00, $30.00. Black: $125.00, $50.00.

Composition Child: All composition girl with sleep eyes, some flirty, open mouth, original clothes and excellent condition. Marked "Ideal" and a number or "Ideal" in a diamond. 14″ - $175.00, $70.00; 18″ - $300.00, $90.00; 22″ - $325.00, $100.00. Cloth body with straight composition legs. 14″ - $145.00, $45.00; 18″ - $195.00, $70.00; 22″ - $225.00, $80.00.

12" "Batgirl" made of all vinyl; same body as posable "Tammy." Green eyes/shadow. Marked "1965/Ideal Toy Corp./W12-3" on head; "1965/Ideal" in oval "2M-12" on hip. Original and a very rare doll. Courtesy Liza Lineberger. 12" - $95.00 up.

15" "Baby Tears" (Betsy Wetsy) in original suitcase with wardrobe. Hard plastic head and vinyl body and limbs. Caracul lamb's wool wig. Marked "Ideal Doll" on head. 15" white - $90.00; in case - $125.00. 15" black - $135.00; in case - $200.00.

Composition Baby: Composition head and limbs with cloth body and closed mouth. Sleep eyes (allow more for flirty eyes), original and in excellent condition. 18" - $145.00, $65.00; 22" - $165.00, $75.00; 25" - $185.00, $80.00. Flirty eyes: 16" - $185.00, $70.00; 18" - $200.00, $100.00.

Cricket: Of Crissy family. 18" - $60.00, $30.00. Black: $85.00, $40.00. Look-a-round: $60.00, $30.00.

Crissy: 18" - $60.00, $20.00. Black: $85.00, $40.00. Look-a-round: $60.00, $25.00. Talking: $80.00, $35.00. First (floor length hair): $145.00, $60.00. Moving: $75.00, $30.00.

Daddy's Girl: 42" - $850.00, $300.00.

Deanna Durbin: All composition. 14" - $425.00, $175.00; 17" - $485.00, $185.00; 21" - $585.00, $300.00; 24" - $725.00, $325.00; 27" - $900.00, $400.00.

Dianna Ross: Plastic/vinyl. 18" - $165.00, $80.00.

Dina: Of Crissy family. 15" - $90.00, $40.00.

Dodi: Of Tammy family. Marked "1964-Ideal-D0-9E." 9" - $40.00, $10.00.

Flexies: Composition and wire, soldier, children, Fanny Brice, etc. 12" - $285.00, $100.00.

Flossie Flirt: Composition/cloth. Flirty eyes: 22" - $285.00, $90.00. Black: $385.00, $125.00.

Giggles: Plastic/vinyl. 16" - $50.00, $20.00; 18" - $85.00, $35.00. Black: 18" - $150.00, $75.00. Baby: 16" - $50.00, $20.00.

Goody Two Shoes: 18" - $125.00, $45.00. Walking/talking: 27" - $225.00, $70.00.

Harriet Hubbard Ayer: Hard plastic/vinyl. 14½" - $200.00, $50.00; 18" - $300.00, $90.00.

Joan Palooka: 1952. 14" - $65.00, $30.00.

Joey Stivic (Baby): One-piece body and limbs. Sexed boy. 15" - $50.00, $25.00.

Jiminy Cricket: Composition/wood. 9" - $285.00, $100.00.

Judy Garland: All composition. 14" - $1,000.00, $400.00; 18" - $1,200.00 up, $500.00. Marked with backward "21": 21" - $500.00, $200.00.

Judy Splinters: Cloth/vinyl/latex, yarn hair, painted eyes. 18" - $100.00, $35.00; 22" - $150.00, $50.00; 36" - $300.00, $100.00.

Kerry: Of Crissy family. 18" - $75.00, $35.00.

King Little: Composition/wood. 14" - $285.00, $100.00.

Kiss Me: See Blessed Event.

Kissy: 22" - $60.00, $30.00. Black: $175.00, $60.00.

Kissy, Tiny: 16" - $55.00, $25.00. Black: $100.00, $50.00.

Liberty Boy: 1918. 12" - $285.00, $100.00.

Little Lost Baby: Three-faced doll. 22" - $75.00, $40.00.

Magic Lips: Vinyl coated cloth/vinyl. Lower teeth. 24" - $85.00, $40.00.

Mama Style Dolls: Composition cloth. 18" - $200.00, $85.00; 23" - $275.00, $100.00. Hard plastic/cloth: 18" - $85.00, $35.00; 23" - $125.00, $45.00.

Mary Hartline: All hard plastic. 15" - $250.00, $90.00; 21-23": $375.00 up, $145.00.

Mary Jane or Betty Jane: All composition, sleep and/or flirty eyes, open mouth. Marked "Ideal 18": 18" - $300.00 up, $100.00.

Mia: Of Crissy family. 15½" - $75.00, $30.00.

Miss Curity: Hard plastic. 14" - $250.00 up, $90.00. Composition: 21" - $400.00, $100.00.

Miss Ideal: Multi-jointed. 25" - $350.00 up, $90.00; 28" - $400.00, $145.00.

Miss Revlon: 10½" - $95.00, $40.00. 17" - $175.00 up, $80.00. 20" - $225.00, $95.00. In box or trunk: 20" - $450.00, $125.00.

Mitzi: Teen. 12" - $60.00, $30.00.

Mortimer Snerd and Other Flexie Dolls: Composition and wire. 12" - $285.00, $100.00.

13" "Bonnie Braids" (in dress) has hard plastic body and limbs and vinyl head with two braids through holes in head. Sleep eyes, open mouth with three painted teeth. Marked "1951 Chicago Tribune." Baby "Bonnie Braids" shown in box has painted eyes and "magic skin" body and limbs. ("Bonnie Braids" is the daughter of comic strip detective "Dick Tracy.") Courtesy Jeannie Mauldin. 13" - $60.00; Baby - $50.00; In box - $100.00.

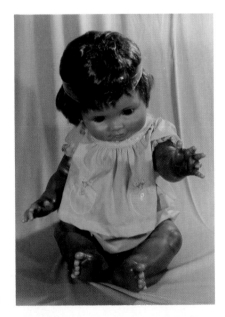

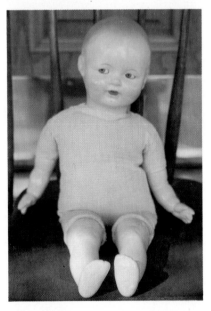

24" white "Crissy Baby" - first issue #1110-6. This doll was kept mint in box and the arms and legs (except ends of toes and fingers) turned dark green. Head remained original color. Doll has been placed in window for year and is gradually returning to normal. Courtesy Marie Ernst.

15" "Flossie Flirt" with molded hair was made 1932-1933. Also came with wigs and larger cut eyes. Cloth body and composition limbs and head. Has dimples in cheeks. Marked "Ideal" on head. Head designed by Bernard Lipfert. Courtesy Kay Bransky. 15" - $200.00.

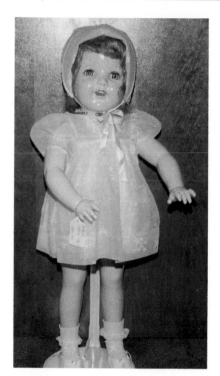

26" all composition and fully jointed. Open, smiling mouth with four teeth and marked "Ideal Doll Made in U.S.A." on back. Has glassene eyes so must have been made in late 1940's. Courtesy Jeannie Mauldin. 26" - $350.00.

17" "Katie Kachoo" represents a child with a cold. She has a red nose hanky in right hand and her left hand raises as she sneezes. Plastic and vinyl, battery operated, all original. Marked "1966 Ideal Toy Co." Courtesy Jeannie Mauldin. 17" - $45.00.

Patti Playpal: 30" - $175.00, $90.00; 36" - $265.00, $100.00. Black: 30" - $350.00, $150.00; 36" - $450.00, $200.00.

Pebbles: Plastic/vinyl and all vinyl. 8" - $15.00, $6.00; 12" - $25.00, $10.00; 15" - $35.00, $20.00.

Penny Playpal: 32" - $185.00, $90.00.

Pepper: 1964. Freckles. Marked "Ideal - P9-3." 9" - $30.00, $15.00.

Pete: 1964. Freckles. Marked "Ideal - P8." 7½" - $30.00, $15.00.

Peter Playpal: 38" - $365.00, $150.00.

Pinocchio: Composition/wood. 11" - $285.00, $100.00; 21" - $600.00, $200.00.

Posey: Hard plastic/vinyl head, jointed knees. Marked "Ideal VP-17." 17" - $100.00, $45.00.

Sandy McCall: See Betsy McCall section.

Sara Ann: Hard plastic. Marked "P-90." Saran wig: 14" - $245.00 up, $90.00. 21" marked "P-93": $400.00 up, $150.00.

Saralee: Cloth/vinyl. Black. 18" - $265.00, $125.00.

Saucy Walker: 16" - $125.00, $50.00; 19" - $165.00, $60.00; 22" - $185.00, $70.00. Black: 18" - $265.00, $100.00.

Shirley Temple: See that section.

Snoozie: Composition/cloth, molded hair, sleep eyes, open yawning

19" "Plassie" is made of hard plastic head and has sleep eyes, molded hair, and cloth body with composition limbs. Original marks "Ideal Doll/Made in U.S.A./Pat. No. 2252077" on head. Original price tag - $7.50. 19" mint - $175.00; 19" soiled - $65.00.

This 14" "Plassie" is made of all hard plastic with curly molded hair, sleep eyes and is all original. Marked "Ideal Doll/Made in U.S.A." on head; "Ideal Doll/14" on body. Original price tag - $5.98. 14" mint - $185.00; 14" soiled - $60.00.

mouth. Marked "B Lipfert." 13" - $150.00, $50.00; 16" - $195.00, $80.00; 20" - $250.00, $120.00.

Snow White: All composition, black wig, on marked Shirley Temple body, sleep and/or flirty eyes. 12" - $475.00, $200.00; 18" - $500.00, $200.00. Molded hair, eyes painted to side: 14" - $185.00, $85.00; 18" - $450.00, $145.00.

Sparkle Plenty: 15" - $60.00, $25.00.

Suzy Playpal: Fat, chubby, vinyl body and limbs. Marked "Ideal O.E.B. 24-3." 24" - $165.00, $60.00.

16" "Saucy Walker" is made of all hard plastic with pin-jointed hips. All original with sleep eyes and open mouth. Marked "Ideal Doll/W 16" on head. 16" - $125.00 up.

18" "Sara Ann" was named for saran, a material used for wigs. Made of all hard plastic, has sleep eyes, and uses the "Toni" doll. Marked "P.92/Ideal Doll/Made in U.S.A." on head and "Ideal P-91" on body. All original. Original price tag: $7.98. 18" - $325.00 up.

Tara: Grows hair. Black. 16" - $50.00, $25.00.

Tammy: 1962. 9" - $45.00, $20.00; 12" - $50.00, $20.00. Black: $60.00, $25.00. Grown-up: 12" - $45.00, $20.00.

Tammy's Mom: 1963. Eyes to side. Marked: "Ideal W-18-L." 12" - $55.00, $30.00.

Ted: Tammy's brother. Molded hair. Marked "Ideal B-12-U-2." 1963. 12½" - $50.00, $25.00.

Thumbelina: Kissing: 10½" - $20.00, $8.00. Tearful: 15" - $30.00, $12.00. Wake Up: 17" - $45.00, $20.00. Black: 10½" - $50.00, $20.00.

Tickletoes: Composition/cloth. 15" - $175.00, $85.00; 21" - $285.00, $100.00.

Tiffany Taylor: Top of head swivels to change hair color. 18" - $80.00, $35.00. Black: 18" - $95.00, $50.00.

Tippy or Timmy Tumbles: 16" - $35.00, $15.00. Black: $50.00, $25.00.

Toni: 14" - $250.00 up, $100.00. Walker: $265.00 up, $100.00; 21" - $350.00 up, $150.00.

Tressy: Of Crissy family. 18" - $75.00, $35.00. Black $125.00, $45.00.

Velvet: Of Crissy family. 16" - $60.00, $20.00. Black: $125.00, $45.00. Look-a-round: $70.00, $30.00. Talking: $70.00, $35.00. Moving: $65.00, $20.00.

22" "Little Lost Baby" has a foam body, plastic legs and stuffed arms. Vinyl three-sided head. Lever at base of neck controls turning head. Battery-operated talker. Made by Ideal in 1968. Courtesy Jeannie Mauldin. 22" - $75.00.

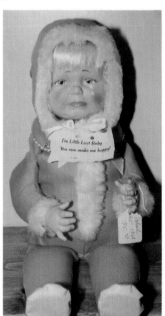

13" "Busy Timmy" is all vinyl with sleep eyes and marked "Jolly Toys 1962" on head. Designed by Eloise Wilkins who also illustrated the Little Golden Book shown with doll. All original except replacement shoes. Courtesy Cheryl and Wayne Koenig. 13" - $75.00 up.

KENNER

First prices are for mint condition dolls; second prices are for played with, dirty or missing clothing and accessories.

Baby Bundles: 16" - $20.00, $10.00. Black: $28.00, $15.00.

Baby Yawnie: Cloth/vinyl, 1974. 15" - $20.00, $10.00.

Big Foot: All rigid vinyl. 13" - $18.00, $7.00.

Butch Cassidy or Sundance Kid: 4" - $15.00, $6.00 each.

Blythe: 1972. Pull string to change the color of eyes. 11½" - $40.00, $20.00.

Charlie Chaplin: All cloth with walking mechanism. 1973. 14" - $75.00, $45.00.

Cover Girls (Darcie, Erica, Dana, etc.): 12½" White: $35.00, $12.00. Black: $40.00, $15.00.

Crumpet: 1970. Plastic/vinyl. 18" - $40.00, $15.00.

Dusty: 11½". $25.00, $10.00.

Gabbigale: 1972. 18" - $40.00, $15.00. Black: $50.00, $20.00.

Garden Gals: 1972. Hand bent to hold watering can. 6½" - $10.00, $4.00.

Hardy Boys: 1978. Shaun Cassidy and Parker Stevenson. 12" - $20.00, $8.00.

Jenny Jones and Baby: All vinyl, 1973. 9" Jenny and 2½" baby: $15.00, $6.00. Set: $25.00, $8.00.

Skye: Black doll. 11½ - $25.00, $10.00.

Sleep Over Dolly: And minature doll. 17" - $35.00, $10.00. Black: $40.00, $15.00.

Star Wars: Large size figures. R2-D2: 7½" - $85.00 up, $25.00. C-3PO: 12" - $85.00 up, $25.00. Darth Vader: 15" - $90.00 up, $25.00. Boba Fett: 13" - $125.00 up, $30.00. Jawa: 8½" - $55.00, $20.00. IG-88: 15" - $100.00 up, $30.00. Stormtrooper: 12" - $85.00 up, $25.00. Leia: 11½" - $90.00 up, $25.00. Hans Solo: 12" - $85.00, $25.00. Luke Skywalker: 13½" - $85.00, $25.00. Chewbacca: 15" - $85.00 up, $25.00. Obi Wan Kenobi: 12" - $90.00, $30.00.

Strawberry Shortcake: $8.00 each up. Sleep eyes: $25.00 each.

Steve Scout: 1974. 9" - $20.00, $8.00. Black: $30.00, $10.00.

Sweet Cookie: 1972. 18" - $25.00, $12.00.

16" "Big Foot" was made in 1978 by Kenner. Has painted features and jointed shoulders and hips. Courtesy Renie Culp. 16" - $22.00.

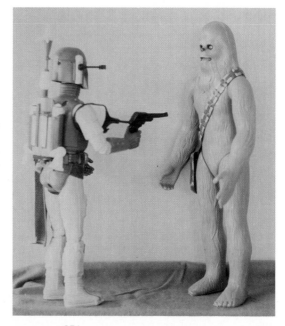

15" "Chewbacca" and 13" "Boba Fett." are made of all rigid vinyl. Both are from the large set of Star Wars figures. Courtesy Karen Heidemann. 15" with weapons - $85.00; 13" with weapons - $125.00.

18" "Gabbigale" is made of plastic and vinyl with rooted hair. Battery operated, pull string in chest and doll repeats anything you say. Painted features. Both dolls are original. Marked "1972/Kenner Products Co/99" on head. Courtesy Jeannie Mauldin. 18" - $40.00; Black - $50.00.

KEWPIE

First prices are for mint condition dolls; second prices are for dolls played with, crazed or cracked, dirty, soiled or not original.

Bisque Kewpies: See antique Kewpie section.

All Composition: Jointed shoulder only. 9" - $135.00, $50.00; 14" - $195.00, $70.00. Jointed hips, neck and shoulder: 9" - $200.00, $80.00; 14" - $300.00, $125.00.

Talcum Powder Container: 7-8" - $195.00.

Celluloid: 2" - $45.00; 5" - $85.00; 9" - $165.00. Black: 5" - $125.00.

Bean Bag Body: 10" - $45.00, $15.00.

Cloth Body: Vinyl head and limbs. 16" - $200.00, $95.00.

Kewpie Gal: With molded hair/ribbon. 8" - $65.00, $25.00.

Hard Plastic: One-piece body and head. 8" - $95.00, $25.00; 12" - $225.00, $95.00; 16" - $350.00, $145.00. Fully jointed at shoulder, neck and hips: 12-13" - $385.00, $175.00; 16" - $500.00, $225.00.

Ragsy: Vinyl one-piece, molded-on clothes with heart on chest. 1964. 8" - $60.00, $28.00. Without heart, 1971: 8" - $45.00, $19.00.

Thinker: One-piece vinyl, sitting down. 4" - $12.00, $5.00.

Kewpie: Vinyl, jointed at shoulder only. 9" - $55.00, $15.00; 12" - $85.00, $20.00; 14" - $100.00, $30.00. Jointed at neck, shoulders and hips: 9" - $75.00, $25.00; 12" - $125.00, $35.00; 14" - $175.00, $50.00; 27" - $300.00, $165.00. Not jointed at all: 9" - $35.00, $10.00; 12" - $50.00, $15.00; 14" - $65.00, $20.00. Black: 9" - $50.00, $15.00; 12" - $75.00, $25.00; 14" - $125.00, $45.00.

Ward's Anniversary: 8" - $75.00, $25.00.

All Cloth: Made by Kreuger. All one-piece including clothing. 12" - $175.00, $80.00; 16" - $285.00, $100.00; 20" - $425.00, $175.00; 25" - $800.00, $300.00. Removable dress and bonnet: 12" - $225.00, $85.00; 16" - $350.00, $145.00; 20" - $565.00, $200.00; 25" - $1,000.00, $400.00.

Kewpie Baby: With hinged joints. 15" - $195.00, $80.00; 18" - $265.00, $95.00.

Kewpie Baby: With one-piece stuffed body and limbs. 15" - $145.00, $60.00; 18" - $165.00, $65.00.

Plush: Usually red with vinyl face mask and made by Knickerbocker. 1960's. 6" - $60.00, $20.00; 10" - $85.00, $25.00.

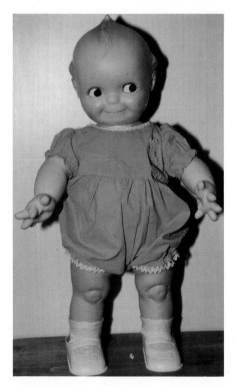

Large 27" "Kewpie" made by Cameo Doll Co. Jointed neck, shoulders and hips on "Skootles" body. Original clothes. Courtesy Jeannie Mauldin. 27" - $300.00.

8½" "Ragsy Kewpie" is jointed at neck only and has molded-on clothes. 13" "Kewpie" is jointed at neck, shoulders, and hips and has original dress. Courtesy Gloria Anderson. 8½" - $60.00; 13" - $100.00.

Roldan, made in Spain and imported by Rosenfeld Imports. This is one of the dolls that was made before Effanbee began to do the importing and the name was changed to "Klumpy." These wonderful characters are fun to collect. Courtesy Martha Gragg. 11" - $65.00.

8" "Sea Captain" Klumpy made after the Effanbee Doll Company began to import them. Ca. 1960's. Stockenette with wire armature throughout so doll is very posable. Clothes are not removable. Price not available.

All prices are for mint condition dolls.

Bozo Clown: 14" - $40.00; 24" - $75.00.

Cinderella: With two heads; one sad; the other with tiara. 16" - $25.00.

Clown: Cloth. 17" - $30.00.

Composition Child: Bent right arm at elbow. 15" - $200.00 up.

Flintstones: 17" - $45.00 each.

Kewpie: See Kewpie section.

Levi Rag Doll: All cloth. 15" - $20.00.

Little House on the Prairie: 1978. 12" - $18.00 each.

Lord of Rings: 5" - $20.00 each.

Mickey Mouse: 1930- 1940's. 18" - $1,600.00.

Pinocchio: All plush and cloth. 13" - $135.00 up. All composition: 13" - $300.00 up.

Scarecrow: Cloth. 23½" - $95.00.

Seven Dwarfs: 10", all composition. Each - $225.00 up.

Sleeping Beauty: All composition, bent right arm. 15" - $250.00 up.

Snow White: All composition, bent right arm. Black wig. 15" - $250.00 up; 20" - $325.00 up.

Soupy Sales: Vinyl and cloth, non-removeable clothes. 13" - $145.00.

Two-headed Dolls: Vinyl face masks; one crying, one smiling. 12" - $20.00.

14" "Dagwood" and 9" "Alexander" are both made of all composition and are marked "Knickerbocker Toy" on heads. Painted features and removable clothes, except shoes and socks on "Alexander" which are molded and painted. Courtesy Shirley Bertrand. 14" - $600.00; 9" - $400.00.

20" "I Dream of Jeannie" is made of plastic and vinyl with sleep eyes and rooted hair. She came in green and rose. Represents Barbara Eden of TV series. Head marked "4.1966/Libby." Box marked "Sidney Sheldon Productions, Inc. 1966 Libby Majorette Doll Corp./Exclusive Mfg." 20" - $50.00; 20" in box - $80.00.

MAKER UNKNOWN

9" beautiful unmarked baby with large painted eyes. Original dress and bonnet. Shown with 7" all celluloid baby with flirty eyes and has open mouth/nurser. Courtesy Gloria Anderson. 9" - $45.00; 7" - $25.00.

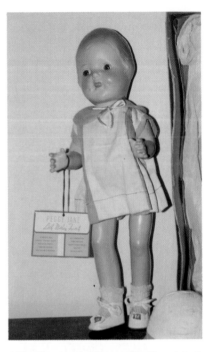

Unmarked with cloth body, composition head and lower limbs. Painted features and original clothes. Little doll is all celluloid. Courtesy Gloria Anderson. 22" - $90.00.

16" all composition and all original. "Patsy" look-a-like. Tagged "Peggy Jane." Sleep eyes, open mouth and dimples. Ca. 1935. Courtesy Gloria Anderson. 16" - $165.00.

10" unmarked all composition baby with extended forefinger on one hand. Painted features and all original. Courtesy Gloria Anderson. 10" - $60.00.

First prices are for mint condition dolls; second prices are for dolls that have been played with, are dirty, soiled, not original and/or do not have accessories.

Allen: 12" in box - $200.00 up.

Baby First Step: 18" - $30.00, $10.00. Talking: $45.00, $15.00.

Baby Go Bye Bye: 12" - $20.00, $10.00.

Baby's Hungry: 17" - $35.00, $12.00.

Baby Pataburp: 13" - $35.00, $12.00.

Baby Say 'n See: 17" - $30.00, $10.00.

Baby Secret: 18" - $45.00, $15.00.

Baby Small Talk: 11" - $18.00, $8.00. As Cinderella: $25.00, $10.00. Black: $35.00, $15.00.

Baby Tenderlove: Newborn. 13" - $10.00, $5.00.

Baby Walk 'n Play: 11" - $25.00, $10.00.

Baby Walk 'n See: 18" - $30.00, $15.00.

Barbie: 1958-1959: #1, holes in feet with metal cylinders. $2,500.00 in box. Doll only: $1,500.00 up. **1960:** #3, curved brows, marked 1959 body. $300.00 up. **1961:** #4, marked "Pat. Pend. 1961." $250.00 up. **1963:** Fashion Queen with 3 wigs. $200.00 up. **1964:** Ponytail with swirl bangs. No curly bangs. $200.00 up. **1965:** Color 'n Curl, 2 heads and accessories. $450.00 up. **1968:** Spanish Talking - $200.00 up. **1969:** Twist 'n Turn - $90.00 up. **1971:** Growing Pretty Hair, bendable knees. $250.00 up. **1972:** Ward Anniversary - $200.00 up.

#850 "Barbie" is mint in her box. This is one of the #3 "Barbie" dolls. Courtesy Gloria Anderson. $300.00 up.

#982 "Solo In The Spotlight" with #3 "Barbie" in bubblecut hairdo. Dressed dolls in original boxes are rare. Courtesy Pat Timmons. $300.00 up.

Left: "New Living Barbie" in original box and dates 1969. Right: "Royal Barbie" from 1979 and "My First Barbie" from 1980. Courtesy Gloria Anderson. "New Living" - $125.00 up; "Royal" - $200.00 up; "My First" - $20.00 up.

"Angel Face Barbie" of 1982, "Great Shape Barbie" and "Sun Gold Barbie" from 1983. Courtesy Gloria Anderson. All dolls - $20.00 up.

Left: Black "Crystal Barbie" dates from 1983. Right: "Barbie" dolls shown in original boxes. Both date from 1985. Courtesy Gloria Anderson. "Crystal" - $25.00 up. "Tropical" - $15.00 up; "Music Lovin' " - $25.00 up.

Special 1989 Edition of "Barbie" made by Mattel. The 1988 "Holiday Barbie" was dressed in red. Courtesy Gloria Anderson. $40.00 up.

1973: Quick Curl - $95.00 up. **1974:** Newport - $45.00 up. Sun Valley - $75.00 up. Sweet Sixteen - $85.00 up. **1975:** Free Moving - $65.00 up. Funtime - $65.00 up. Gold Medal Skater - $50.00 up. **1976:** Ballerina - $50.00 up. Deluxe Quick Curl - $45.00. Free Moving - $55.00 up. **1978:** Super Size Barbie - $95.00. **1979:** Pretty Changes - $45.00 up. **1980:** Beauty Secrets - $30.00 up. **1981:** Western - $30.00 up. **1983:** Twirly Curls - $30.00 up.

Barbie Items: Car Roadster - $265.00 up. Sports car - $150.00. Dune Buggy - $80.00 up. Clock - $40.00. Family House - $65.00. Watches - $20.00-40.00. Airplane - $500.00. Horse "Dancer" (brown) - $100.00 up. Wardrobe - $45.00. First Barbie stand (round with two prongs) - $165.00.

Bozo: 18" - $45.00, $15.00.

Buffie: With Mrs. Beasley. 6" - $65.00, $12.00. 10" - $85.00, $20.00.

Capt. Lazer: 12½" - $250.00, $50.00.

Casey: 1975, 11½". $145.00 up.

Casper, The Ghost: 16" - $40.00, $20.00.

Gift set of "Barbie," "Ken," and "Midge" Majorette outfits. Any of the gift sets are rare. Courtesy Pat Timmons. $300.00 up.

Wedding gift set includes "Skipper," "Ken," "Barbie," and "Midge" and is very rare. Courtesy Pat Timmons. Boxed set - $450.00 up.

Charming Chatty: 25" - $125.00, $40.00.

Chatty Brother, Tiny: 15" - $40.00, $10.00. Baby: $40.00, $10.00. Black: $55.00, $20.00.

Chatty Cathy: 20" - $85.00, $40.00. Brunette/brown eyes: $100.00, $50.00. Black: $225.00, $55.00.

Cheerleader: 13" - $15.00, $7.00.

Cheerful Tearful: 13" - $25.00, $8.00. Tiny: 6½" - $15.00, $6.00.

Christie: 1968, Black doll. 11½" - $95.00 up.

Cynthia: 20" - $50.00, $25.00.

Dancerina: 24" - $50.00, $20.00. Black: $70.00, $30.00. Baby: Not battery operated. $40.00, $15.00. Black: $60.00, $25.00.

Dick Van Dyke: 25" - $100.00, $50.00.

Fluff: 9" - $60.00 up.

25" "Charmin' Chatty" made of plastic and vinyl. Both are all original. Side glancing sleep eyes. Record fits into slot in back of doll and she "talks" to you. Pull string operated. Marked "1961 Mattel Inc." Courtesy Jeannie Mauldin. 25" - **$125.00.**

"Francie" with original box and "Francie" with "Growing Pretty Hair." 1969. Courtesy Gloria Anderson. "Twist 'n Turn" - $150.00 up; "Growing Pretty Hair" - $150.00 up.

Francie: 11½" - $85.00 up. Black: $400.00 up. Malibu: $30.00.

Grandma Beans: 11" - $20.00, $9.00.

Gorgeous Creatures: Mae West style body/animal heads, 1979. $25.00 each, $10.00.

Guardian Goddesses: 11½", each - $175.00 up.

Hi Dottie: 17" - $30.00, $12.00.

Herman Munster: 16" - $45.00, $15.00.

Hush Lil Baby: 15" - $15.00, $5.00.

Jamie Walker with Dog: 1969. 11½" - $295.00 up.

Julia: 11½" nurse - $185.00 up. Talking: $225.00 up.

Lil Big Guy: 13" - $10.00, $5.00.

Ken: Flocked hair - $125.00 up. Molded hair/non-bending knees - $125.00 up. Malibu - $30.00 up. Live Action - $60.00 up. Mod hair - $30.00 up. Busy - $45.00 up. Talking - $150.00 up.

Kiddles: With cars - $45.00 up. With planes - $50.00 up. In ice cream cones - $20.00 up. In jewelry - $30.00 up. In perfume bottles - $20.00 up. In bottles - $20.00 up. With cup and saucer - $100.00 up. Storybooks with accessories - $100.00 up. Baby Biddle in carriage - $175.00 up. Santa - $50.00 up. Animals - $40.00

Midge: 11½", freckles. $150.00 up. Bendable legs, 1965: $85.00 up.

3½" "Lavender Lace Tea Party Kiddle" from 1969. All vinyl, painted features, original. Came packaged with cup and saucer. Set - $100.00.

Mother Goose: 20" - $50.00, $20.00.

Mrs. Beasley: Talking, 16". $50.00, $20.00.

Peachy & Puppets: 17" - $25.00, $10.00.

Randy Reader: 19" - $35.00, $15.00.

Real Sister: 14" - $20.00, $14.00.

Ricky: 1965, red hair and freckles. $100.00 up.

Rockflowers: 6½" - $30.00, $10.00.

Rose Bud Babies: 6½" - $25.00, $10.00.

Saucy: 16" - $65.00. Black: $95.00.

Scooby Doo: 21" - $85.00, $30.00.

Skediddles: 4" - $50.00 up. Disney - $125.00 up.

Skooter: 1963, freckles. $65.00 up.

Skipper: 1963 - $95.00 up. Growing up, 1976: $50.00 up.

Sister Belle: 17" - $50.00, $20.00.

Stacy, Talking: $125.00.

Swingy: 20" - $40.00, $15.00.

Tatters: 10" - $40.00, $15.00.

Teachy Keen: 17" - $35.00, $12.00.

Teeners: 4" - $45.00, $10.00.

A rare "Ken" dressed as "King Arthur." Original in box, #0773. Molded and painted hair. Courtesy Gloria Anderson. $300.00 up.

Tinkerbelle: 19" - $45.00, $15.00.
Tippy Toes: 16" - $25.00, $9.00.
Tricycle or horse: $20.00, $5.00.
Truly Scrumptious: 11½" - $250.00 up. Doll only: $175.00 up.
Tutti: 6" - $60.00 up. Packaged sets: $50.00 up.
Todd: 6" - $60.00 up.
Twiggy: 11" - $145.00 up.

"P.J." dates 1969 and "Sun Lovin' P.J." is from 1978. Courtesy Gloria Anderson. $75.00 up.

Mattel's "Shrinking Violet" is made of all cloth. Her mouth and eyes move and she has pull string talker. All original. Courtesy Jeannie Mauldin. $50.00 up.

First prices are for mint condition dolls; second prices are for ones that are dirty or not original.

Batman: Action figure. 8" - $15.00, $6.00.

Cher: 12" - $15.00 up, $6.00. Dressed in Indian outfit: $20.00, $10.00.

Dianna Ross: 12½" - $45.00 up, $15.00.

Dinah Mite: 7½" - $15.00, $6.00. Black: $20.00, $9.00.

Happy Days Set: Fonzie - $14.00, $6.00. Others - $9.00, $3.00.

Joe Namath: 12" - $75.00, $20.00.

1979 "Fashion Candi" in original box. Made by Mego. Courtesy Gloria Anderson. 18" - $45.00.

18" "Candi" made by Mego and in extra jeans outfit made for her. Shown with boxed "Candi" sold as "Lady Linda." Doll is of excellent quality. Courtesy Marie Ernst. 18" - $45.00.

Our Gang Set: Mickey - $22.00, $10.00. Others - $12.00, $6.00.

Planet of Apes: 8" - $15.00, $7.00.

Pirates: 8" - $50.00, $15.00.

Robin Hood Set: $45.00, $10.00.

Sir Lancelot Set: 8" - $50.00, $15.00.

Star Trek Set: 8" - $30.00, $10.00.

Soldiers: 8" - $15.00, $4.00.

Sonny: 12" - $20.00 up, $9.00.

Starsky or Hutch: $10.00, $5.00. Captain or Huggy Bear: $15.00, $7.00.

Super Women: Action figures. 8" - $10.00, $3.00.

Waltons: 8" - $15.00, $6.00.

Wizard of Oz: Dorothy - $25.00, $9.00. Munchkins - $15.00, $6.00. Wizard - $20.00, $8.00. Others - $10.00 - $4.00. 15" size: $100.00, $40.00.

First prices are for mint condition dolls; second prices are for crazed, cracked, dirty dolls or ones without original clothes.

Mollye Goldman of International Doll Company and Hollywood Cinema Fashions of Philadephia, PA made dolls in cloth, composition, hard plastic and plastic and vinyl. Only the vinyl dolls will be marked with her name, the rest usually have paper wrist tag. Mollye purchased unmarked dolls from many other firms and dressed them to be sold under her name. She designed clothes for many makers, including Horsman, Ideal and Eegee (Goldberger).

Airline Doll: Hard plastic. 14" - $200.00 up, $75.00; 18" - $300.00 up, $125.00; 23" - $385.00 up, $100.00; 28" - $500.00 up, $200.00.

Babies: Composition. 15" - $150.00, $65.00; 21" - $225.00, $95.00. Composi-tion/cloth: 18" - $85.00, $40.00. All composition toddler: 15" - $175.00, $80.00; 21" - $250.00, $100.00. Hard plastic: 14" - $95.00, $65.00; 20" - $165.00, $90.00. Hard plastic/cloth: 17" - $95.00, $55.00; 23" - $165.00, $85.00. Vinyl: 8½" - $15.00, $7.00; 12" - $20.00, $8.00; 15" - $35.00, $12.00.

Cloth: Children: 15" - $125.00, $50.00; 18" - $185.00, $75.00; 24" - $225.00, $80.00; 29" - $300.00, $100.00. Young ladies: 16" - $185.00, $80.00; 21" - $275.00, $100.00. Internationals: 13" - $90.00 up, $40.00; 15" - $150.00 up, $50.00; 27" - $275.00 up, $85.00.

Composition: Children: 15" - $150.00, $45.00; 18" - $185.00, $75.00. Young lady: 16" - $365.00, $100.00; 21" - $525.00, $150.00. Jeanette McDonald: 27" - $800.00 up, $250.00. Bagdad Dolls: 14" - $275.00, $85.00; 19" - $475.00, $125.00. Sultan: 19" - $650.00, $200.00. Subu: 15" - $600.00, $200.00.

18" all original cloth Mollye doll with pressed face mask and oil-painted features. Yarn hair. Courtesy Gloria Anderson. 18" - $185.00.

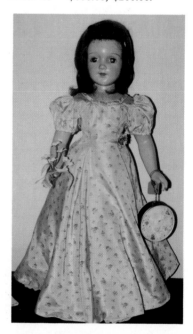

20" all original and all composition. Dress tagged "Mollye Dolls." Tin sleep eyes, closed mouth. Courtesy Gloria Anderson. 20" - $500.00.

Vinyl Children: 8" - $25.00, $9.00; 11" - $40.00, $15.00; 16" - $65.00, $20.00.

Hard Plastic: Young ladies. 17" - $200.00 up, $85.00; 20" - $250.00 up, $100.00; 25" - $300.00, $125.00.

Little Women: Vinyl, 9". $35.00, $10.00.

Lone Ranger/Tonto: Hard plastic/latex. 22" - $200.00, $75.00.

Raggedy Ann or Andy: See that section.

Beloved Belinda: See Raggedy Ann section.

MONICA STUDIOS

15-16" "Monica" is made of all composition with human hair embedded into scalp. Painted eyes. Original except shoes. No marks. Courtesy Jeannie Mauldin. Composition: 10½" - $275.00; 17" - $475.00; 21" - $550.00. Hard plastic: 14" - $365.00; 17" - $550.00.

The painted bisque Nancy Ann Dolls will be marked "Storybook Doll U.S.A." and the hard plastic dolls marked "Storybook Doll U.S.A. Trademark Reg." The only identity as to who the doll represents is a paper tag around wrist with the doll's name on it. The boxes are marked with the name, but many of these dolls are found in the wrong box.

Bisque: 5" - $50.00-60.00 up; 7½-8" - $60.00 up. Jointed hips: 5" - $70.00 up; 7½-8" - $75.00 up. Swivel neck: 5" - $75.00 up; 7½-8" - $80.00 up. Swivel neck and jointed hips: 5" - $75.00; 7½-8" - $85.00. Black: 5" - $125.00 up; 7½-8" - $150.00 up.

Plastic: 5" - $45.00 up; 7½-8" - $50.00. Black: $65.00.

Bisque Bent Leg Baby: 3½-4½" - $125.00 up.

Plastic Bent Leg Baby: 3½-4½" - $85.00 up.

Judy Ann: Incised with name on back. 5" - $200.00 up.

Audrey Ann: 6" heavy doll, toddler legs, marked "Nancy Ann Storybook 12." $1,000.00 up.

Margie Ann: 6" bisque, in school dress. $135.00 up.

Debbie: Name on wrist tag/box. Hard plastic in school dress. $125.00 up.

Debbie: Hard plastic with vinyl head. $85.00.

Debbie: In dressier type Sunday dress and all hard plastic. $150.00. Same with vinyl head. $100.00.

Teen Type (Margie Ann): Marked "Nancy Ann." All vinyl. 10½" - $90.00 up.

Muffie: 8", all hard plastic. Dress: $165.00 up. Ballgown: $185.00 up. Riding Habit: $185.00 up.

Muffie: 8" hard plastic, reintroduced doll. $85.00 up.

Nancy Ann Style Show Doll: 17-18" unmarked. All hard plastic. All in ballgown. $500.00 up.

6½" all bisque Nancy Ann Storybook dolls that are all original and marked. Courtesy Gloria Anderson. 6½" - $60.00 up.

Left: 5" "Pirate Storybook Doll" incised on back "Storybook Dolls USA." Earrings are attached to bandana and he wears an eye patch. Boots are painted on with oil cloth tops slipped onto legs. Right: 5" "Judy Ann Storybook Doll" incised on back "Judy Ann USA." Dressed in winter oufit. Dress has round gold tag "Storybook Dolls." Coat is knit, lined in white. Leggings are knit as is hat with white pompom. Boots are painted white. Courtesy Lynn Motter. 5" doll, each - $300.00 up.

8" "Muffie" is made of all hard plastic and a non-walker. No eyebrows and painted lashes over eyes. Courtesy Bessie Carson. 8" - $165.00.

8" "Muffie" is made of all hard plastic. Walker, head turns. Marked "Storybook Doll California Muffie." All original. 8" - $185.00.

NATURAL DOLL CO.

20" "Angela Cartwright" representing TV actress Linda Williams from the Danny Thomas Show. Vinyl and plastic, four molded teeth. Box marked "1961 Materto and Natural Doll Co." There is also a 30" size of this doll. This doll's face has "fallen in" due to weight of eyes against soft vinyl as she was stored face up in box. Courtesy Jeannie Mauldin. 20" - $95.00; 30" - $165.00.

9" "Court Man & Woman" made of all felt with cloth bodies. Jointed shoulders and hips. Removable clothes. Mohair wigs, painted features. Marked "Old Cottage Doll/Hand made in Great Britain." Courtesy Marge Meisinger. 9" - $95.00 up each.

8" "School Girl" made of all felt with jointed shoulders and hips. Painted features. Tagged "Old Cottage Doll/Hand made in Great Britain." Courtesy Marge Meisinger. 9" - $95.00 up.

First prices are for mint condition dolls; second prices are for played with, dirty, missing clothes or redressed dolls.

Designed by Johnny B. Gruelle in 1915, these dolls are still being made. Early dolls will be marked "Patented Sept. 7, 1915." All cloth, brown yarn hair, tin button eyes (or wooden ones), painted lashes below eyes and no outline of white of eyes. Some are jointed by having knees or elbows sewn. Features of early dolls are painted on cloth. 15-16" - $775.00 up, $300.00; 23-24" - $900.00 up, $400.00; 30" - $1,000.00, $500.00.

Averill, Georgene: Red yarn hair, painted features and have sewn cloth label in side seam of body. Mid-1930's to 1963. 15" - $125.00 up - $45.00.

Beloved Belinda: Black doll. 15" - $900.00 up, $500.00.

Mollye Dolls: Red yarn hair and printed features. Will be marked in printed writing on front of torso "Raggedy Ann and Andy Doll/Manufactured by Mollye Doll Outfitters. 15" - $700.00 up, $185.00; 22" - $900.00 up, $200.00.

Knickerbocker Toy Co.: Printed features, red yarn hair. Will have tag sewn with name of maker. 1963-1982. 12" - $40.00, $10.00; 17" - $55.00, $20.00; 24" - $95.00, $40.00; 26" - $185.00, $70.00; 36" - $250.00, $100.00.

Vinyl Dolls: 8½" - $12.00, $3.00; 12" - $18.00, $6.00; 16" - $22.00, $8.00; 20" - $28.00, $10.00.

Applause Dolls: Will have tag sewn in seam. Still available.

Volland "Raggedy Ann and Andy." All original. "Raggedy Ann" is stamped "Patent Set. 7, 1915." "Raggedy Andy" is from 1920. Courtesy Candy Brainard. 15" "Ann" - $1,500.00; 18" "Andy" - $900.00.

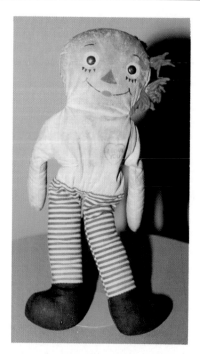

10" "Asleep and Awake Raggedy Ann." Has metal button eyes and blue/white striped legs. Just part of red yarn hair remains. Date unknown. Maker most likely Knickerbocker. 10" in this condition - $50.00; 10" in excellent condition - $125.00.

18" Georgene Novelties "Raggedy Ann and Andy." Tagged 1947. "Andy" has unusual vertical striped legs. Courtesy Candy Brainard. 18" - $150.00 each.

16" "Raggedy Ann and Andy" from the 1960's. Made by Knickerbocker and are in mint condition in boxes. Courtesy Candy Brainard. 16" pair - $400.00.

15" Knickerbocker "Talking Raggedy Ann" in original box. 1960's. Courtesy Candy Brainard. 15" - $250.00.

12" 1974 Knickerbocker "Talking Raggedy Ann." Courtesy Candy Brainard. 12" - $35.00.

15" "Beloved Belinda" made by Knickerbocker in 1965. Doll is in mint condition with box. Courtesy Candy Brainard. 15" in box - $400.00.

REMCO

First prices are for mint condition dolls; second prices are for played with, dirty or not original dolls.

Addams Family: 5½" - $12.00, $4.00.

Baby Crawlalong: 20" - $25.00, $10.00.

Baby Grow A Tooth: 14" - $25.00, $10.00. Black: $35.00, $12.00.

Baby Know It All: 1969. 17" - $30.00, $15.00.

Baby Laugh A Lot: 16" - $20.00, $7.00. Black: $30.00, $15.00.

Baby Sad or Glad: 14" - $25.00, $15.00.

Dave Clark 5: 4½" - $50.00, $20.00.

Heidi: 5½" - $9.00, $3.00. Herby: 4½" - $12.00, $5.00. Spunky (glasses): 5½" - $14.00, $5.00.

Winking Heidi: $10.00, $4.00.

Jeannie, I Dream Of: 6" - $15.00, $5.00.

Jumpsy: 14" - $20.00, $8.00. Black: $22.00, $10.00.

Laura Partridge: 19" - $50.00, $20.00.

L.B.J.: Portrait, 5½" - $25.00, $10.00.

Little Chap Family: Set of four. $185.00, $60.00. Dr. John: 14½" - $50.00, $20.00. Lisa: 13½" - $40.00, $12.00. Libby: 10½" - $30.00, $10.00. Judy: 12" - $30.00, $10.00.

Mimi: Battery operated singer. 19" - $40.00, $15.00. Black: $60.00, $20.00.

Orphan Annie: Plastic and vinyl. 15" - $40.00, $15.00.

Tumbling Tomboy: 1969. 16" - $20.00, $8.00.

Rainbow and Computer: 1979. 8½" - $45.00, $10.00.

16" "Baby Laugh A Lot." Cloth body and limbs with vinyl head and gauntlet hands. 1970. Battery operated, push button and she laughs. Painted features. 16" - $20.00.

14" "Jumpsy" made by Remco in 1970. Plastic with vinyl head, painted eyes and rooted hair. Battery operated and jumps rope. Marked on head "Remco, Inc. 1970." Courtesy Jeannie Mauldin. 14" - $20.00.

SASHA

Sasha dolls were made by Trenton Toys, Ltd., Reddish, Stockport, England from 1965 to 1986, when they went out of business. The original designer of these dolls was Sasha Morgenthaler in Switzerland. The dolls are made of all rigid vinyl with painted features. The only marks will be a wrist tag.

Boy: "Gregor" - $195.00.
Girl: $195.00.
Black Girl: "Cora" - $250.00.
Black Boy: "Caleb" - $225.00.
Black Baby: $200.00.
White Baby: $165.00.
Sexed Baby: $195.00.
Limited Edition Dolls: Limited to 5,000, incised #763, dressed in navy velvet. **1981:** $250.00. **1982:** Pintucks dress: $300.00. **1983:** Kiltie Plaid. $300.00. **1985:** Prince Gregor. $350.00. **1986:** Princess. $1,600.00. **1986:** Dressed in sari from India. $1,000.00 up.

16" Sasha doll from 1974. All rigid vinyl with painted features. Original. Courtesy Gloria Anderson. 16" - $195.00.

1974 "Gregor" designed by Sasha. All rigid vinyl and has painted features. Courtesy Gloria Anderson. 16" - $195.00.

Last doll to be made by Sasha Company and called "Princess." Courtesy Shirley Bertrand. $1,600.00 up.

One of the last dolls sold by the Sasha firm before going out of business. The "Sari" outfit came in three colors. Courtesy Shirley Bertrand. $1,000.00 up.

SHINDANA

First prices are for mint condition dolls; second prices are for played with, dirty dolls or not original ones. Dolls will be marked "Div. of Operation Bootstraps, Inc. U.S.A. (year) Shindana." They were in business from about 1968-1980.

Baby Janie: 1968. 13" - $35.00, $12.00.

Dr. J (Julius Erving): Full action figure, 1977. 16" - $35.00, $10.00.

Flip Wilson/Geraldine: All cloth, talker, 1970. 16" - $20.00, $10.00.

J.J. (Jimmie Walker): All cloth talker. 15" - $20.00, $10.00; 23" - $25.00, $12.00.

Kim: Young lady in ballgown, 1969-1972. 16" - $50.00, $25.00.

Lea: Cloth/vinyl face mask and gauntlet hands. 1973. 11" - $20.00, $10.00.

Malaika: Young lady, 1969. 15" - $25.00, $15.00.

O.J. Simpson: Full action figure. 9½" - $35.00, $12.00.

Rodney Allen Rippy: 1979, all cloth talker. 16½" - $20.00, $10.00.

Tamu: Cloth/vinyl talker, 1969. 15" - $25.00, $12.00.

Wanda: 11½": Nurse - $30.00, $10.00. Ballerina - $20.00, $8.00. Disco - $25.00, $10.00. Airline Stewardess: $40.00, $10.00.

Zuri: Sculptured hair baby. All vinyl, 1972. 11½" - $30.00, $15.00.

SHINDANA

Left: 13" "Baby Janie" made of plastic and vinyl. Open mouth/nurser with painted teeth. Made in 1968 by Shindana Division of Operation Bootstraps; Watts, California. Right: White version of 12" "Baby Zuri" which also came in black with molded hair. Made in 1972. Both have painted eyes. Courtesy Jeannie Mauldin. 13" - $35.00; 12" - $35.00.

SHIRLEY TEMPLE

First prices are for mint condition dolls; second prices are for played with, dirty, cracked or crazed or not original dolls. Allow extra for special outfits such as "Little Colonel," "Cowgirl," "Bluebird," etc.

All Composition:
11" - $700.00, $425.00. 11" Cowgirl: $725.00, $475.00.

13" - $650.00, $400.00.

16" - $625.00, $425.00.

17-18" - $685.00, $500.00.

20" - $750.00, $500.00.

22" - $785.00, $550.00.

25" - $900.00, $550.00. 25" Cowgirl: $950.00, $565.00.

27" - $1,000.00, $650.00. 27" Cowgirl: $1,200.00, $400.00.

Vinyl of 1950's: Allow more for flirty eyes in 17" and 19" sizes.

12" in box - $200.00; Mint, not in box - $165.00; Played with, dirty - $35.00.

15" in box - $300.00; Mint, not in box - $265.00; Played with, dirty - $85.00.

17" in box - $400.00; Mint, not in box - $350.00; Played with, dirty - $95.00.

19" in box - $475.00; Mint, not in box - $425.00; Played with, dirty - $100.00.

36" in box - $1,800.00; Mint, not in box - $1,400.00; Played with, dirty - $600.00.

1972: Reissue from Montgomery Ward. In box - $200.00; Mint, not in box - $165.00; Dirty - $45.00.

1973: Has box with many pictures of Shirley on it. Doll in red polka dot dress. 16" in box - $150.00; Mint, no box - $100.00; Played with, dirty - $25.00. Boxed outfits for this doll - $35.00 each.

Shirley Display Stand: Mechanical doll. $2,000.00 up.

"Hawaiian": Marked Shirley Temple (but not meant to be a Shirley Temple.) 18" - $825.00, $350.00.

Pin Button: Old 1930's doll pin. $90.00. Others - $15.00.

Statuette: Chalk in dancing dress. 7-8" - $245.00.

Japan: All bisque (painted) with molded hair. 6" - $200.00. Composition: 7-8" - $245.00.

Trunk: $145.00 up. Tagged 1930's dress: $100.00 up. Gift set/doll and clothes: 1950's - $300.00 up.

Babies: Marked on head, open mouth with upper and lower teeth, flirty, sleep eyes. 16" - $950.00, $565.00; 18" - $1,000.00, $650.00; 22" - $1,200.00, $700.00; 25" - $1,400.00, $800.00; 27" - $1,600.00, $900.00.

19" all composition "Shirley Temple," fully marked. All original except ribbon. 16" cloth and composition "Shirley Temple" baby with flirty tin sleep eyes and open mouth. Courtesy Frasher Doll Auctions. 19" - $700.00; 16" - $950.00.

20" "Little Colonel," 18" "Our Little Girl," 17" "Ranger," 16" "Curly Top," 13" "Little Colonel" and 11" "Curly Top." All are composition. Courtesy Glorya Woods. See listing for prices.

26" "Shirley Temple" made of all composition and is original with original pin. Flirty sleep eyes. Courtesy Gloria Anderson. 26" - $950.00.

25" "Shirley Temple" made of all composition and is fully marked. Shown with new reproduction blue glassware. Courtesy Glorya Woods. 25" - $900.00.

12" "Shirley Temple" made of all vinyl with molded teeth. Shown in four of the many costumes available in 1958. Courtesy Frasher Doll Auctions. 12" - $35.00-165.00.

"Shirley Temple" baby buggy, ca. 1935. Wooden with decal of Shirley on each side. Metal frame, rubber wheels and hubs marked with "Shirley Temple" in script. Folding leather hood. To top of handle it measures 26". Courtesy Frasher Doll Auctions. 26" - $350.00 up.

17" "Shirley Temple" made of all vinyl and from 1973. All original. Courtesy Gloria Anderson. 17" - $100.00.

19" "Shirley Temple" copy, excellent quality. Unmarked. Vinyl with long rooted hair, open/closed mouth with four painted teeth. Cheek dimples. Courtesy Marie Ernst. 19" - $165.00 up.

9" and 8" Sun Rubber babies. Left: Squeeze toy made of all vinyl with painted features, molded-on clothes. Right: "So Wee" from 1951. All vinyl, inset eyes, nurser. Courtesy Gloria Anderson. 8-9" - $35.00-45.00; Squeeze toy - $10.00.

TERRI LEE

First prices are for mint condition dolls, which could be higher due to the outfit on the doll. Second prices are for soiled, poor wig or not original.

Terri Lee: Composition: $325.00, $95.00. Hard plastic: Marked "Pat. Pend." $285.00, $100.00. Others: $250.00, $80.00. Black: $500.00 up, $200.00. Vinyl: $200.00, $75.00. Talking: $475.00, $165.00. Mint in box: $400.00-475.00.

Jerri Lee: 16" hard plastic, caracul wig. $300.00, $185.00. Black: $500.00, $250.00. Mint in box: $450.00-500.00.

Tiny Terri Lee: 10" - $165.00, $85.00.

Tiny Jerri Lee: 10" - $195.00, $95.00.

Connie Lynn: 19" - $365.00 up, $200.00.

Gene Autry: 16" - $1,200.00 up, $600.00.

Linda Baby: (Linda Lee) 10-12" - $185.00 up, $95.00.

So Sleepy: 9½" - $200.00 up, $100.00.

Clothes: Ballgown - $100.00 up. Riding Habit - $100.00 up. Skaters - $100.00 up. School Dresses - $50.00 up. Coats - $35.00 up. Brownie Uniform - $40.00 up.

Clothes for Jerri Lee: Two-piece pants suit - $100.00 up. Short pants suits - $100.00 up. Western shirt/jeans - $70.00 up.

Mary Jane: Plastic walker, Teri Lee look-alike with long molded eyelids. 16" - $250.00 up.

16" "Terri Lee" and 10" "Tiny Jerri Lee." Both are all original. She has painted features and he has sleep eyes with lashes and a caracul wig. Courtesy Frasher Doll Auctions. 16" - $250.00; 10" $195.00.

16" "Jerri Lee and Terri Lee." Painted features and both are all original. Courtesy Frasher Doll Auctions. 16" "Terri" - $250.00; 10" "Jerri" - $300.00.

16" "Terri Lee" in all original ballerina outfit. Courtesy Marie Ernst. 16" - $250.00.

19" "Connie Lynn" is made of all rigid vinyl, sleep eyes with lashes and caracul wig. 10" "Linda Baby" is all original and has painted features. Original tagged clothes. Courtesy Frasher Doll Auctions. 19" - $365.00; 10" - $185.00.

Left: 16" "Pattie Jo" is a Jackie Ormes comic character made by Terri Lee company. Wears an original Terri Lee dress. Features are different and wig is hard wiry strands. Marked "Terry Lee." Courtesy Marie Ernst. 16" - $600.00. Right: 16½" "Mary Jane" is an all hard plastic walker. Head turns, flirty sleep eyes with long lashes, unmarked. Patterned after Jackie Ormes comic character and is a "Terri Lee" look-a-like. Courtesy Margaret Biggers. 16½" - $250.00.

13" "Grandma and Grandpa." All vinyl and original. Marked "Dam Troll 1977" on backs. **Courtesy June Schultz.** 13" - $65.00 up; 7" - $40.00 up; 6" - $25.00 up; 3" - $15.00 up.

UNEEDA

First prices are for mint condition dolls; second prices are for soiled, dirty or not original dolls.

Anniversary Doll: 25" - $60.00, $25.00.

Baby Dollikins: 21" - $40.00, $20.00.

Baby Trix: 16" - $20.00, $10.00.

Ballerina: Vinyl. 14" - $20.00, $7.00.

Blabby: $25.00, $9.00.

Bare Bottom Baby: 12" - $25.00, $12.00.

Dollikins: 8" - $15.00, $6.00; 11" - $20.00, $8.00; 19" - $35.00, $15.00.

Fairy Princess: 32" - $90.00, $40.00.

Freckles: 32" - $90.00, $35.00.

Freckles Marionette: 30" - $65.00, $30.00.

Lucky Lindy: (Lindbergh) Composition. 14" - $300.00, $175.00.

Pollyanna: 10½" - $30.00, $9.00; 17" - $45.00, $15.00; 31" - $100.00, $50.00.

Pri-Thilla: 12" - $20.00, $8.00.

Rita Hayworth: Composition. 14" - $350.00, $165.00.

Serenade: Battery-operated talker. 21" - $50.00, $15.00.

Suzette: 10½" - $45.00, $20.00; 11½" - $45.00, $20.00; 11½" Sleep eyes: $60.00, $30.00.

Tiny Teens: 5" - $8.00.

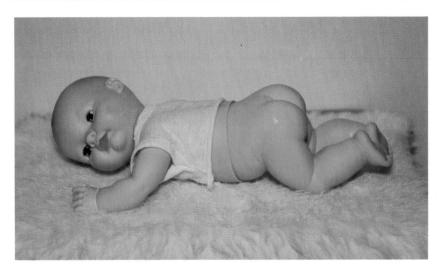

12" "Bare Bottom Baby." Painted hair, sleep eyes, jointed at waist and bottom part on doll molded in one piece. Neck jointed so head will tilt. Marked "Uneeda Doll Co. Inc./1983." Courtesy Jeannie Mauldin. 12" - $25.00.

15" "Purty" is made of all vinyl and came with painted and rooted hair, inset eyes, and open mouth/nurser. Squeeze stomach and eyes squint. Marked "Uneeda" on head and "516-42/Uneeda" on back. Courtesy Jeannie Mauldin. 15" - $30.00.

First prices are for mint condition dolls; second prices are for played with, dirty, crazed, messed up wig or not original.

Baby Dear: 12" - $55.00, $20.00; 17" - $95.00, $40.00. 1964: 12" - $50.00, $20.00.

Baby Dear One: 25" - $185.00, $85.00.

Baby Dear Two: 27" - $195.00, $95.00.

Brickette: 22" - $95.00, $40.00.

Ginny: Composition "Toddles": $265.00 up, $90.00.

Ginny: 8" hard plastic, strung, painted eyes. $350.00 up, $100.00.

Ginny: 8" hard plastic, sleep eyes, painted lashes and strung. $300.00 up, $100.00.

Ginny: Caracul (lamb's wool) wig. Child, not baby. $365.00 up, $185.00.

Ginny: Painted lashes, sleep eyes, hard plastic walker. $265.00 up, $95.00.

Ginny: Hard plastic molded lash walker. $185.00 up, $80.00.

Ginny: Hard plastic, jointed knee, molded lash walker. $165.00 up, $70.00.

Ginny Queen: $1,500.00 up, $500.00.

Ginny Crib Crowd: Bent leg baby with caracul (lamb's wool) wig. $650.00 up, $300.00.

Crib Crowd Easter Bunny: $1,200.00 up, $600.00.

Ginny: All vinyl Internationals. $50.00 up. Other: $35.00 up.

Ginny Gym: $275.00 up.

Ginny Pup: Steiff. $165.00 up.

Hug A Bye Baby: 16" - $35.00, $15.00. Black: $45.00, $20.00.

Jan: 12" - $75.00, $25.00.

Jeff: 10" - $50.00, $20.00.

Jill: 10" - $95.00, $35.00. In box/ ballgown - $250.00 up.

Lil Imp: 11" - $65.00, $30.00.

Love Me Linda: 15" - $45.00, $15.00.

Star Bright: 18" - $100.00, $40.00. Baby: 18" - $65.00, $25.00.

Welcome Home or Welcome Home Baby Turns Two: 20-24" - $75.00, $30.00.

Wee Imp: 8", red wig. $400.00 up, $100.00.

25" "Baby Dear One" with cloth body and vinyl head and limbs. Rooted hair and two lower teeth. Marked high on right leg "E. Wilkins (designer) 1961" and "1961 E. Wilkins/Vogue Dolls" on head. Courtesy Jeannie Mauldin. 25" - $185.00.

8" walker "Ginny" with painted lashes and poodle-cut lamb's wool wig. All original. Courtesy Sandy Johnson-Barts. 8" - $365.00 up.

8" walker "Ginny" with painted lashes. #21 "Kindercrowd", original. Courtesy Sandy Johnson-Barts. 8" - $285.00 up.

8" "Crib Crowd" with painted eyes. All original "Toodles." Courtesy Sandy Johnson-Barts. 8" - $650.00 up.

8" "Jack & Jill" Toodles. All composition, mohair wigs, painted eyes and marked "Vogue." Jack is missing his hat. Courtesy Glorya Woods. 8" - $265.00 each.

Both dolls are 11" "Littlest Angel" dolls. Made of plastic and vinyl with sleep eyes and all original. Clothes tagged "Vogue Dolls Made in USA." Head: "Vogue Doll/1965." Wrist tag: "Melrose. Mass." 11" - $25.00.

14" "Lil Imp" is all original and shown with original box and pamphlet. Courtesy Glorya Woods. 14" - $65.00.

15" "Cleopatra, Queen of Egypt" from 1984. Marked on head "1984 World Doll." One in set of three "Heroines of History" and limited to 5,000 pieces. Slim vinyl body, flat feet, rooted hair and sleep eyes. Jeweled tiara is metal. Courtesy Marie Ernst. 15" - $185.00.

8" "Bonnie Blue" made in 1989 for the 50th anniversary of "Gone With The Wind." Only the very first dolls shipped had the hands painted red (meant to be gloves) and due to cost, the remainder marketed were left flesh toned. Vinyl with rooted hair. Courtesy Shirley Bertrand. Red hands - $85.00; flesh hands - $40.00.

INDEX

NUMBERS

LETTERS AND SYMBOLS

Schroeder's Antiques
Price Guide

Schroeder's Antiques Price Guide has become THE household name in the antiques and collectibles field. Our team of editors work year around with more than 200 contributors to bring you our #1 best-selling book on antiques and collectibles.

With more than 50,000 items identified and priced, *Schroeder's* is a must for the collector and dealer alike. If it merits the interest of today's collector, you'll find it in *Schroeder's.* Each subject is represented with histories and background information. In addition, hundreds of sharp original photos are used each year to illustrate not only the rare and unusual, but the everyday "fun-type" collectibles as well – not postage stamp pictures, but large close-up shots that show important details clearly.

Our editors compile a new book each year. Never do we merely change prices. Each category is thoroughly checked to spot inconsistencies, listings that may not be entirely reflective of actual market dealings, and lines too vague to be of merit. Only the best of the lot remains for publication. You'll find *Schroeder's Antiques Price Guide* the one to buy for factual information and quality.

8½x11", 608 Pages   **$12.95**

COLLECTOR BOOKS
A Division of Schroeder Publishing Co., Inc.